Lecture Notes in Artificial Intelligence   3899

Edited by J. G. Carbonell and J. Siekmann

Subseries of Lecture Notes in Computer Science

W0112633

Simone Frintrop

VOCUS: A Visual Attention System for Object Detection and Goal-Directed Search

 Springer

Series Editors

Jaime G. Carbonell, Carnegie Mellon University, Pittsburgh, PA, USA
Jörg Siekmann, University of Saarland, Saarbrücken, Germany

Author

Simone Frintrop
Kungliga Tekniska Högskolan (KTH)
Computer Science and Communication (CSC)
Computational Vision and Active Perception Laboratory (CVAP)
10044 Stockholm, Sweden
E-mail: frintrop@csc.kth.se, simone.frintrop@web.de

This work was carried out at
Fraunhofer Institute for Autonomous Intelligent Systems (AIS)
St. Augustin, Germany
and accepted as PhD thesis at the University of Bonn, Germany

Library of Congress Control Number: 2006921341

CR Subject Classification (1998): I.2.10, I.2.6, I.4, I.5, F.2.2

LNCS Sublibrary: SL 7 – Artificial Intelligence

ISSN   0302-9743
ISBN-10   3-540-32759-2 Springer Berlin Heidelberg New York
ISBN-13   978-3-540-32759-2 Springer Berlin Heidelberg New York

Springer is a part of Springer Science+Business Media

springer.com

© Springer-Verlag Berlin Heidelberg 2006
Printed in Germany

Typesetting: Camera-ready by author, data conversion by Scientific Publishing Services, Chennai, India
Printed on acid-free paper   SPIN: 11682110   06/3142   5 4 3 2 1 0

Foreword

In humans, more than 30% of the brain is devoted to visual processing to allow us to interpret and behave intelligently as part of our daily lives. Vision is by far one of the most versatile and important sensory modalities for our interaction with the surrounding world. Consequently, it is not surprising that there is a considerable interest in endowing artificial systems with similar capabilities. Computational vision for embodied cognitive agents offers important competencies in terms of navigating in everyday environments, recognition of objects for interaction and interpretation of human actions as part of cooperative interaction.

One problem in terms of use of vision is computational complexity. It is well known that tasks such as search and recognition in principle might have NP complexity. At the same time, for use of vision in natural environments there is a need to operate in real-time, and thus to bound computational complexity to ensure timely response. The study of visual attention is very much the design of control mechanisms to limit complexity. Using a rather coarse classification one might divide visual processing into data- and model/goal-driven processing. In data-driven processing, the areas of an image to be processed are selected based on their saliency and offered to other modules in a system for higher-level tasks as, for example, recognition and description. So this is very much the "What is out there?" type of processing. In model-driven processing, the processing is driven by a desire to answer questions such as "Is there a cup in the image?". The selection of which regions to process and how to fuse different image descriptors is then performed according to criteria of optimality in the sense of discrimination.

Visual attention has been widely studied for at least a century, and over the last 25 years rich models of visual attention in primates have been developed. This is not to say that a complete model is available; in fact, a number of competing models have been reported in the literature. However, there are well-formulated models from biology which can be adopted for computational systems.

The present volume is an excellent example of how such computational models can be adopted for artificial systems and how we can study these models empirically using robots. Simone Frintrop has chosen to base her research on the popular model by Koch and Ullman, which is based on the psychological work by Treisman termed the "feature-integration-theory". The model uses saliency maps in combination with a winner-take-all selection mechanism. Once a region has been selected for processing, it is inhibited to enable other regions to compete for the available resources. The Koch-Ullman model has primarily been studied for data-driven/bottom-up processing. The framework presented in the present volume — the VOCUS (Visual Object Detection with a Computational Attention System) — presents a modification of the Koch-Ullman model to enable both data-driven and model-driven integration of features. Through adaption of a hybrid model it is possible to integrate the control strategies for search and recognition into a single attentional mechanism.

VOCUS includes a strategy for direct learning of object models for later recognition. It is well suited for design of artificial systems to be used in application, for example, in cognitive systems or in robotics. The volume contains not only a basic design of the hybrid attention model, but the new method has also been tested on detection and recognition of objects in everyday scenarios such as indoor office navigation and recognition of objects on a cluttered tabletop. VOCUS has in addition been evaluated for detection of objects using laser range data, which represents an extreme version of a dense disparity field. Using such diverse sets of feature representations, highly efficient strategies for both search and recognition have been reported.

Simone Frintrop has thus achieved significant progress on several fronts. First of all, the new model represents a major step forward on integration of data and model-driven mechanisms for studies of visual attention. In addition, the model has been empirically evaluated using a diverse set of visual scenes to clearly characterize the new model. It is highly encouraging to see this synthesis of earlier results from primate attention work into a joint model and to see the application of the attention model in the context of robotic applications for navigation and scene modeling.

Henrik I. Christensen
Stockholm, December 2005.

Abstract

Visual attention is a mechanism in human perception which selects relevant regions from a scene and provides these regions for higher-level processing as object recognition. This enables humans to act effectively in their environment despite the complexity of perceivable sensor data. Computational vision systems face the same problem as humans: there is a large amount of information to be processed and to achieve this efficiently, maybe even in real-time for robotic applications, the order in which a scene is investigated must be determined in an intelligent way. A promising approach is to use computational attention systems that simulate human visual attention.

This monograph introduces the biologically motivated computational attention system VOCUS (Visual Object detection with a CompUtational attention System) that detects regions of interest in images. It operates in two modes, in an exploration mode in which no task is provided, and in a search mode with a specified target. In exploration mode, regions of interest are defined by strong contrasts (e.g., color or intensity contrasts) and by the uniqueness of a feature. For example, a black sheep is salient in a flock of white sheep. In search mode, the system uses previously learned information about a target object to bias the saliency computations with respect to the target. In various experiments, it is shown that the target is on average found with less than three fixations, that usually less than five training images suffice to learn the target information, and that the system is mostly robust with regard to viewpoint changes and illumination variances.

Furthermore, we demonstrate how VOCUS profits from additional sensor data: we apply the system to depth and reflectance data from a 3D laser scanner and show the advantages that the laser modes provide. By fusing the data of both modes, we demonstrate how the system is able to consider distinct object properties and how the flexibility of the system increases by considering different data. Finally, the regions of interest provided by VOCUS serve as input to a classifier that recognizes the object in the detected region. We show how and in which cases the classification is sped up and how the detection quality is improved by the attentional front-end. This approach is especially useful if many object classes have to be considered, a frequently occurring situation in robotics.

VOCUS provides a powerful approach to improve existing vision systems by concentrating computational resources to regions that are more likely to contain relevant information. The more the complexity and power of vision systems increase in the future, the more they will profit from an attentional front-end like VOCUS.

Acknowledgments

First, I would like to express my profound gratitude to my advisor, Prof. Joachim Hertzberg, who supported my work with many valuable hints and suggestions and who always took the time to answer my questions and to comment on my writings. I was also deeply impressed by his skills and I am indebted to him for enabling me to study the here presented subject in depth; without this, I never would have been able to finish this thesis so rapidly. Special thanks go to Erich Rome, who supported this work with many useful suggestions and who was available each time I asked for his help. I am also grateful to Prof. Armin B. Cremers, who kindly took on the task to co-advise this thesis. Furthermore, Prof. Wolfgang Förstner's valuable suggestions, which helped me to seriously improve my work, are greatly appreciated. I was impressed by his bright scientific mind and by his strong enthusiasm for science.

I am also deeply grateful to Prof. John Tsotsos for his kind advice. He contributed to my work with very helpful ideas and always kept me going; I particularly enjoyed our inspiring e-mail discussions. Furthermore, I want to thank Gerriet Backer for the fruitful discussions on many aspects of this thesis. His helpful comments regarding the psychological background on attention and suggestions concerning computational realizations contributed considerably to my work.

I also would like to thank all my colleagues for supporting me in various ways, especially Andreas Nüchter, Kai Pervölz, Matthias Hennig, Sara Mitri, Uwe Weddige, and Hartmut Surmann, for the fruitful collaboration and the pleasant working atmosphere. Several people kindly provided me with their image data or experimental results. Special thanks go to Jens Pannekamp, Bernd Schönwälder, Fred Hamker, Vidhya Navalpakkam, and Laurent Itti.

Finally, I want to sincerely thank Henrik for his enduring patience when I started to discuss my topic after work or at weekends, for showing interest in my work, and for constantly encouraging me and cheering me up during the tough times. I am also grateful to my friends with whom I had an enjoyable life beyond work. Last but not least, my very special thanks go to my mother and, in loving memory, to my father. Both have always believed in me and permanently supported me in every way. Without their help, love, and faith I never would have been able to even start this work.

Contents

List of Acronyms

CODE	COntour DEtector theory for perceptual grouping
CTVA	CODE Theory of Visual Attention
DAM	Distributed Associative Memory
FEF	Frontal Eye Fields
FIT	Feature Integration Theory
fMRI	functional Magnetic Resonance Imaging
FOA	Focus Of Attention
IOR	Inhibition Of Return
IPL	Inferior Parietal Lobule
IT	Infero Temporat cortex
LGN	Lateral Geniculate Nucleus
LIP	Lateral IntraParietal area
MFG	Middle Frontal Gyrus
MSR	Most Salient Region
MT	Middle Temporal area (V5)
NE	NorepinEphrine system
NVT	Neuromorphic Vision Toolkitt
PO	Parieto Occipale area
PP	Posterior Parietal cortex
ROI	Region Of Interest
RT	Reaction Time
SC	Superior Colliculus
SPL	Superior Parietal Lobule
SAIM	Selective Attention for Identification Model
SEF	Supplementary Eye Field
SERR	SEarch via Recursive Rejection
SLAM	SeLective Attention Model
TVA	Theory of Visual Attention
V1	primary visual cortex, striate cortex
V2 - V5	regions of extrastriate cortex
VOCUS	Visual Object detection with a CompUtational attention System
WTA	Winner Take All network

1

Introduction

1.1 Motivation

Imagine the following scenario: you are visiting the street carnival in Cologne, Germany for the first time. Fascinated by the colorful and imaginative costumes of the people around you, your gaze wanders from one exciting spot to the next: here a clown with a fancy dress, there a small boy masqueraded as Harry Potter. But not only visual cues capture your attention: over there a band starts to play the new hit of the year and the smell of fresh cookies from the right also revives your interest. Suddenly you remember that you did not come here alone: where has your friend gone? You start to look around, finding her is not easy in the crowd. You remember that she wears a yellow hat, a clue that could make the search easier and you start to watch out for yellow hats. After your gaze has been distracted by some other yellow spots, you detect the hat, recognize your friend who is just dancing with a group of witches, and you start to push through the crowd to join them.

This scenario gives an insight into the complexity of human perception. A wealth of information is perceived at each moment, much more than can be processed efficiently by the brain. Nevertheless, detection and recognition of objects usually succeed with little conscious effort. In contrast, in computer vision and robotics the detection and recognition of objects is one of the hardest problems [Forsyth and Ponce, 2003]. There are several sophisticated systems for specialized tasks such as the detection of faces [Viola and Jones, 2004] or pedestrians [Papageorgiou et al., 1998] – although even these approaches usually fail if the target is not viewed frontally – but developing a general system able to match the human ability to recognize thousands of objects from different viewpoints, under changing illumination conditions and with partial occlusions seems to lie remotely in the future. Suggesting therefore to improve the performance of technical systems is to seek for inspiration from biological systems and to simulate their mechanisms – the brain is the proof that solving the task is possible.

One of the mechanisms that make humans so effective in acting in everyday life is the ability to extract the relevant information at an early processing stage, a mechanism called *selective attention*. The extracted information is then directed to higher brain areas where complex processes such as object recognition take place. Restricting these processes to a limited subset of the sensory data enables efficient processing.

One of the main questions when determining the *relevant* information is the problem of what is relevant. There is no general answer since the relevance of information depends on the situation. With no special goal except exploring the environment, certain cues with strong contrasts attract our attention, for example the clown in the fancy dress. The saliency also depends on the surrounding: the clown is much more salient in a crowd of black witches than among other clowns. In addition to these *bottom-up cues*, the attention is also influenced by *top-down cues*, that means cues from higher brain areas like knowledge, motivations and emotions. For example, if you are hungry the smell of fresh cookies might capture your attention and cause you to ignore the clown. Even more demanding is a goal: when you start to search for the yellow hat of your friend you concentrate on yellow things on the heads of the people around you. Other cues, even if salient, lose importance. Both bottom-up and top-down cues compete for attention and direct your gaze to the most interesting region. The choice of this region is not only based on visual cues but, as suggested in the carnival example, sounds, smells, tactile sensations, and tastes also compete for attention.

In computer vision and robotics, object detection and recognition is a field of high interest. Applications in computer vision range from video surveillance, traffic monitoring, driver assistance systems, and industrial inspection to human computer interaction, image retrieval in digital libraries and medical image analysis. In robotics, the detection of obstacles, the manipulation of objects, the creation of semantic maps, and the detection of landmarks for navigation profit considerably from object recognition.

The further the development of such systems proceeds and the more general their tasks will be, the more urgent is the need for a pre-selecting system that sorts out the bulk of irrelevant information and helps to concentrate on the currently relevant data. A system that meets these requirements is the visual attention system VOCUS (Visual Object detection with a CompUtational attention System) that will be presented in this work.

1.2 Scope

In this monograph, a computational attention system, VOCUS, is presented, which detects regions of potential interest in images. First, fast and rough mechanisms compute saliencies according to different features like intensity, color, and orientation in parallel. If target information is available, the features are weighted according to the properties of the target. Second, the resulting information is fused and the most salient region is determined, yielding the focus of attention. Finally, the focus region is provided for complex processes like object recognition, which are usually costly and time consuming. By restricting the complex tasks to small portions of the input data, the system is able to achieve considerable performance gains.

The introductory example presented above already contains the four main aspects of the monograph which are examined in the four main chapters: first, VOCUS detects regions of interest from bottom-up cues such as strong contrasts and uniqueness (e.g., the fancy clown); second, top-down influences such as goal-dependent properties influence the processing and enable goal-directed search (e.g., the yellow hat); third, information from different sensor modes attracts the attention and is fused to yield a single focus of attention (as the music and the smell of cookies compete for attention with the visual cues) and finally, after directing the focus of attention to a region of interest, object recognition takes place (e.g., recognition of the hat).

Now some words to categorize the present work. There are two objectives usually aspired by computational attention systems. The first is to better understand human perception and provide a tool that is able to test whether the psychological models are plausible. The second objective is to build a technical system which represents a useful front-end for higher-level tasks as object recognition and thus assists to yield a faster and more robust recognition system. This monograph concentrates on the second objective, that means the aim of the work is to build a system that improves the recognition performance in computer vision and robotics.

1.3 Contributions

This monograph presents a new approach for robust object detection and goal-directed search in images. The work is based on a well-known and widely accepted bottom-up attention system [Itti et al., 1998]. This architecture is extended and improved in several aspects, the major one being extending the system to deal with top-down influences and perform goal-directed search. A detailed discussion on the delimitation to existing work follows in the respective chapters, here we present a short summary of the main contributions:

- Introduction of the computational attention system VOCUS which extends and improves one of the standard approaches of computational attention systems [Itti et al., 1998] by several aspects, ranging from implementation details to conceptual revisions. These improvements enable a considerable gain in performance and robustness (chapter 4, also published in [Mitri et al., 2005, Frintrop et al., 2005c, Frintrop et al., 2005b]).
- Presentation of a new top-down extension of VOCUS to enable goal-directed search. Learning of target-specific properties as well as searching for the target in a test scene are performed by the same attention system. Detailed experiments and evaluations of the method illustrate the

behavior of the system and demonstrate its robustness in various settings. This is the main contribution of the monograph (chapter 5, also published in [Frintrop et al., 2005a, Mitri et al., 2005, Frintrop et al., 2005b]).

- Extension of the attention model to enable operation on different sensor modes. Application of the system to range and reflection data from a 3D laser scanner and investigation of the advantages of the respective sensor modes (chapter 6, also published in [Frintrop et al., 2005c, Frintrop et al., 2003a, Frintrop et al., 2003b]).

- Combination of the attention system with a classifier that enables object recognition. Evaluation of the time and quality performance that is achieved by combining the systems (chapter 7, also published in [Frintrop et al., 2004b, Frintrop et al., 2004a, Mitri et al., 2005]).

Several aspects of these contributions have been done in cooperation with some of my colleagues: the data acquisition with the laser scanner (chapter 6 and 7) has been performed by Andreas Nüchter and Hartmut Surmann. The object recognition with the classifier (chapter 7) has been done in cooperation with Andreas Nüchter, Sara Mitri and Kai Pervölz. Some of the experiments concerning goal-directed search (chapter 5) have been performed by Uwe Weddige. Furthermore, many valuable hints and suggestions were given by Joachim Hertzberg, Erich Rome, and Gerriet Backer.

1.4 Outline

The remainder of this monograph is structured into six chapters. The first two are concerned with the psychological and neuro-scientific background of visual attention (chapter 2) and with the state of the art of computational attention systems (chapter 3), whereas the following four chapters each deal with one of the main contributions of this work:

Chapter 4 introduces the computational attention system describing the details that enable the computation of a region of interest. Particular emphasis is placed on the improvements with respect to other systems and on the discussion of how bottom-up systems of attention may be evaluated.

Chapter 5 elaborates on top-down influences as a new approach to bias the processing of visual input according to the properties of a target object. It is shown how these properties are learned from one or a small selection of training images, and how the learned information is used to find the target in a test scene. A wide variety of experiments on artificial as well as on real-world scenes show the effectiveness of the system.

Chapter 6 examines the extension of VOCUS to several sensor modes. The application of the attention system to range and reflection data from a 3D laser scanner illustrates how the information may be processed separately and finally fused into a combined representation from which a single focus of attention is computed. The advantages of each sensor mode are discussed and the differences between saliencies in laser and camera data are highlighted.

Chapter 7 combines the attention system with a fast and powerful classifier to enable recognition on the region of interest. It is shown how the time and quality performance improves when combining the two systems. Finally, chapter 8 concludes the work by summarizing the main concepts, discussing the strengths and limitations, and giving an outlook on future work.

2

Background on Visual Attention

Visual attention is, as mentioned in the introduction, the selective process that enables us to act effectively in our complex environment. The term *attention* is common in everyday language and familiar to everyone. Nevertheless — or even therefore — it is necessary to clarify and define the term properly. Since visual attention is a concept of human perception, it is important to understand the underlying visual processing in the brain and to know about the psychophysical and neuro-biological findings in this field.

In this chapter, we first describe what we understand by attention and which concepts are important in this field (section 2.1). Then, we discuss the neural processes that underlie visual processing and attention in the human brain (section 2.2). Next, we introduce in section 2.3 several psychophysical models of visual attention that form the basis for many current computer models of attention and finally, we bridge the gap between biology and models by discussing which neuro-biological correlates exist for current attention models in psychology and computer science (cf. section 2.4). We conclude this chapter with a discussion in section 2.5.

2.1 Concepts of Visual Attention

In this section, we discuss several concepts of visual attention. First, we define the term attention, then we introduce the concepts of overt versus covert attention as well as of bottom-up versus top-down attention, and finally, we elaborate on visual search, its efficiency, pop-out effects, and search asymmetries.

2.1.1 What Is Attention?

The concept of selective attention refers to a fact that was already mentioned by Aristoteles: "It's not possible to perceive two things in one and the same indivisible time". Although we usually have the impression to retain a rich representation of our visual world and that large changes to our environment will attract our attention, various experiments reveal that our ability to detect changes is usually highly overestimated. Only a small region of the scene is analyzed in detail at each moment: the region that is currently attended. This is usually but not always the same region that is fixated by the eyes. That other regions than the attended one are usually ignored is shown, for example, in experiments on *change blindness* [Simons and Levin, 1997, Rensink et al., 1997]. In these experiments, a significant change in a scene remains unnoticed, that means the observer is "blind" for this change. One convincing experiment on this topic is described in [Simons and Levin, 1998]: an experimenter approaches a pedestrian to ask for directions. During their conversation, two people carrying a door pass between the experimenter and the pedestrian and during that interruption, the first experimenter is replaced by a second experimenter. Even though subjects engaged in an interaction with both the first and the second experimenter and the second person was also wearing different clothing, 50% of the subjects did not notice the person change.

The reason why people are nevertheless effective in every-day life is that they are usually able to automatically attend to regions of interest in their surrounding and to scan a scene by rapidly changing the focus of attention. The order in which a scene is investigated is determined by the mechanisms of *selective attention*. A definition is given for example in [Corbetta, 1990]: "Attention defines the mental ability to select stimuli, responses, memories, or thoughts that are behaviorally relevant among the many others that are behaviorally irrelevant". Although the term attention is also often used to refer to other psychological phenomena (e.g., the ability to perform two or more tasks at the same time, or the ability to remain alert for long periods or time), for the purposes of this work, attention shall refer exclusively to perceptual selectivity.

If attention is needed to perform higher tasks in the human brain, and there are mechanisms that perform the attentional selection, this yields to a dichotomy of visual perception: one part is responsible for selecting the region of interest, the other one investigates the selected regions further [Neisser, 1967]. The mechanisms involved in the first task are called *pre-attentive* whereas the mechanisms operating on the selected data are called *attentive*. At which point this separation actually takes place is subject of the *early selection, late selection debate* which is discussed in [Pashler, 1997].

2.1.2 Covert Versus Overt Attention

Usually, directing the focus of attention to a region of interest is associated with eye movements (*overt attention*). However, this is only half of the truth. As early as in 1890, William James posited that we are able to attend to peripheral locations of interest without moving our eyes [James, 1890]; this is referred to as *covert attention*. This mechanism should be well known to each of us when we "look out of the corner of our eyes".

There is evidence that simple manipulation tasks can be performed without overt attention [Johansson et al., 2001]. On the other hand, there are cases in which an eye movement is not preceeded by covert attention: Findlay and Gilchrist [Findlay and Gilchrist, 2001] found that in tasks like reading and complex object search, *saccades* (rapid eye movements) were made with such frequency that covert attention could not have scanned the scene first. Even though, covert attention and saccadic eye movements usually work together: the focus of attention is directed to a region of interest followed by a saccade that fixates the region and enables the perception with a higher resolution. That covert and overt attention are not independent was shown by Deubel and Schneider [Deubel and Schneider, 1996]: it is not possible to attend to one location while moving the eyes to a different one.

An advantage of covert attention is that it is independent of motor commands. Neither the eyes nor the head have to be moved to concentrate on a certain scene region. Therefore, the process is much faster than overt attention. Nevertheless, many experiments on visual attention investigate mainly overt attention since this can be easily measured with eye trackers. Covert attention is more difficult to investigate. Posner [Posner, 1980] proposes several methods to analyze covert attention: psychological investigations include the measuring of the reaction time to detect a target, neuro-biological methods include for example the measurement of the evoked potential amplitude or of changes in firing rates of single cells.

2.1.3 Bottom-Up Versus Top-Down Attention

Shifting the focus of attention can be initiated by two general categories of factors: *bottom-up factors* and *top-down factors* [Desimone and Duncan, 1995]. Bottom-up factors are derived solely from the conspicuousness of regions in a visual scene, for example by strong contrasts. Beside *bottom-up attention*, this attentional mechanism is also called exogenous, automatic, reflexive, or peripherally cued [Egeth and Yantis, 1997].

On the other hand, *top-down attention* is driven by the "mental state" of the subject, that means by information from "higher" brain areas such as knowledge, expectations and current goals [Corbetta and Shulman, 2002]. That means, car holders are more likely to see the petrol stations in a street whereas bikers notice if there are cycle tracks. And if looking for a yellow highlighter on your desk, yellow regions attract the view more easily than other regions. Only parts of top-down processing are investigated by now, usually the parts concerning the knowledge about a target to be found. Other top-down influences like motivations, expectations, and emotions are much more difficult to control and to analyze and therefore much less is known on these aspects.

In psychophysics, top-down influences are often investigated by so called *cuing experiments*. In these experiments, a "cue" directs the attention to the target. Cues may have different characteristics: they may indicate *where* the

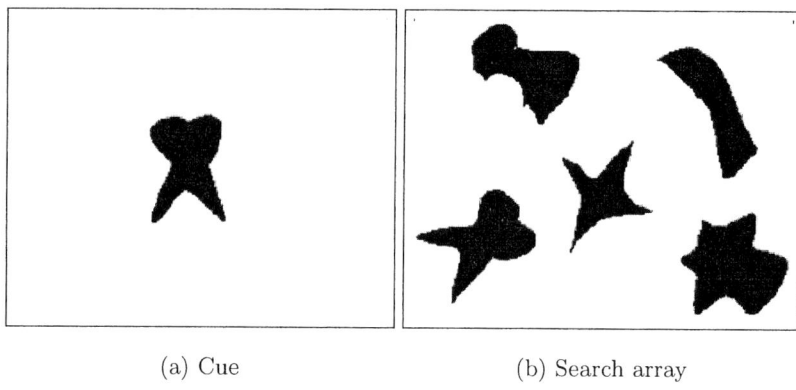

(a) Cue   (b) Search array

Fig. 2.1. Cuing experiment: **(a)** a cue is presented for 200 ms. Thereafter, human subjects had to search for the cued shape in a search array **(b)**. The reaction time is usually faster when the cue matches the target exactly than when the cue was rotated (Fig. reprinted with permission from [Vickery et al., 2005]. ©2005 The Association for Research in Vision and Ophthalmology (ARVO))

target will be, for example by a central arrow that points into the direction of the target [Posner, 1980, Styles, 1997], or *what* the target will be, for example the cue is a (similar or exact) picture of the target or a word (or sentence) that describes the target ("search for the black, vertical line") [Vickery et al., 2005, Wolfe et al., 2004] (cf. Fig. 2.1). A cue speeds up the search if it matches the target exactly and slows down the search if it is invalid. Deviations from the exact match slow down search speed, although they lead to faster speed compared with a neutral cue or a semantic cue [Vickery et al., 2005, Wolfe et al., 2004]. Other terms for top-down attention are *endogenous* [Posner, 1980], *voluntary* [Jonides, 1981], or *centrally cued* attention.

Evidence from neuro-physiological studies indicates that two independent but interacting brain areas are associated with the two attentional mechanisms [Corbetta and Shulman, 2002]. During normal human perception, both mechanisms interact. As per Theeuwes [Theeuwes, 2004], the bottom-up influence is not voluntary suppressible: a highly salient region "captures" the focus of attention regardless of the task; for example if there is an emergency bell, you will probably stop reading this text, regardless of how engrossed in the topic you were. This effect is called *attentional capture* (cf. Fig. 2.2).

Bottom-up attention is much better investigated. One reason is that the data-driven stimuli are easier controlled than the mental state that includes knowledge and expectations. Even less is known on the interaction of both processes.

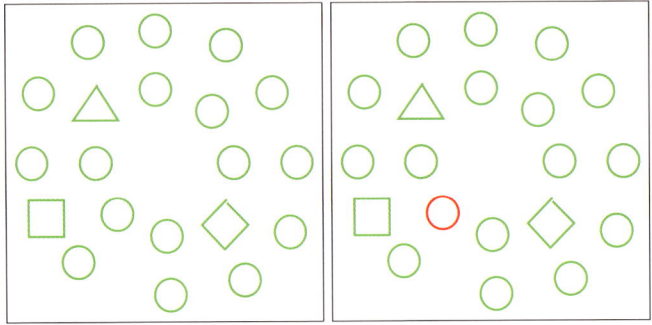

Fig. 2.2. Attentional capture: in both displays, human subjects had to search for the diamond. Although they knew that color was unimportant in this search task, the red circle in the right display slowed down the search about 65 ms (885 vs 950 ms) [Theeuwes, 2004]. That means, the color pop-out "captures" the attention independent of the task (Fig. adapted from [Theeuwes, 2004])

2.1.4 Visual Search and Pop-Out

An important tool in research on visual attention is *visual search* [Neisser, 1967, Styles, 1997, Wolfe, 1998a]. The general question of visual search is: given a target and a test image, is there an instance of the target in the test image? We perform visual search all the time in every-day life. Finding your friend in a crowd as discussed in the introductory example of this monograph is such a visual search task. In psychophysical experiments, the scene for a visual search task is usually an artificial composition of several items with different features such as color, orientation, shape, or size (cf. Fig. 2.2). The computational complexity of visual search has been investigated in [Tsotsos, 1990, Tsotsos, 2001]. *Unbounded visual search* (no target is given or it cannot be used to optimize search — for example, if the command is to find the odd-man-out) is proven to be *NP-complete*[1]. This is due to the fact that all subsets of pixels must be considered to find the target in a worst case. In contrast, the *bounded visual search* (the target is explicitly known in advance) requires linear time. Also, psychological experiments on visual search with known targets report that the search performance has linear time complexity and not exponential, thus the computational nature of the problem strongly suggests that attentional top-down influences play an important role during the search.

In psychophysical experiments, one measure of the *efficiency* of visual search is the *reaction time* or *response time (RT)* that a subject needs to detect the target. The RT is measured, for example, by pressing one button

---

[1] Problems that are *NP-complete* belong to the hardest problems in computer science. No polynomial algorithm is known for this class of problems and they are expected to require exponential time in the worst case [Garey and Johnson, 1979].

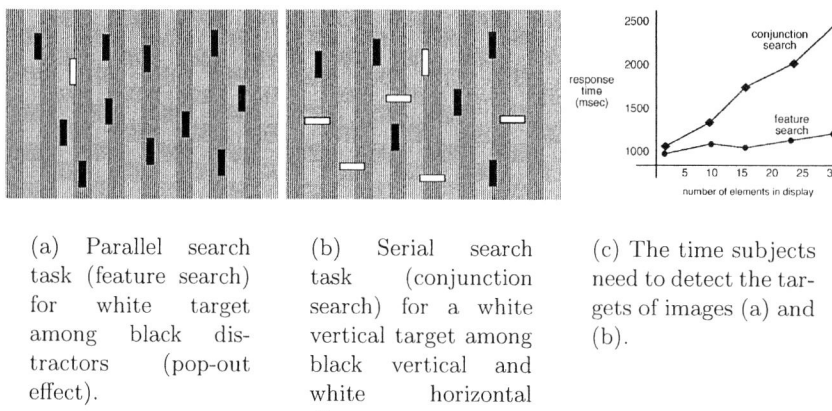

(a) Parallel search task (feature search) for white target among black distractors (pop-out effect).

(b) Serial search task (conjunction search) for a white vertical target among black vertical and white horizontal distractors.

(c) The time subjects need to detect the targets of images (a) and (b).

Fig. 2.3. The reaction time (RT) a subject needs to detect a target depends on the complexity of the search task (**c**). If the target differs only in one feature from the distractors, the search time is almost constant with respect to the number of elements in the display (feature search); the target seems to pop out of the scene (**a**). If the target is defined by a conjunction of features (conjunction search), the reaction time increases linearly with the number of distractors (**b**) (Fig. from [URL, 01])

if the target was detected and another if it is not present in the scene or by reporting a detail of the target. The efficiency is represented as a function that relates RT to the number of *distractors* (the elements that differ from the target) (cf. Fig. 2.3 (c)).

The searches vary in their efficiency: the flatter the slope of the function, the more efficient the search. Two extremes hereby are *serial* and *parallel* search. Parallel search means that the slope is near zero, i.e., there is no significant variation in reaction time if the number of distractors changes and a target is found immediately without the need to perform several shifts of attention. This effect occurs when the target differs in exactly one feature from the distractors, therefore the search is also called *feature search*. Already in the 11th century, Ibn Al-Haytham (English translation: [Sabra, 1989]) found that "some of the particular properties of which the forms of visible objects are composed appear at the moment when sight glances at the object, while others appear only after scrutiny and contemplation". This effect is nowadays referred to as *pop-out effect*, according to the subjective impression that the target leaps out of the display to grab attention (cf. Fig. 2.3 (a)). Scenes with pop-outs are sometimes also referred to as *odd-man-out* scenes, one example is the well known black sheep in a white herd. Parallel search is often but not always accompanied by pop-out [Wolfe, 1994]. Usually, pop-out effects only occur when the distractors are homogeneous, for example, the target is red

and the distractors are green. Instead, if the distractors are green and yellow, there is parallel search but no pop-out effect.

Serial search instead occurs if the reaction time increases with the number of distractors. This is usually the case in *conjunction search tasks* in which the target is defined by several features, for example, finding a white, vertical line among white, horizontal and black, vertical ones (cf. Fig. 2.3 (b)). The strict separability of serial and parallel search is doubted nowadays. Experiments by Wolfe indicate that the increase in reaction time seems to be a continuum [Wolfe, 1998b].

There has been a multitude of experiments on visual search and many settings have been designed to find out which features enable parallel search and which do not. There have been several quite interesting experiments not only showing that there is parallel search for red among green or vertical among horizontal items, but also for numbers among letters, for mirrored letters among normal ones, for the silhouette of a "dead" elephant (legs to the top) among normal elephants [Wolfe, 2001a], and for the face of another race among faces of the same race as the test subject [Levin, 1996]. An interesting experiment was done by Jonides [Jonides and Gleitman, 1972]: the search for an O among letters is fast if subjects are told to search for the "zero" and slow if they are told to search for the letter "O" although the same setting was used in both experiments. This indicates that the pure semantic meaning of the element already influences visual search. Interesting is also that the search for a novel element among familiar ones is parallel [Wang et al., 1994]. This is an important effect that helps humans to ignore known things and focus processing on the new, most informative, sensory data.

The idea behind all these experiments is to find out the *basic features* of human perception, that means the features which are early and pre-attentively processed in the human brain. Testing the efficiency of visual search helps to investigate this since parallel search is said to take place if the target is defined by a single basic feature and the distractors are homogeneous [Treisman and Gormican, 1988]. Thus, finding out that a red blob pops out among green ones indicates that color is a basic feature. Opinions on what are basic features are controversial. There appear to be about a dozen [Wolfe, 1998a]. In [Treisman and Gormican, 1988] the following features are named: colors, different levels of contrast (intensity), line curvature, line tilt (orientation) or misalignment, terminators, closure, direction of movement, stereoscopic disparity (depth) and quantitative values like length and number or proximity. Several findings indicate that basic features may also be learned. For example, Neisser mentions that finding special letters in a text is much more difficult for young children and illiterates than for people able to read [Neisser, 1967]. Anyone who has ever played the computer game Tetris for quite some time might also know this: after some time of playing, one seems to see the Tetris blocks everywhere in the environment[2]. Features not meeting the parallel search criterion are, for

---

[2] Annotation of J. Hertzberg: "This works also for Tangram!"

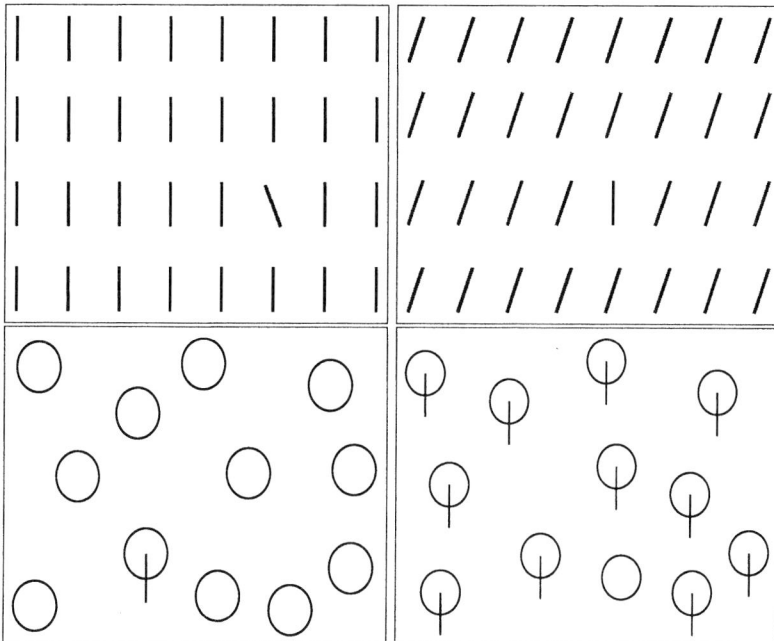

Fig. 2.4. Search asymmetries: it is easier to detect a tilted line among vertical distractors than vice versa (top) and to find a circle with a line among circles than vice versa (bottom)

example, line arrangements like intersection, juncture, and angles, topological properties like connectedness and containment, and relational properties like height-to-width ratio.

An important aspect in visual search tasks are *search asymmetries*, that means a search for stimulus A among distractors B produces different results from a search for B among As. An example is that finding a tilted line among vertical distractors is easier than vice versa (cf. Fig. 2.4). An explanation is proposed in [Treisman and Gormican, 1988]: the authors claim that it is easier to find deviations among canonical stimuli than vice versa. Given that vertical is a canonical stimulus, the tilted line is a deviation and may be detected fast. Therefore, by investigating search asymmetries it is possible to determine the canonical stimuli of visual processing which might be identical to feature detectors. For example, Treisman suggests that for color the canonical stimuli are red, green, blue, and yellow, for orientation, they are vertical, horizontal, and left and right diagonal, and for luminance there exist separate detectors for darker and lighter contrasts [Treisman, 1993]. Especially when building a computational model of visual attention this is of high interest: if it is clear which feature detectors are there in the human brain, it might be adequate to focus on the computation of these features and unnecessary to compute more.

2.2 The Neurobiology of Vision and Attention

Since visual attention is a concept of human perception, it is worth to regard the human visual system in more detail to get an insight into the nature of this concept. In this section, we first introduce the basic mechanisms that are involved in the processing of the visual information (section 2.2.1). Thereafter, we mention in section 2.2.2 the processes involved in assigning visual attention to regions of interest. While being far from an exhaustive explanation of the mechanisms in the human brain, we focus on describing the parts that are necessary for understanding the visual processing involved in selective attention. Further literature on this topic can be found, for example, in [Palmer, 1999, Kandel et al., 1996] and [Zeki, 1993].

2.2.1 The Human Visual System

Before going into the details of the mechanisms involved in the processing of visual information, let us briefly summarize the whole process in a few sentences [Palmer, 1999] (cf. Fig. 2.5): The light that achieves the eye is projected onto the retina and from there the optic nerve transmits the visual information to the optic chiasm. From there, two pathways go to each brain hemisphere: the collicular pathway leading to the Superior Colliculus (SC) and, more important, the retino-geniculate pathway, which transmits about 90% of the visual information and leads to the Lateral Geniculate Nucleus (LGN). From the LGN, the information is transferred to the primary visual cortex (V1). Up to here, the processing stream is also called *primary visual pathway*. From V1, the information is transmitted to the "higher" brain areas V2 – V4, infero temporal cortex (IT), the middle temporal area (MT or V5) and the posterior parietal cortex (PP). In the following, we discuss the processing in detail.

The Eye

The light that enters the eye through the *pupil* passes through the *lens*, travels through the clear *vitreous humor* that fills the central chamber of the eye and finally reaches the *retina* at the back of the eye (cf. Fig. 2.6, left). The retina is a light-sensitive surface and is densely covered with over 100 million photosensitive cells. The task of the photoreceptors is to change the electromagnetic energy of photons into neural activity that is needed as input by neurons.

There are two categories of photoreceptor cells in the retina: *rods* and *cones*. The rods are more numerous, about 120 million, and are more sensitive to light than the cones. However, they are not sensitive to color. The cones (about 8 million) provide the eye's color sensitivity: among the cones,

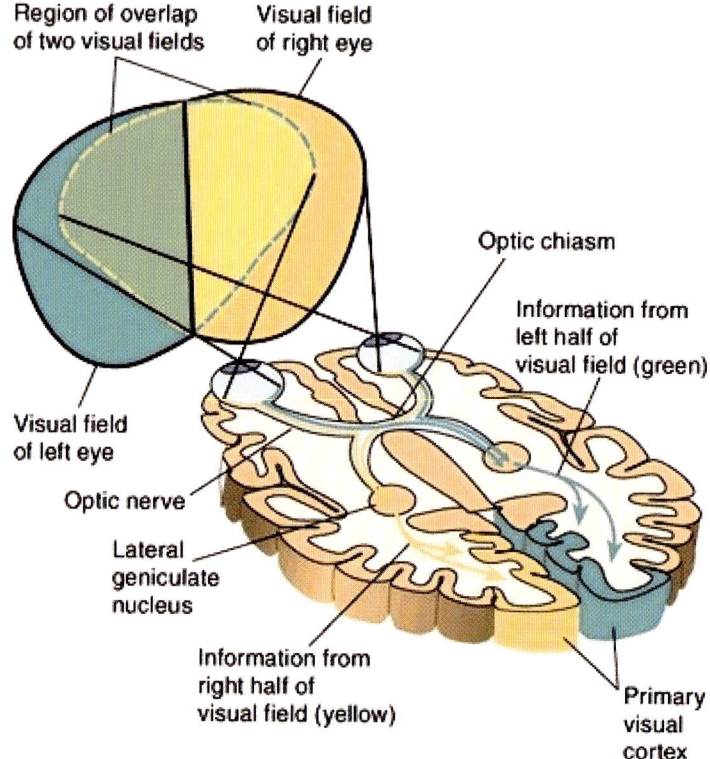

Fig. 2.5. The *primary visual pathway* in the human brain. The visual information enters the brain at the eye and is transmitted via the optic nerve to the optic chiasm. From here, most of the information is transmitted to the Lateral Geniculate Nucleus (LGN) and then to the Primary Visual Cortex (V1). From V1 the information is transmitted to "higher" brain areas (Fig. from: [URL, 02])

there are three different types of color reception: long-wavelength cones (L-cones) which are sensitive primarily to the red portion of the visible spectrum (64%), middle-wavelength cones (M-cones) sensitive to the green portion (32%), and short-wavelength cones (S-cones) sensitive to the blue portion (2%) (cf. Fig. 2.7 (a)). The cones are much more concentrated in the central yellow spot known as the *macula*. In the center of that region is the *fovea centralis* or briefly just *fovea*, a 0.3 mm diameter rod-free area with very thin, densely packed cones. It is the center of the eye's sharpest vision. This arrangement of cells has the effect that we do not perceive every part of the visual scene with the same resolution, but instead perceive the small region currently fixated in a high resolution and the whole surrounding only diffuse and coarse. An example of a scene as we perceive it is shown in Fig. 2.6, right.

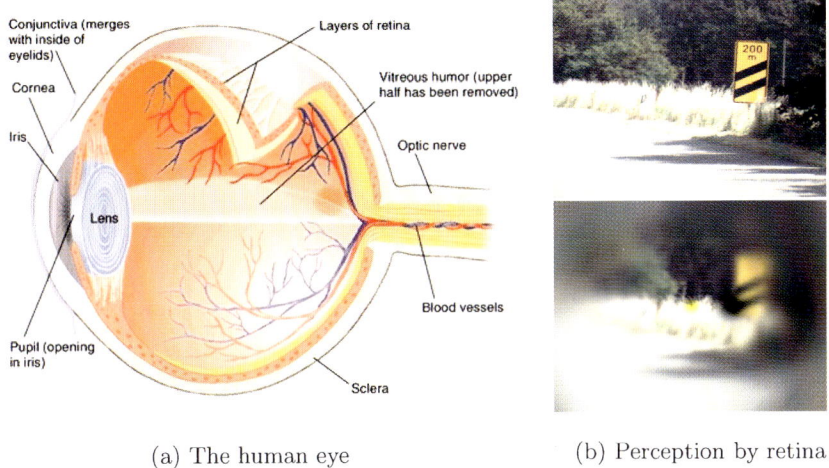

(a) The human eye   (b) Perception by retina

Fig. 2.6. (a) the human eye. The incoming light traverses the lens and the vitreous humor and finally reaches the retina. From there the visual information is transmitted via the optic nerve to the brain for further processing (Fig. from: [URL, 02]); **(b)** the cells on the retina are concentrated in one region, the fovea centralis. This is the region with the eye's sharpest vision. Regions in the surrounding are perceived only diffuse as is visualized in this example. The upper image shows the original image, the lower one depicts the scene as perceived by the retina (Images from: [URL, 05])

The photoreceptors are connected via bipolar cells with the ganglion cells (cf. Fig. 2.7 (a)). Whereas photoreceptors and bipolar cells respond by producing graded potentials, the ganglion cells are the first cells which produce spike discharges and so transform the analog signal into a discrete one.

The receptive field of a ganglion cell is circular and separated into two areas: a center area and a surround area (cf. Fig. 2.7 (b)). There are two different types of cells: *on-center cells* which respond excitatorily to light at the center and *off-center cells* which respond inhibitorily to light at the center. The area surrounding the central region always has the opposite characteristic [Palmer, 1999]. There are small ganglion cells (P ganglion cells, parvus = small) and large ones (M ganglion cells, magnus = large). P ganglion cells receive their input just from the cones and are more sensitive to color than to black and white, whereas the M ganglion cells receive input from both rods and cones and are more sensitive to luminance contrasts [Palmer, 1999].

An important question now is: how is the color opponency (red-green and blue-yellow) derived from the outputs of the three-cone system? The red-green contrast is derived from combining the excitatory input from the L-cones and the inhibitory input from the M-cones, essentially subtracting the signals from the L- and M-cones to compute the red-green component of the

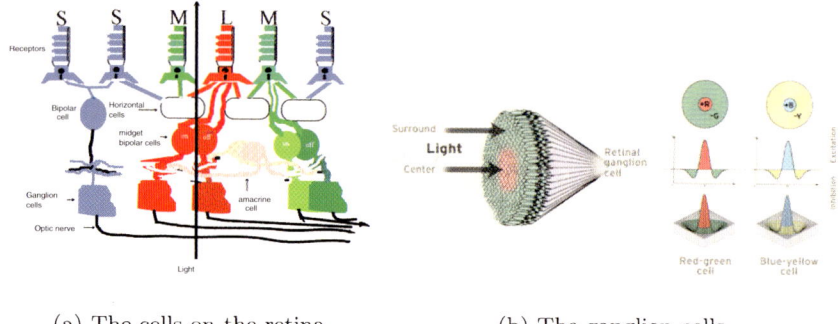

(a) The cells on the retina   (b) The ganglion cells

Fig. 2.7. (a) there are the three different types of cones in the retina: L-cones ("red"), M-cones ("green") and S-cones ("blue"). They transmit the visual information to the bipolar cells which send it to the ganglion cells (Fig. from: [Kaiser, 1996], copyright ©1996-2004 Peter K. Kaiser); **(b)** the ganglion cells are separated into on-center cells, which respond excitatorily to light at the center and off-center cells, which respond inhibitorily to light at the center. For colors, there is a red-green and a blue-yellow antagonism resulting in red-green, green-red, blue-yellow, and yellow-blue cells (Fig. from: [URL, 03])

stimulus $(L - M)$. The green-red contrast is equally determined by $(M - L)$. The blue-yellow contrast is derived from the excitatory output of S-cones and the inhibitory sum of the M- and L-cones $(S - (L + M))$ and the yellow-blue contrast is determined by the excitatory sum of the M- and L-cones and the inhibitory output of the S-cones $((M+L)-S)$. Finally, the luminance contrast is derived by summing the excitation from all three cone types $(S + M + L)$ (on-off contrast) or by summing their inhibitory output $(-S - M - L)$ (off-on contrast) [Palmer, 1999].

The Optic Chiasm

The axons of the ganglion cells leave the eye via the optic nerve, which leads to the *optic chiasm*. Here, the information from the two eyes is divided and transferred to the two hemispheres of the brain: one half of each eye's information is crossed over to the opposite side of the brain while the other remains on the same side. The effect is, that the left half of the visual field goes to the right half of the brain and vice versa.

From the optic chiasm, two pathways go to each hemisphere: the smaller one goes to the *superior colliculus*, which is e.g. involved in the control of eye movements. The more important pathway goes to the LGN of the thalamus and from there to higher brain areas.

The Lateral Geniculate Nucleus (LGN)

The *Lateral Geniculate Nucleus (LGN)* consists of six main layers composed of cells that have center-surround receptive fields similar to those of retinal ganglion cells but larger and with a stronger surround. Four of the LGN layers consist of relatively small cells, the *parvocellular cells*, the other two of larger cells, the *magnocellular cells*. The parvocellular cells process mainly the information from the P-cells of the retina and are highly sensitive to color, especially to red-green contrasts [Gegenfurtner, 2003], whereas the magnocellular cells transmit information from the M-cells of the retina and are highly sensitive to luminance contrasts. Below those six layers lie the koniocellular sub layers, which respond mainly to blue-yellow contrasts [Gegenfurtner, 2003]. From the LGN, the visual information is transmitted to the *primary visual cortex* at the very back of the brain.

The Primary Visual Cortex (V1)

The *primary visual cortex* is with some 200 million cells the largest cortical area in primates and is also one of the best-investigated areas of the brain. It is known by many different names. Besides the primary visual cortex, the most common ones are *V1* (the abbreviated form) and the *striate cortex* (due to its striped appearance).

V1 is essentially a direct map of the field of vision, organized spatially in the same fashion as the retina itself. In other words, any two adjacent areas of the primary visual cortex contain information about two adjacent areas of the retinal ganglion cells. However, V1 is not exactly a point-to-point map of the visual field. Although spatial relationships are preserved, the densest part of the retina, the fovea, takes up a much smaller percentage (1%) of the visual field than its representation in the primary visual cortex (25%).

The primary visual cortex contains six major layers, giving it a striped appearance. The cells in V1 can be classified into three types: *simple cells*, *complex cells*, and *hypercomplex cells*. As the ganglion cells, the simple cells have an excitatory and an inhibitory region. Most of the simple cells have an elongated structure and, therefore, are orientation selective, that means, they fire most rapidly when exposed to a line or edge of a particular direction [Palmer, 1999]. Complex cells take input from many simple cells. They have larger receptive fields than the simple cells and obtain responses from every part of the receptive field. Furthermore, they are highly nonlinear and sensitive to moving lines or edges. Hypercomplex cells, in turn, receive as input the signals from complex cells. These neurons are capable of detecting lines of a certain length or lines that end in a particular area.

The Extrastriate Cortex and the Visual Pathways

From the primary visual cortex, a large collection of neurons sends information to higher brain areas. These areas are collectively called *extrastriate cortex*, in opposite to the striped architecture of V1. The areas belonging to the extrastriate cortex are V2, V3, V4, the infero-temporal cortex (IT), the middle temporal area (MT or V5) and the posterior-parietal cortex (PP). The notation V1 to V5 comes from the former belief that the visual processing would be serial.

On the extrastriate areas, much less in known than on V1. It was not before the 1980's that these areas were examined in detail since at this time the advent of functional imaging methodologies has opened the way for closer examination of cortical areas in the intact human brain. One of the most important findings was that the processing of the visual information is not serial — that means the information is not transmitted from one area to the next — but highly parallel. Recently, many authors have claimed that the extrastriate areas are functionally separated [Kandel et al., 1996, Zeki, 1993, Livingstone and Hubel, 1987, Palmer, 1999]. Some of the areas process mainly color, some form, and some motion. The functional separation already started in the retina with the M-cells and P-cells and results in several pathways leading to different brain areas in the extrastriate cortex. The statements on the number of existing pathways differ: the most common belief is that there are three main pathways, one color pathway, one form pathway, and one motion pathway which is also responsible for depth processing [Kandel et al., 1996]. Other researchers mention four pathways by separating the motion pathway into one motion and one depth pathway [Livingstone and Hubel, 1987, Palmer, 1999] whereas some mention one color, one motion and two form pathways [Zeki, 1993]. The reason for this discordance is that firstly the pathways are not completely isolated and secondly the investigation of the extrastriate cortex has only started several years ago and its functionality is still not completely understood.

The color and form pathways result from the P-cells of the retina and the parvocellular cells of the LGN, go through V1, V2, and V4 and end finally in IT, the area where the recognition of objects takes place. In other words, IT is concerned with the question of "what" is in a scene. Therefore, the color and form pathway together are also called the *what pathway*. Other names are the *P pathway* or *ventral stream* because of its location on the ventral part of the body. The motion (and depth) pathway result from the M-cells of the retina and the magnocellular cells of the LGN, go through V1, V2, V3, MT (V5), and the parieto occipale area (PO) and end finally in PP, responsible for the processing of motion and depth. Since this area is mainly concerned with the question of "where" something is in a scene, this pathway is also called *where pathway*. Other names are the *M pathway* or *dorsal stream* because it is considered to lie dorsally. The distinction into "where" and "what" pathway traces back to [Ungerleider and Mishkin, 1982]; a visualization of these pathways is shown in Fig. 2.8.

Newer findings even propose that there is much less segregation of feature computations than suggested by these different pathways. It is indicated that luminance and color are not separated but there is a continuum of cells,

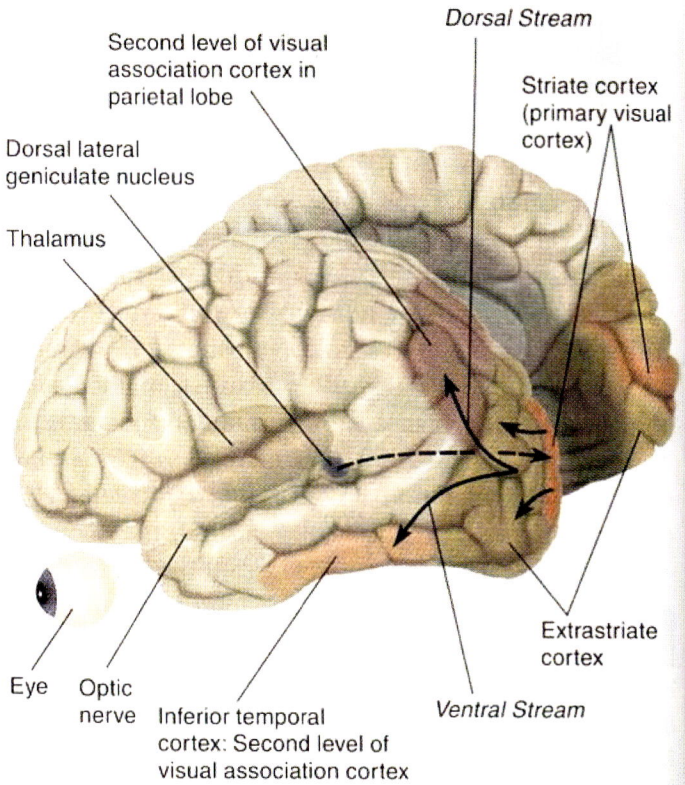

Fig. 2.8. The visual processing is divided functionally: the *ventral stream* leads to the inferior temporal cortex (IT) where object recognition takes place ("what" pathway) whereas the *dorsal stream* leads to the parietal lobe where motion and depth are processed ("where" pathway) (Fig. from: [URL, 04])

varying from cells that respond only to luminance, to a few cells that do not respond to luminance at all [Gegenfurtner, 2003]. Furthermore, neurons in the cortex can have a chromatic preference not only for red, green, yellow, or blue, but for any hue [Lennie et al., 1990], and V4, usually claimed to be the "color center" of the brain, processes also many other aspects of spatial vision. Additionally, the form processing is not clearly segregated from the processing of color since most cells that respond to oriented edges respond also to color contrasts. So a more correct view, at least as it is seen currently, is that some cells respond more to one kind of feature than to another one and certain brain areas have a prevalence of processing certain features but a clear segregation does not exist.

Finally, it is worth to mention that although the processing of the visual information was so far described in a feed-forward manner, it is usually bi-directional. Top-down connections from higher brain areas influence the processing and go down as far as LGN. Also lateral connections combine the different areas, for example, there are connections between V4 and MT, showing that the "what" and "where" pathway are not completely separated. The simplification of the last sections shall help to get an impression of the overall concept, but it should not be forgotten that the whole processing is much more complex and not yet completely understood at all.

2.2.2 Attentional Mechanisms in the Human Brain

The mechanisms of selective attention in the human brain still belong to the unsolved problems in the field of research on perception. Perhaps the most prominent outcome of new neuro-physiological findings on visual attention is that there is no single brain area guiding the attention, but neural correlates of visual selection appear to be reflected in nearly all brain areas associated with visual processing [Maunsell, 1995].

The more specific attentional mechanisms are carried out by a network of anatomical areas [Corbetta and Shulman, 2002]. Important areas of this network are PP, SC, the Lateral IntraParietal area (LIP), the Frontal Eye Field (FEF) and the pulvinar. Regarding the question which area fulfills which task, the opinions fall apart. We review several findings here.

[Posner and Petersen, 1990] describe three major functions concerning attention: first, orienting of attention, second, target detection, and third, alertness. They claim that the first function, the orienting of attention to a salient stimulus, is carried out by the interaction of three areas: the PP, the SC, and the pulvinar. The PP is responsible for disengaging the focus of attention from its present location (inhibition of return), the SC shifts the attention to a new location, and the pulvinar is specialized in reading out the data from the indexed location. Posner et al. call this combination of systems the *posterior attention system*. The second attentional function, the detection of a target, is carried out by what the authors call the *anterior attention system*. They claim that the anterior cingulate gyrus in the frontal part of the brain is involved in this task. Finally, they state that the alertness to high priority signals is dependent on activity in the norepinephrine system (NE) arising in the locus coeruleus.

Brain areas involved in guiding the movements of the eyes are the FEF, an area of the prefrontal cortex, and the SC. Furthermore, [Bichot, 2001] claims that the FEF is the place where a kind of *saliency map* is located which derives information from bottom-up as well as from top-down influences. Other groups locate the saliency map at different areas, e.g. at LIP [Gottlieb et al., 1998], at SC [Findlay and Walker, 1999], or, in most recent findings, at V4 [Mazer and Gallant, 2003].

Recently, there has been evidence that the source of top-down biasing signals may derive from a network of areas in parietal and frontal cortex. According to [Kastner and Ungerleider, 2001], these areas include the superior parietal lobule (SPL), the frontal eye fields (FEF), and the supplementary eye field (SEF), and, less consistently, areas in the inferior parietal lobule (IPL), the lateral prefrontal cortex in the region of the middle frontal gyrus (MFG), and the anterior cingulate cortex. The results from [Corbetta and Shulman, 2002], which show that two independent but interacting brain areas are associated with bottom-up and top-down attentional mechanisms, support these findings.

To sum up, at the current time it is known that there is not a single brain area that controls attention but a network of areas. Several areas have been verified to be involved into attentional processes but the accurate task and behavior of each area as well as the interplay among them still remain an open question.

2.3 Psychophysical Models of Attention

In the field of psychology, there exists a wide variety of models on visual attention. Their objective is to simulate behavioral data and thereby to explain and better understand human perception. There are descriptive models and models that are computationally implemented. The latter ones are especially well suited for comparison with psychophysical data obtained from experiments with humans. A review on computational models with a psychological objective is found in [Heinke and Humphreys, 2004]. In contrast to the models presented in this chapter, the computational systems of the next chapter intend to improve computer vision systems. However, there is an overlap of psychologically and technically motivated models and some of the mentioned approaches might be categorized in this as well as in the next chapter.

Here we describe two psychophysical models in detail because they belong to the best-known models in the field and have the greatest impact on this work. The first, introduced in section 2.3.1, is the *Feature Integration Theory* of Treisman and the second one is the *Guided Search Model* of Wolfe, described in section 2.3.2. In section 2.3.3, we mention several additional models.

2.3.1 Treisman's Feature Integration Theory

The *Feature Integration Theory (FIT)* of Treisman is one of the best known and most accepted theories in the field of visual attention. The theory was first introduced in 1980 [Treisman and Gelade, 1980] but it was steadily modified and adapted to current research findings. An overview of the theory is found in [Treisman, 1993], a model of FIT is depicted in Fig. 2.9.

The theory claims that "different features are registered early, automatically and in parallel across the visual field, while objects are identified separately and only at a later stage, which requires focused attention" [Treisman

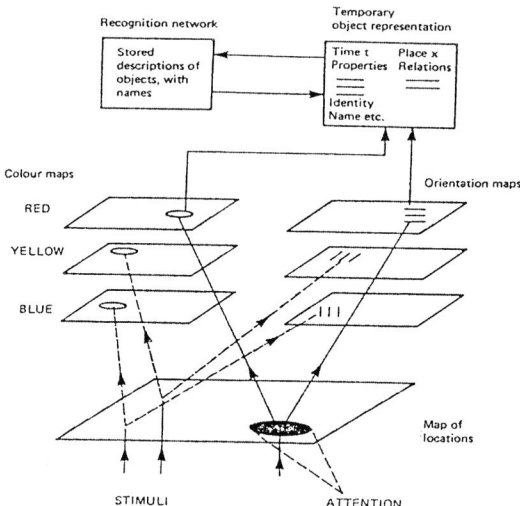

Fig. 2.9. Model of the *Feature Integration Theory (FIT)* of Treisman. Features such as color and orientation are coded automatically, pre-attentively, and in parallel. Each feature dimension consists of several *feature maps* such as red, yellow, and blue for color. The saliencies of the feature maps are coded in the *master map of locations*. When attention is focused on one location in this map, it allows retrieval of the features that are currently active at that location and creates a temporary representation of the object in an *object file* (Fig. reprinted with permission from [Treisman and Gormican, 1988]. ©1988 American Psychological Association (APA))

and Gelade, 1980]. Information from the resulting *feature maps* — topographical maps that highlight saliencies according to the respective feature — is collected in a *master map of location*. This map specifies *where* in the display things are, but not *what* they are. Scanning serially through this map focuses the attention on the selected scene regions and provides this data for higher perception tasks.

One of the main statements of the feature integration theory is that a target is detected easily, fast, and in parallel (pop-out) if it differs from the distractors in exactly one feature and the distractors are homogeneous. If it differs in more than one feature (conjunctive search) focal attention is required resulting in serial search. In later work, Treisman pointed out that information about the target object, represented in so called *object files*, , influences the search task by inhibiting the feature maps [Treisman, 1993].

Finally, it may be mentioned that Treisman uses the notation *feature* for intra-dimensional characteristics like red or horizontal and the notation *dimension* for supersets of these features, for example, color or orientation. In other approaches, the term feature is used for the dimensions.

2.3.2 Wolfe's Guides Search

Beside Treisman's Feature Integration Theory, the *Guided Search Model* of Wolfe is among the most important work in the field of psychophysical models of visual attention. Originally, the model was created as an answer to some criticism on early versions of the FIT. During the years, a competition arose between Treisman's and Wolfe's work, resulting in continuously improved versions of the models.

The basic goal of the model is to explain and predict the results of visual search experiments. There has been also a computer simulation of the model [Cave and Wolfe, 1990, Wolfe, 1994]. As Treisman's work, the model has been continuously developed further over the years. According to versions of software, the different versions of the system have been denoted with Guided Search 1.0 [Wolfe et al., 1989], Guided Search 2.0 [Wolfe, 1994], Guided Search 3.0. [Wolfe and Gancarz, 1996], and Guided Search 4.0 [Wolfe, 2001b]. Here, we focus on Guided Search 2.0 since this is the best elaborated description of the model. Versions 3.0 and 4.0 contain minor changes, for example, in 3.0 eye movements are included into the model and in 4.0 the implementation of memory for previously visited items and locations is improved.

The architecture of the model is depicted in Fig. 2.10. It shares many concepts with the FIT, but is more detailed in several aspects which are necessary for computer implementations. Alike FIT, it models several feature maps but unlike FIT it does not follow the idea that there are separate maps for each *feature type* (red, green, ...). There is only one map for each *feature dimension* (color, orientation, ...) and within each map, different feature types are represented. However, Wolfe mentions that there is evidence for differences between features. For example, there may be multiple color maps but only one orientation map [Nothdurft, 1993]. The features considered in the implementation are color and orientation.

Comparable to the *master map of location* in FIT, there is an *activation map* in Guided Search in which the feature maps are fused. But in contrast to at least the early versions of FIT, in Guided Search the attentive part profits from the results of the pre-attentive one. The fusion of the feature maps is done by summing up.

Additionally to this bottom-up behavior, the model also considers the influence of top-down information. To realize this, for each feature there is not only a bottom-up but also a top-down map. The latter map selects the feature type which distinguishes the target best from its distractors. This is not necessarily the feature with the highest activation for the target. Note that only one feature type is chosen, that means for an orange target the image regions with red portions are highlighted. It is not considered that a target might have different feature types, for example, 70% red and 30% yellow.

Basic Components of Guided Search

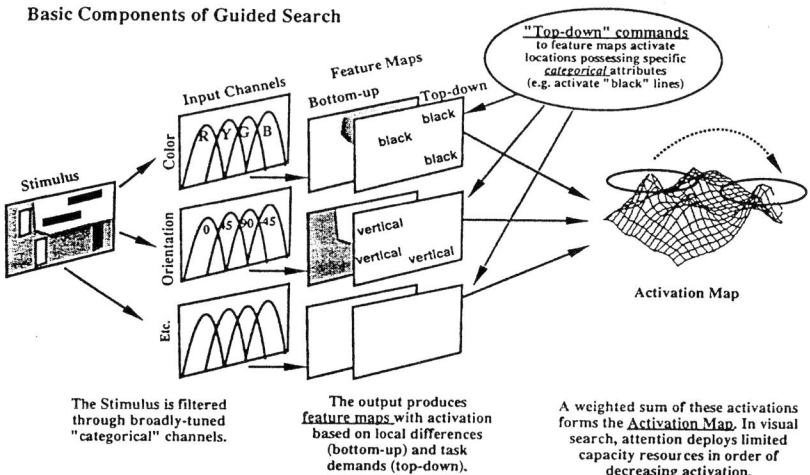

Fig. 2.10. The *Guided Search model* of Wolfe. One map for each feature dimension codes the properties of a scene concerning several feature types. Additionally to these bottom-up maps, top-down maps highlight the regions with task-specific attributes. A weighted sum of these activations forms the *activation map* (Fig. reprinted with permission from [Wolfe, 1994]. ©1994 Psychonomic Society)

2.3.3 Additional Models

Besides the Feature Integration Theory of Treisman and the Guided Search Model of Wolfe, there is a wide variety of psychophysical models on visual attention. The often used metaphor of attention as a *spotlight* comes from the *zoom lens model* [Eriksen and James, 1986]. In this model, the scene is investigated by a spotlight with varying size. Many attention models fall into the category of connectionist models, that means models based on neural networks. They are composed of a large number of processing units connected by inhibitory or excitatory links. Examples are the *dynamic routing circuit* [Olshausen et al., 1993], and the models MORSEL [Mozer, 1987], SLAM (SeLective Attention Model) [Phaf et al., 1990], SERR (SEarch via Recursive Rejection) [Humphreys and Müller, 1993], and SAIM (Selective Attention for Identification Model) [Heinke et al., 2002].

A formal mathematical model is presented in [Logan, 1996]: the CODE Theory of Visual Attention (CTVA). It integrates the COntour DEtector (CODE) theory for perceptual grouping [van Oeffelen and Vos, 1982] with the Theory of Visual Attention (TVA) [Bundesen, 1990]. The theory is based on a *race model* of selection. In these models, a scene is processed in parallel and selected is the element that first finishes processing (the winner of the race). That means, a target is processed faster than the distractors in a scene. Newer work concerning CTVA can be found, for example, in [Bundesen, 1998].

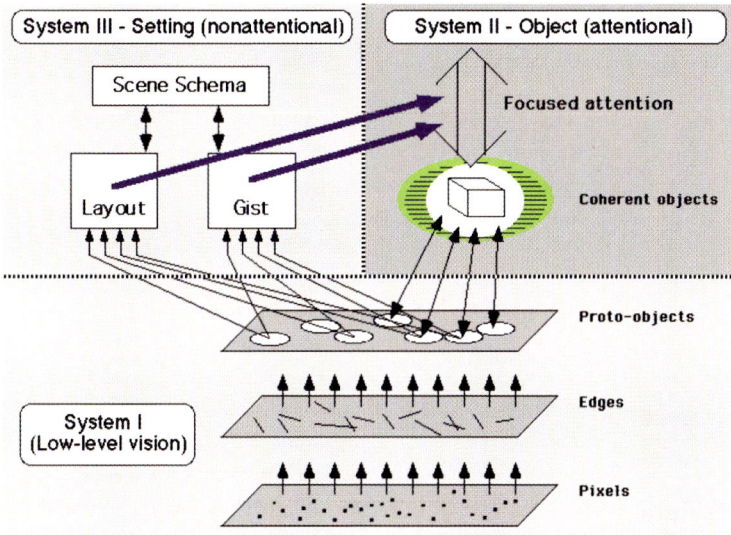

Fig. 2.11. The *triadic architecture* of Rensink suggests that visual perception is carried out via the interaction of three different systems: in the low level system, early level processes produce volatile proto-objects rapidly and in parallel. In system II, focused attention grabs these objects and in system III, setting information guides the attention to various parts of the scene (Fig. reprinted with permission from [Rensink, 2000]. ©2000 Psychological Press)

Recently, an interesting theoretical model has been introduced in [Rensink, 2000, Rensink, 2002]. His *triadic architecture* is very detailed and fits well for simulating it in a computer implementation (cf. Fig. 2.11). This was partially considered in [Navalpakkam et al., 2005]. The architecture consists of three parts: first a low-level vision system which produces *proto-objects* rapidly and in parallel. The proto-objects result from linear and not-linear processing of the input scene and are "quick and dirty" representations of objects or object parts that are limited in space and time.

Second, a limited-capacity attentional system forms these structures into stable object representations. Finally, a non-attentional system provides setting information, for example, on the *gist* — the abstract meaning of a scene, e.g., beach scene, city scene, etc. — and on the *layout* — the spatial arrangement of the objects in a scene. This information influences the selection of the attentional system, for example, by restricting the search for a person on the sand region of a beach scene and ignoring the sky region. Whereas the first two aspects resemble the traditional approaches of a pre-attentive and an attentive processing stage, the third part of the model is new and seems to be a promising extension of existing models.

2.4 From Biology to Models: Biological Correlates for Attentional Mechanisms

In this section, we will discuss to which extent the concepts usually used by psychological and computational models of attention are supported by neuro-biological evidence. Some of these (computational) concepts will be introduced not until the next chapter but we discuss the correlation here since often the neuro-biological evidence forms the basis for these mechanisms.

Feature Maps

In rather all psychological and computational models of attention the processing of distinct features is parallelized in separate feature channels. This separation is much stricter than the processing in the human brain suggests: there are different neurons and also different brain areas specialized for the processing of certain features but the whole processing is much more intertwined than posited by most models [Gegenfurtner, 2003]. However, the distinction into several pathways for color, form, motion, and depth coincides to some extent with the distinct feature channels. Even if these pathways may not exist in their pure forms, they nevertheless refer to the bias of certain brain regions.

However, there is usually no one-to-one mapping between the psychological features and the biological pathways. Whereas psychological findings claim that there are about a dozen basic features [Wolfe, 1998a], the biological pathways are argued to be limited to three or four [Palmer, 1999]. Interestingly, three of the suggested neural pathways usually coincide each with one psychological feature channel, namely motion, color, and depth, whereas there are several psychological feature channels concerning form processing: there are feature maps for line curvature, line tilt or misalignment, terminators, and closure. Since newer findings suggest that there is no separate form pathway but many cells are responsible for edge detection as well as for color processing [Gegenfurtner, 2003], the psychological feature channels seem to correspond to several brain areas.

Center-Surround Mechanisms

The center-surround mechanisms that are used in most computational models of attention and in several psychological ones to determine the feature contrast regarding intensity or color have their neuro-physiological correlates on many different places in the brain: already the ganglion cells in the retina are separated into on-center and off-center cells. Later, cells in the LGN, V1, and the extrastriate cortex continue in responding to contrasts with these mechanisms.

Worth to mention is that some computational models combine the center-surround differences for on-off and for off-on instead of computing both [Itti et al., 1998, Ouerhani et al., 2004]. This is not only contrary to the processing in the human brain, it also leads to problems: several pop-out effects are not achieved and top-down guidance for particular feature types is not possible. We discuss this in detail in section 4.1.1 (page 59).

Color Perception

As mentioned before, the perception and processing of color starts in the retina with different types of photoreceptors. There are three types of receptors with preferences for the colors red, green, and blue. Later, the processing is extended from this trichromatic architecture to the opponent processing with the color opponencies red-green and blue-yellow.

Psychological models often do not touch the question of how the color feature is processed in detail and if they do they usually focus on a three-color or double opponency approach but do not consider both. Computational models usually take RGB images as input. This correlates to the three-cone system in the retina. The further computation of colors differs strongly in different systems. Most use directly the RGB input whereas some first convert the image to a different color space. Most systems consider the red-green and blue-yellow opponency, but often it is not considered that there are separated mechanisms for red-green and for green-red as well as for blue-yellow and yellow-blue. Instead, the computation is combined, what leads to problems in combination with the center-surround mechanisms concerning several pop-out effects and top-down guidance for particular feature types (see section 4.1.1, page 59 for details).

The Saliency Map

Until recently, the opinions on whether there is a "saliency map" in the brain that collects the saliencies of the feature channels and directs the focus of attention were highly controversial. Several groups believed in such a saliency map, whereas others declined this view. Recently, there is increasing evidence that there is a structure in the brain representing a retinotopic saliency map that guides exploratory eye movements and is influenced by bottom-up as well as by top-down cues. As mentioned before, the opinions on which brain area fulfills this part are controversial. Candidates are the FEF [Bichot, 2001], LIP [Gottlieb et al., 1998], SC [Findlay and Walker, 1999], and, most recently, V4 [Mazer and Gallant, 2003].

It remains to mention that the organization of such a neurological "saliency map" is different from the saliency maps in most psychological and computational models. In the brain, this map is rather a collection of neurons, each with its own specialized behavior, than a map with the same behavior for each element.

Bottom-Up Versus Top-Down

Although there is agreement that top-down cues play an important role in the processing of visual information and it is known that there are numerous connections from higher brain areas to the areas of basic processing, the details of these processes are still not known at all. As mentioned before, in [Corbetta and Shulman, 2002] the authors claim that two independent but interacting brain areas are associated with the two attentional mechanisms, which interact during normal human perception. The areas involved in top-down biasing are as per [Kastner and Ungerleider, 2001] the superior parietal lobule (SPL), the frontal eye fields (FEF), and the supplementary eye field (SEF), and, less consistently, areas in the inferior parietal lobule (IPL), the lateral prefrontal cortex in the region of the middle frontal gyrus (MFG), and the anterior cingulate cortex. However, which part fulfills which task and how these areas interact is still not known.

Most psychological and computational models focus on bottom-up processing since this part is better investigated and, for the computational systems, easier to realize. Some existing models which include top-down information weight the features with target-specific weights, some influence only the feature dimensions, and some influence the processing not until the saliency map that means they consider those regions that are salient in this map and are also task-relevant. The latter approaches are far from the biological analogue since in the brain top-down cues influence all parts of the processing down to early feature computations. A detailed, well evaluated system including top-down cues does not exist currently.

2.5 Discussion

In this chapter, we have reviewed the background that is important in the field of visual attention. We introduced several notations that are relevant in this field, for example, the distinction of *overt* and *covert attention* as well as *bottom-up* and *top-down influences*. The psychophysical paradigm of visual search was introduced and explained in detail. We furthermore sketched the processing flow of visual information in the human brain and discussed which processes and brain areas are involved in the attentional mechanisms. Then, we have introduced several psychophysical models of visual attention, ahead the Feature Integration Theory by Treisman and the Guided Search model by Wolfe. Finally, we related these topics by discussing which biological processes correlate to which mechanisms in current attention models.

This chapter shows that the research on visual attention is a highly interdisciplinary field. The different disciplines attack the problem from different sides: the psychologists regard the brain as a black box. In various experiments, they investigate human behavior on different tasks and try to conclude from the outcome of the experiments on the content of the black box.

The result are usually psychophysical theories or models. The neuro-biologists instead take a view directly into the brain. With new techniques like functional Magnetic Resonance Imaging (fMRI) it is visualized which brain areas are active under certain conditions. Again another practice is pursued by the computer scientists: they usually take over what they consider useful from psychological and biological findings and combine this with technical methods to build improved systems for computer vision or robotics applications.

In the last years, the different disciplines have highly profited from each other. Psychologists refer to neuro-biological findings to improve their attention models and neuro-biologists consider psychological experiments to interpret their data. Additionally, more and more psychologists start to implement their models computationally to verify if the behavior of the systems on example scenes equals human perception. These findings help to improve the understanding of the mechanisms and eventually lead to improved attention systems. The further the theory on visual attention proceeds, the better get also the computational systems and the more useful they are in applications in computer vision and robotics.

3

State of the Art
of Computational Attention Systems

The increased interest on research on visual attention together with the increased power of computers and the resulting ability to realize complex computer vision systems has led to a wide variety of computational systems on visual attention. In this chapter, we will review the most influential work in this field. We already considered models of visual attention in the previous chapter. Although several of them are also implemented computationally, their focus is on the psychological aspect of visual attention more than on the technical aspect: the models of the previous chapter try to explain and better understand human perception whereas the systems in this chapter usually have the aim to improve vision systems for applications in computer vision and robotics. Of course, there is an overlap of the objectives and there are psychological models that might be useful in computational applications and technical systems well suited to explain psychophysical data.

In this chapter, we will first introduce several of the most important computational systems on visual attention (section 3.1). Then, we discuss several characteristics that distinguish the different approaches, for example which features are implemented or whether top-down cues are considered (section 3.2). Next, we present several applications of attentional systems in computer vision and robotics in section 3.3 and finally we conclude and discuss the limitations of current approaches (section 3.4).

3.1 Computational Models of Visual Attention

In this section, we will introduce some of the most important computational attention systems, especially those with the highest impact on our work. We start be introducing the model of Koch & Ullman, which laid the theoretical basis for many current attention systems [Koch and Ullman, 1985]. Next, we describe the system of Milanese, since it was one of the first implementations of an attention model and introduced several useful mechanisms that were later adopted by other approaches [Milanese, 1993]. Then, one of the currently

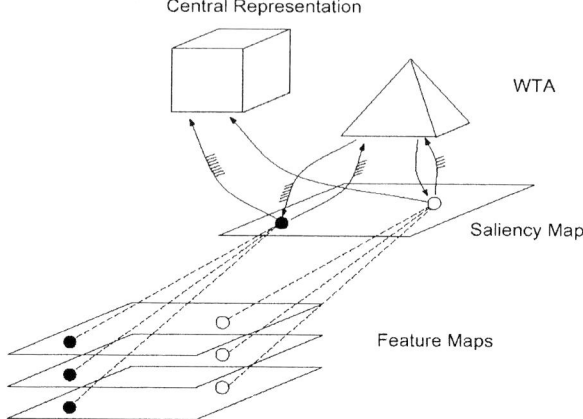

Fig. 3.1. The Koch-Ullman model. Different features are computed in parallel and their conspicuities are represented in several *feature maps*. A central *saliency map* combines the saliencies of the features and a *winner take all network (WTA)* determines the most salient location. This region is routed to the *central representation* where complex processing takes place (Fig. reprinted with permission from [Koch and Ullman, 1985]. ©1985 Springer)

best-known attention systems is presented: the *Neuromorphic Vision Toolkit (NVT)* of Itti et al. [Itti et al., 1998]. It will be described in some detail since it had the greatest impact on our work. Worth mentioning in this context is a derivative of the NVT that includes top-down information on target objects [Navalpakkam et al., 2005]. Another system that is able to cope with top-down information is the one of Hamker [Hamker, 2005]. After describing these attention systems explicitly, we mention in section 3.1.5 several additional approaches that emphasize other important aspects and are worth mentioning.

3.1.1 Koch & Ullman

The first approach for a computational architecture of visual attention was introduced by Koch and Ullman [Koch and Ullman, 1985] (see Fig. 3.1). When it was first published, the model was not yet implemented, but it provided the algorithmic reasoning serving as a foundation for later implementations and for many current computational models of visual attention. The idea is that several features are computed in parallel and their conspicuities are collected in a *saliency map*. A *Winner-Take-All network (WTA)* determines the most salient region in this map, which is finally routed to a *central representation*. Here, complex processing takes place restricted to the region of interest.

The model is based on the *Feature Integration Theory* by Treisman [Treisman and Gelade, 1980] (cf. chapter 2.3.1): the idea of feature maps that represent in parallel different features as well as the idea of a central map of attention — Treisman's *master map of location* — are adopted. The saliency computations are also influenced by rules called *proximity* and *similarity preferences*, which favor regions that are close or similar to the last focused region. However, newer findings claim that distance has no effect on attentional shifts, that means there is no proximity effect [Remington and Pierce, 1984, Kröse and Julesz, 1989].

An important contribution of Koch and Ullman's work is the WTA network — a neural network that determines the most salient region in a topographical map — and a detailed description of its implementation. It may be noted that the WTA network shows how the selection of a maximum is implementable by neural networks, that means by single units which are only locally connected. This approach is strongly biological motivated and shows how such a mechanism might be realized in the human brain. However, for a technical system a WTA is certainly an overhead since there are much easier ways to compute a maximum from a saliency map. Nevertheless, many computational attention systems take over the idea of a WTA.

After selecting the most salient region by the WTA, this region is routed into a *central representation* which at any instant contains only the properties of a single location in the visual scene. Due to this routing, the approach is also referred to as *selective routing model*. How the routing is performed and what happens with the information in the central representation is not mentioned; the idea is that more complex vision tasks are restricted to the selected information. Finally, the authors suggest a mechanism for inhibiting the selected region causing an automatic shift towards the next most conspicuous location *(inhibition of return (IOR))*.

The idea of a central representation in this form is hardly plausible from a biologically point of view: simple and complex processing of visual information in the brain is thought to be more intertwined than suggested by this model. But from a computational point of view the method is suggestive since it enables a modular assembling of different systems: an attentional system for the detection of regions of interest and a recognition system for the detailed investigation of these regions.

The proposed architecture is merely bottom-up; it is not discussed how top-down influences from higher brain areas may contribute to the selection of salient regions.

3.1.2 Milanese

One of the earliest implementations of a visual attention system was introduced by Milanese [Milanese, 1993, Milanese et al., 1994]. It is based on the Koch-Ullman model [Koch and Ullman, 1985] and uses filter operations for the computation of the feature maps. Hence, it is one of the first in the group of *filter-based models*. These models are especially well-suited to be applied to real-world scenes since the filter operations — used frequently in computer vision — provide useful tools for the efficient detection of scene properties like contrasts or oriented edges.

The idea of the feature maps and the saliency map was taken over from the Koch-Ullman model. As features, Milanese considers two color opponencies — red-green and blue-yellow —, 16 different orientations, local curvature and, if no color information is available, intensity. To compute the feature-specific saliency, he proposes a *conspicuity operator* which compares the local values of the feature maps to their surround. This operator is motivated from the on-off and off-on cells in the cortex and is also a common technique for detecting contrasts in images; it is usually referred to as *center-surround mechanism* or *center-surround difference*. The resulting contrasts were collected in so called *conspicuity maps*, a term that was since then frequently used to denote feature-dependent saliency.

The conspicuity maps are integrated into the saliency map by a relaxation process that identifies a small number of convex regions of interest. The output of the system is the saliency map that shows a few regions of interest. A process determining the order in which to select regions from this map is not mentioned. A drawback of the system is its high computational complexity that results from the many filter operations on different scales and by the relaxation process which, as per Milanese, usually requires about a dozen iterations. Although this drawback is nowadays no longer as significant as when the system was developed, the approach is still too computationally demanding for real-world applications.

In a derivative [Milanese et al., 1994], Milanese includes top-down information from an object recognition system realized by *distributed associative memories (DAMs)*. The idea is that object recognition is applied to a small number of regions of interest that are provided by the bottom-up attention system. The results of the object recognition are displayed in a top-down map which highlights the regions of recognized objects. This map competes with the conspicuity maps for saliency resulting in a saliency map combining bottom-up and top-down cues. The effect is that known objects appear more salient than unknown ones. It may be doubted if this is consistent with human vision, on the contrary, humans tend to pay more attention to unknown objects [Wang et al., 1994]. Nevertheless, for a technical system this might be an interesting approach, the more so as it is possible to provide the DAM only with a single object and thus highlight this object in a scene. This would correspond to visual search. Not mentioned is if there is an advantage of this system over pure object recognition.

Note that the top-down information only influences the conspicuity maps (feature dimensions) and not the feature maps (feature types). Therefore, it is not possible to strengthen properties like "red" or "vertical". Furthermore, the system depends strongly on the object recognition system. It is not able to learn the features of an object independently. Nevertheless, the system provides an interesting approach and has set benchmarks for several techniques which are used in computational attention models until today. Unfortunately, this promising system was not further developed since 1994.

3.1.3 Itti et al.

One of the currently best known attention systems is the *Neuromorphic Vision Toolkit (NVT)*, a derivative of the Koch-Ullman model [Koch and Ullman, 1985], that is steadily kept up to date by the group around Laurent Itti [Itti et al., 1998,Itti and Koch, 2001a,Miau et al., 2001,Itti and Koch, 2001b,Navalpakkam et al., 2005]. Their model as well as their implementation serve as a basis for many research groups; one reason for this is the good documentation and the availability of the source code for download, allowing other researchers to experiment and further develop the system [URL, 05].

Fig. 3.2 shows the basic structure of the model. The ideas of the feature maps, the saliency map, the WTA and the IOR were adopted from the Koch-Ullman Model, the approaches of using linear filters for the computation of the features, of determining contrasts by center-surround differences and the idea of the conspicuity maps were probably adopted from Milanese [Milanese, 1993]. The main contributions of this work are detailed elaborations on the realization of theoretical concepts, a concrete implementation of the system and the application to artificial and real-world scenes. The authors describe in detail how the feature maps for intensity, orientation, and color are computed: all computations are performed on *image pyramids*, *Image pyramid* a common technique in computer vision that enables the detection of features on different scales. Additionally, they propose a weighting function for the weighted combination of the different feature maps by promoting maps with few peaks and suppressing those with many ones. This technique is computationally much faster than the relaxation process of Milanese and yields good results. Since the suggested weighting function still suffered from several drawbacks, they introduced an improved procedure in [Itti and Koch, 2001b].

The system contains several details that were chosen for efficiency reasons or because they represent a straight-forward solution to complex requirements. This approach may lead to some problems and inaccurate results in several cases. For example, the center-surround mechanism is realized by the subtraction of different scales of the image pyramid, a method that is fast but not very precise (cf. page 61). Then, the conspicuity of the feature intensity is collected in a single intensity map, although neuro-biological findings show that there are cells both for on-off and for off-on contrasts [Palmer, 1999] and psychological work suggests considering separate detectors for darker and lighter contrasts [Treisman, 1993]. This simplification leads to some non-plausible results in certain pop-out experiments and in the top-down guidance of attention (cf. page 60). The same is true for the computation of the color-opponency maps: one red-green and one blue-yellow map are computed instead considering red-green as well as green-red and blue-yellow as well as yellow-blue contrasts separately. Furthermore, the chosen color space RGB represents colors

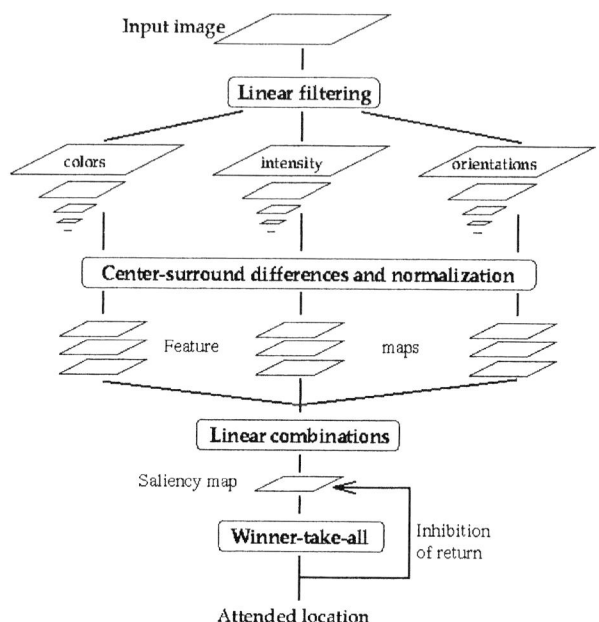

Fig. 3.2. Model of the *Neuromorphic Vision Toolkit (NVT)* by Itti et al. From an input image, three features are computed: color, intensity, and orientation. For each feature, an *image pyramid* is built to enable computations on different scales. *Center-surround mechanisms* determine the conspicuities concerning the features which are collected in a *central saliency map*. A *winner take all network* determines the most salient location in this map which yields the focus of attention. *Inhibition of return* inhibits this region in the saliency map and enables the computation of the next focus (Fig. reprinted with permission from [Itti et al., 1998]. ©1998 IEEE)

differently to human perception, which seems not appropriate for a system simulating human behavior and leads to implausible results, too. Although these are details, considering them in the implementation results in significant improvements in performance as will be shown in this work.

Some of these drawbacks were already pointed out by Draper and Lionelle [Draper and Lionelle, 2003] who showed that the NVT lacks robustness according to 2D similarity transformations like translations, rotations, and reflections. They point out that these drawbacks result from weaknesses in implementation rather than from the design of the model itself. To overcome these drawbacks, they introduced an improved version of the system, SAFE, which shows several differences and is more stable with respect to geometric transformations. It may be noted, that although these invariances are important for an object recognition system — the task Draper has in mind — they are not obviously required and maybe not even wanted for a system that aims at simulating human perception since usually human eye movements are not invariant to these transformations, too. Nevertheless, it should be guaranteed that the computations are as correct as possible and that variances result only from the model and not from its implementation. On the other hand, if it is desired to achieve fast computations, time needs to be traded off against precision.

To evaluate the quality of the NVT, a comparison with human behavior was performed in [Parkhurst et al., 2002]. The authors compared how the saliency computed by the system matched with human fixations on the same scenes and found a significant coherence which was highest for the initial fixation. They also found that the coherence was dependent on the kind of scene: for fractals it was higher than for natural scenes. This was explained by the influence of top-down cues in the human processing of natural scenes, an aspect left out in the NVT.

Miau at al. investigated the combination of the NVT with object recognition, considering in [Miau and Itti, 2001, Miau et al., 2001] the simple biologically plausible recognition system HMAX and in [Miau et al., 2001] the recognition with support vector machines. Walther et al. continued these investigations, starting in [Walther et al., 2002] also with a combination with the HMAX model. In a current approach [Walther et al., 2004], they combine the system with the well-known recognition approach of Lowe [Lowe, 2004] and show how the detection results are improved by concentrating on regions of interest.

A test platform for the attention system — the robot platform *Beobot* — was presented in [Chung et al., 2002, Itti, 2002, Itti, 2003]. In [Itti, 2002], it was shown how the processing can be distributed among different CPUs enabling a fast, parallel computation.

Navalpakkam

The NVT in its basic version does concentrate on computing bottom-up attention. The need for top-down influences is mentioned but not realized. In a recent approach, Navalpakkam and Itti introduce a derivative of their bottom-up model which is able to deal with top-down cues [Navalpakkam et al., 2005]. The idea is to learn feature values of a target from a training image in which the target is indicated by a binary mask. Considering the target region as well as a region in the close surrounding — considering 9 locations from a 3×3 grid of fixed size centered at the salient location — the system learns the feature values from the different feature maps on different scales. This yields a 42 component feature vector (red/green, blue/yellow, intensity, and 4 orientations, each on 6 scales). However, it may be doubted if it is useful to learn the scale of a target since during visual search the target should be detected on different scales. During object detection, this feature vector is used to bias the feature maps by multiplying each map with the corresponding weight.

Thereby, exciting and inhibiting as well as bottom-up and top-down cues are mixed and directly fused into the resulting saliency map.

One difficulty with this approach is that it is not clear how bottom-up and top-down cues compete. Desirable for a technical system would be the possibility to adapt the strength of the respective influence according to the state of the system, similar to the approach of Milanese, that means a high or even exclusive concentration to the target's features in one case (task-oriented system state) and a higher influence of diverting bottom-up cues in another case (curious, explorative system state). Additionally, since there is evidence that two distinct brain areas are associated with bottom-up and top-down mechanisms in human perception [Corbetta and Shulman, 2002] (cf. chapter 2), it might be useful to separate the processing also in a computational system.

Unfortunately, a detailed analysis of the quality of the detection has not yet been published. Instead, the results in [Navalpakkam et al., 2005] concentrate on showing that the system detects a target faster when operating in top-down mode than the original bottom-up system. Also of interest would be investigations on how many fixations are needed in average in different visual search tasks and on the robustness of the system concerning changes in viewpoint and illumination. In chapter 5.4.5, we compare our attention system VOCUS in detail with the NVT, pointing out the differences of the models and showing results of comparative experiments.

So far, we have commented only on the aspects of Navalpakkam's approach that regard the main contributions of this monograph and therefore are of most interest here. However, it shall be mentioned that the system has several further aspects, only partially realized at the moment, which are interesting and promising. For example, the knowledge base in which the objects are stored is organized as a graph with entities as vertices and their relationships as edges. An object may be related to another for example by being similar or by being a part of the other object. This information might help in visual search: for example if a hand shall be found and a finger is detected, the knowledge that a finger is a part of a hand implies that the hand has been found.

Another interesting aspect is the idea of extending the model by additional information on the scene by computing the gist and the layout of the scene according to the psychological triadic architecture presented in [Rensink, 2002]. This is not yet realized but is, as per [Navalpakkam et al., 2005], subject for future work.

3.1.4 Hamker

The attention system of Hamker aims mainly at modeling the visual attention mechanism of the human brain [Hamker, 1998, Hamker, 2000, Hamker, 2005]. Its objective is more on explaining human visual perception and gaining insight into its functioning than on providing a technical system. Nevertheless, this approach is discussed here and not in the previous chapter since it is based on current computer models [Koch and Ullman, 1985, Itti et al., 1998] and since it is often presented in the computer vision community. Hamker's model, shown in Fig. 3.3, shares several aspects with the architecture of Itti: he computes contrasts for several features — intensity, orientation, red-green, blue-yellow and additionally spatial resolution — and combines them in feature-conspicuity maps. The conspicuities of these maps are combined in a *perceptual map* that corresponds to the common saliency map. In earlier approaches, Hamker negates the existence of a saliency map in the human brain. But since new findings in neuro-science claim that there is a region in the brain fulfilling the function of collecting salient cues [Mazer and Gallant, 2003], he adopted his system accordingly [Hamker, 2004, Hamker, 2005].

In addition to this bottom-up behavior, the system belongs to the few existing ones that consider top-down influences. It is able to learn a target, that means it remembers the feature values of a presented stimulus. This stimulus is usually presented on a black background; hence, the system concentrates on the target's features but is not able to consider the background of the scene. This means a waste of important information since it is not possible to favor features that distinguish a target well from its background. When searching for a red, vertical bar among red, horizontal ones, the color red is not relevant; in this case, it would be useful to concentrate on orientation. To achieve a stable and robust system behavior, it would be necessary to learn the features of a target from several training images.

After determining the target's features, they are memorized in a *working memory*. From here, they influence the conspicuity of the features in a presented test scene and thus merge the conspicuities of bottom-up and top-down cues. It may be noted that the target information influences the processing of the conspicuity maps, but not the earlier processing of the feature maps. Bottom-up and top-down cues together determine the saliency in the perceptual map. A problem with this approach might be that it is not clear how bottom-up and top-down cues compete. As for the NVT, it might be useful to introduce a factor as the one by Milanese that allows the adaption of the influence of bottom-up and top-down cues.

Hamker distinguishes between covert and overt shifts of attention, the latter corresponding to eye movements. The covert focus of attention is directed to the most salient region in the perceptual map. Whether this region is also a candidate for an eye movement is determined by so called *match detection units* that compare the encoded pattern with the target template. If these patterns are similar, an eye movement is initiated towards this region and the target is said to be detected. The match detection units are an interesting approach in this system. However, it may be noted that this is a very rough kind of object recognition which is only based on a few simple features and does not consider spatial configuration of features. It also recognizes only patterns that are presented with the same orientation as during learning. Therefore, although at the moment this kind of recognition seems to be not sufficient in

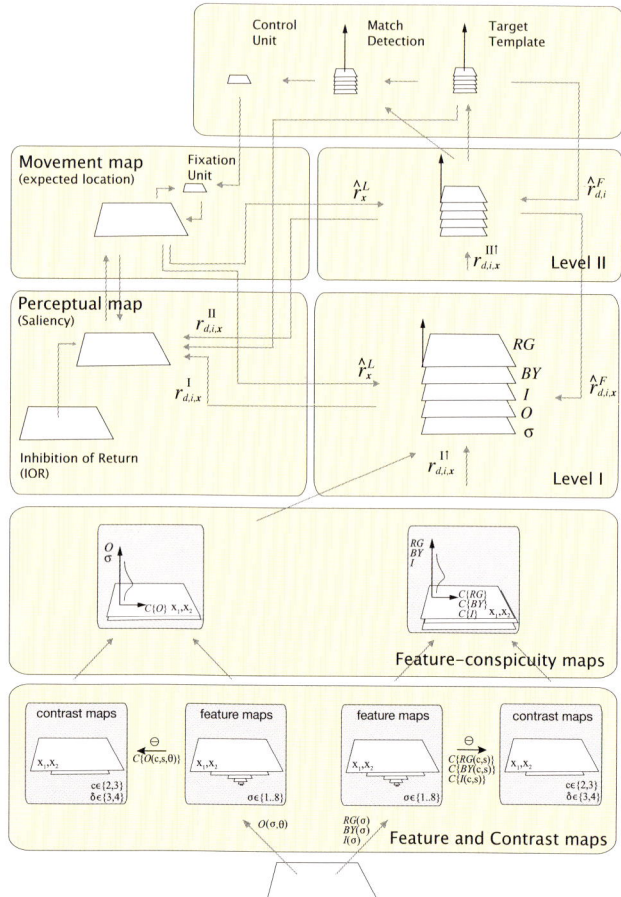

Fig. 3.3. The attention system of Hamker. From the input image, several feature and contrast maps are computed and fused into feature-conspicuity maps and finally into the perceptual map. Additionally, target information influences the processing. Match detection units determine whether a salient region in the perceptual map is a candidate for an eye movement. See text for details (Fig. reprinted from [Hamker, 2005], ©2005, with permission from Elsevier)

detection and false detection rates for a technical system, it is nevertheless an interesting approach and seems to be a step into the right direction.

3.1.5 Additional Attention Systems

Beside the mentioned attention models, there is a wide variety of models in the literature. Many differ only in minor changes from the already described

Fig. 3.4. The attentional shifts performed by the system of Sun and Fisher. First, the house and then the boat are focused on a coarse resolution (left, blue arrows). Second, the boat region is zoomed in and is investigated in more detail, resulting in fixations on the people (red arrows) (Fig. reprinted from [Sun and Fisher, 2003], ©2003, with permission from Elsevier)

approaches, for example, they consider additional features. Here, we mention some of the more important approaches in the field.

Sun and Fisher present in [Sun and Fisher, 2003] a sophisticated approach to hierarchical object-based selection of regions of interest. Regions of interest are computed on different scales, first on a coarse scale and then, if the region is sufficiently interesting, it is investigated on a finer scale. This yields foci of attention of different extents, for example in a landscape image showing a lake, a boat is focused on a coarse scale, then the boat region is further investigated on a finer scale and the people in the boat are focused one after the other (see Fig. 3.4).

Backer presents an interesting model of attention with two selection stages [Backer, 2004, Backer et al., 2001]. The first stage resembles standard architectures like [Koch and Ullman, 1985], but the result is not a single focus but a small number, usually 4, of salient locations. In the second selection stage, one of these locations is selected and yields a single focus of attention. The model explains some of the more unregarded experimental data on multiple object tracking and object-based inhibition of return.

The attention model of Ouerhani et al. is implemented on a highly parallel architecture that allows to meet real-time requirements [Ouerhani, 2003, Ouerhani and Hügli, 2003c]. They have also integrated the rarely considered features depth and motion into their system [Ouerhani and Hügli, 2000, Ouerhani

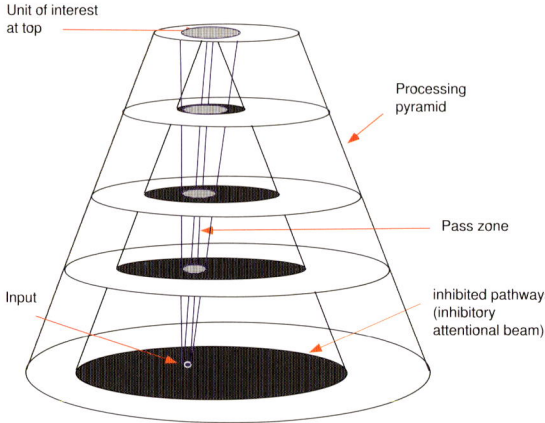

Fig. 3.5. The *inhibitory attentional beam* of Tsotsos et al. The selection process requires two traversals of the pyramid: first, the input traverses the pyramid in a feedforward manner. Second, the hierarchy of WTA processes is activated in a top-down manner to localize the strongest item in each layer while pruning parts of the pyramid that do not contribute to the most salient item (Fig. kindly provided by J. Tsotsos)

and Hügli, 2003b]. Another model which integrates these features is presented by the group of Eklundh [Maki et al., 1996, Maki et al., 2000].

Beside the mentioned models that are based on feature computations with linear filters, there is another important class of attention models: the *connectionist models*. These models process the input data mainly with neural networks. Usually, these models claim to be more biologically plausible than the filter models. Since this approach differs strongly from the approach presented in this thesis, these models will be mentioned only briefly here.

One of the most famous models in the field of *connectionist models* is the *selective tuning model* of visual attention by Tsotsos et al. [Tsotsos, 1990, Tsotsos, 1993, Tsotsos et al., 1995, Tsotsos et al., 2005]. It consists of a pyramidal architecture with an *inhibitory beam* (see Fig. 3.5). This beam is rooted at the selected item at the top of the hierarchy and has a *pass zone* and an *inhibit zone*. The pass zone is the pathway that is selected for further processing; in the inhibit zone, all locations are inhibited that do not belong to the selected item. It is also possible to include target-specific top-down cues into the processing. This is done by either inhibiting all regions with features different from the target features or regions of a specified location. Additional excitation of target features as proposed by [Navalpakkam et al., 2004] is not considered. The model has been implemented for several features, for example luminance, orientation, or color opponency [Tsotsos et al., 1995], and currently in a sophisticated approach also for motion, considering even the direction of movements [Tsotsos et al., 2005]. Note that in each version only one feature dimension is processed; the binding of several feature dimensions has not yet been considered but is, as per Tsotsos, subject for future work.

An unusual adaptation of Tsotsos's model is provided in [Ramström and Christensen, 2002]: the distributed control of the attention system is performed by game theory concepts. The nodes of the pyramid are subject to trading on a market, the features are the goods, rare goods are expensive (the features are salient), and the outcome of the trading represents the saliency.

Another model based on neural networks is the *FeatureGate* Model described in [Cave, 1999]. Beside bottom-up cues it also considers top-down cues by comparing pixel values with the values of a target object; but since the operations only work on single pixels and so are highly sensitive to noise, it seems to be not applicable to real-world scenes.

3.2 Characteristics of Attention Systems

After introducing some of the most influential computational attention systems, we summarize in this section several characteristics of attention systems that distinguish the respective approaches. We start by distinguishing the objectives of the systems concerning psychological or technical issues and continue by discussing which features are computed in the different approaches. Next, we distinguish connectionist and filter models and finally, we examine what kinds of top-down influences exist and how they are realized in several computational attention systems.

3.2.1 Objective

Computational attention systems might be categorized by their objective. As already mentioned, the systems may be firstly designed to simulate and understand human perception or, secondly, to technically improve vision systems. Although systems of both classes may be very similar, this distinction usually has a high impact on the visibility of the systems: whereas the first class of systems is usually well known by the psychological and cognitive science community, the latter class is more familiar in areas like computer vision and robotics. Since each side may highly profit from the knowledge of the other, a better interchange between communities would be desirable.

3.2.2 The Choice of Features

Many computational attention systems focus on the computation of mainly three features: intensity, orientation, and color [Itti et al., 1998, Draper and Lionelle, 2003, Sun and Fisher, 2003, Ramström and Christensen, 2004]. Reasons for this choice are that these features belong to the basic features proposed in psychological and biological work [Treisman, 1993, Wolfe, 1994, Palmer, 1999] and that they are relatively easy to compute. A special case of color computation is the separate computation of skin color [Rae, 2000, Heidemann et al., 2004, Lee et al., 2003]. This is often useful if faces or hand gestures have to be detected. Other features that are considered are for example curvature [Milanese, 1993], spatial resolution [Hamker, 2005], optical flow [Tsotsos et al., 1995, Vijayakumar et al., 2001], or corners [Ouerhani and Hügli, 2004, Fraundorfer and Bischof, 2003, Heidemann et al., 2004]. Several systems compute also higher level features that use approved techniques of computer vision to extract useful image information. Examples for such features are entropy [Heidemann et al., 2004], ellipses [Lee et al., 2003], eccentricity [Backer et al., 2001], or symmetry [Backer et al., 2001, Heidemann et al., 2004, Lee et al., 2003].

Motion is definitely an important feature in human perception (there is a large brain area (MT) mainly concerned with processing motion!). Nevertheless, it is rarely considered in computational models, probably because of the difficulties arising when dealing with dynamics. Some approaches that consider motion as a feature are [Backer and Mertsching, 2000, Maki et al., 2000, Ouerhani and Hügli, 2003b, Itti, 2002, Rae, 2000]. All of these approaches only implement a very simple kind of motion detection: usually, two subsequent images in a video stream are subtracted and the difference codes the feature conspicuity. The most sophisticated approach concerning motion was recently proposed in [Tsotsos et al., 2005]. This approach is highly biologically motivated, it considers the direction of movements, and processes motion on several levels similar to the processing in the brain regions V1, MT, and MST.

Another important aspect in human perception that is rarely considered is depth. In the literature it is not clear whether depth is simply a feature or something else; definitely, it has some unusual properties distinguishing it from other features: if one of the dimensions in a conjunctive search is depth, a second feature can be searched in parallel [Nakayama and Silverman, 1986], a property that does not exist for the other features. Computing depth for an attention system is usually solved with stereo vision [Backer and Mertsching, 2000, Maki et al., 2000]. The data obtained from stereo vision has the drawback that it is usually not very accurate and contains large regions without depth information. Another approach is to use special 3D sensors, as for example the lately appearing 3D cameras [Ouerhani and Hügli, 2000].

Finally, it may be noted that considering more features usually results in more accurate and biologically plausible detection results but also reduces the speed since the parallel architectures are usually implemented sequentially. Furthermore, the concept of the models is the same regardless of the number of features, therefore, most effects can already be shown with a small number of features.

3.2.3 Connectionist Versus Filter Models

As mentioned before, there is a distinction between connectionist models that are based on neural networks and filter models that use classical linear filters to compute features. Usually, the connectionist models claim to be more biologically plausible than the filter models since they have single units corresponding to neurons in the human brain, but it has to be noted that they are still a high abstraction from the processes in the brain. Usually, a single neuron is more complex than a complete computational system. Furthermore, also filter models may be strongly biologically motivated, as the system of Hamker shows [Hamker, 2005].

However, the advantage of connectionist models is that they are — at least theoretically — able to show a different behavior for each neuron whereas in filter models usually each pixel in a map is treated equally. In practice, treating each unit differently is usually too costly and so a group of units shows the same behavior. The advantage of filter models is that they may profit from approved techniques in computer vision and that they are especially well suited for the application to real-world images.

Examples of connectionist systems of visual attention are presented for instance in [Olshausen et al., 1993, Postma, 1994, Tsotsos et al., 1995, Baluja and Pomerleau, 1995, Cave, 1999]. As mentioned in chapter 2, many psychophysical models fall into this category, too, for example [Mozer, 1987, Phaf et al., 1990, Humphreys and Müller, 1993, Heinke et al., 2002]. Examples of linear filter systems of visual attention are presented for instance in [Milanese, 1993, Itti et al., 1998, Rae, 2000, Backer et al., 2001, Ouerhani, 2003, Sun and Fisher, 2003, Heidemann et al., 2004, Hamker, 2005].

3.2.4 Top-Down Cues

The distinction of bottom-up and top-down cues and their significance in human perception was already outlined in section 2.1.3. For a technical attention system, top-down cues are equally important: most systems are not only designed to detect bottom-up salient regions but there are goals to achieve and targets to detect. Although the importance of top-down cues is well known and even mentioned in many articles, most systems consider only bottom-up computations.

Before we discuss which systems consider top-down information, we will first distinguish between different kinds of top-down influences. Top-down information includes all kinds of information that exist at one moment in time concerning the mental state of the subject (or the inner state of the system) and knowledge of the outer world. This includes aspects like prior knowledge of the target, pre-knowledge of the scene or of the objects that might occur in the environment, but also emotions, desires, intentions, and motivations. The latter four aspects are hard to conceptualize and are not realized in any computer system we know about. The interaction of attention, emotions, motivations, and goals is discussed in [Balkenius, 2000, Balkenius, 2002], but in his computer simulation these aspects are not considered.

Top-down information that refers to knowledge of the outer world, that means of the background scene or of the objects that might occur, is considered in several systems. In these approaches, for example all objects of a data base that might occur in a scene are investigated in advance and their most discriminative regions are determined, i.e., the regions that distinguish an object best from all others in the data base [Fritz et al., 2004, Pessoa and Exel, 1999]. Another approach is to regard context information, that means searching for a person in a street scene is restricted to the street region and the sky region is ignored. The contextual information is obtained from past search experiences in similar environments [Oliva et al., 2003, Torralba, 2003].

The kind of top-down information that will be most relevant in this thesis is the prior knowledge of a target that is used to perform visual search. Systems regarding this kind of top-down information use knowledge of the target to influence the computation of the most salient region. This knowledge is usually learned in a preceding training phase but might in simpler approaches also be provided manually by the user.

In the existing systems, the target information influences the processing at different stages: some systems already influence the feature types (usually the feature maps) [Navalpakkam et al., 2005, Tsotsos et al., 1995], some systems influence the feature dimensions (usually the conspicuity maps) [Milanese et al., 1994, Hamker, 2005], and some influence the processing not before the computation of the saliency map [Rao et al., 2002, Lee et al., 2003, Navalpakkam and Itti, 2002]. The latter approach is a very simple one: the bottom-up saliency map is computed and the most salient regions are investigated for target similarity. It can be hardly called top-down influence of processing at all. Only targets that are most salient in a scene can be found with this approach. More elaborated is the tuning of the conspicuity maps, but biologically most plausible and also technically most useful is the approach to already bias the feature types as for example red or horizontal.

There are also different methods for influencing the maps with the target information. Some approaches inhibit the target-irrelevant regions [Tsotsos et al., 1995], whereas others prefer exciting target-relevant regions [Hamker, 2005, Navalpakkam and Itti, 2003]. New findings suggest that inhibition and excitation both play an important rule [Navalpakkam et al., 2004]; this is implemented in [Navalpakkam et al., 2005].

The processing of target-relevant top-down cues in computational attention systems is not yet well investigated. Even the systems that consider top-down cues are seldomly tested on natural scenes or only on hand-picked examples [Hamker, 2005]. The currently best tested system also including natural scenes is presented in [Navalpakkam et al., 2005]. Unfortunately, the quality of the detection results has not yet been published; the mentioned paper focuses on comparing the top-down approach with the previous bottom-up system (merely the improvement factor is indicated not the absolute detection results). Currently, there exists no complete, robust, and well investigated system of top-down visual attention which analyzes the influence of top-down cues systematically for different targets, with changing viewpoints, on different backgrounds, and under changing illumination conditions.

3.3 Applications in Computer Vision and Robotics

While psychological models of visual attention usually aim at describing and better understanding human perception, computational attention systems usually intend to improve technical systems. In this section, we discuss several application scenarios in the field of computer vision and robotics and introduce the approaches that currently exist in this field.

3.3.1 Object Recognition

Probably the most suggesting application of an attention system is object recognition since the two-stage approach of a preprocessing attention system and a classifying recognizer is adapted to human perception [Neisser, 1967]. It is worth mentioning that object recognition may be a subtask of more complex applications like object manipulation in robotics, which will be described later.

One example of a combination of an attentional front-end with a classifying object recognizer is shown in [Miau and Itti, 2001, Miau et al., 2001]. The recognizer is the biologically motivated system HMAX [Riesenhuber and Poggio, 1999]. Since this system focuses on simulating processes in human cortex, it is rather restricted in its capabilities and it is only possible to recognize simple artificial objects like circles or rectangles. In [Miau et al., 2001], the authors replace the HMAX system by a support vector machine algorithm to detect pedestrians in natural images. This approach is much more powerful with respect to the recognition rate but still computationally very expensive and lacks real-time abilities. Walther and colleagues combine in [Walther et al., 2004] an attention system with an object recognizer based on SIFT features [Lowe, 2004] and show that the recognition results are improved by the attentional front-end. In [Salah et al., 2002] an attention system is combined with neural networks and an observable Markov model to do handwritten digit recognition and face recognition. In [Ouerhani, 2003], an attention-based traffic sign recognition system is presented.

All of these systems rely only on bottom-up information and therefore on the assumption that the objects of interest are sufficiently salient by themselves. Non-salient objects are not detected and so they are missed. For some object classes like traffic signs which are intentionally designed salient, this works quite well; for other applications, top-down information would be needed to enable the system to focus on the desired objects.

It may also be mentioned that when combining object recognition with attention, the advantage over pure classification is usually the time saving and not the quality improvement: most classifiers show no improvement if restricted to a region of interest (an exception is the work of Walther et al. [Walther et al., 2004] since the Lowe detector improves if restricted to a region of interest). Since most attention systems are still rather slow and the recognition systems not powerful enough to deal with a wide variety of objects, the advantage of such a combination of attention and classification does usually not yet show of to its best. Currently, there is no existing approach that exhibits a time saving resulting from the combination of attention and classification. However, in future, with more powerful recognition systems and more complex requirements concerning vision systems, an attentional front-end is a promising approach.

A different view on attention for object recognition is presented in [Fritz et al., 2004]: an information-theoretic saliency measure is used to determine discriminative regions of interest in objects. The saliency measure is computed by the conditional entropy of estimated posteriors of the local appearance patterns. That means, regions of an object are considered as salient if they discriminate the object well from other objects in an object data base. A similar approach is presented in [Pessoa and Exel, 1999].

3.3.2 Image Compression

A new and interesting application scenario is presented in [Ouerhani et al., 2001]: *focused image compression*. Here, a color image compression method adaptively determines the number of bits to be allocated for coding image regions according to their saliency. Regions with high saliency have a higher reconstruction quality with respect to the rest of the image.

3.3.3 Image Matching

Image matching is the task to redetect a scene, or part of a scene, in a newly presented image. This is often done by matching relevant key points. An approach that uses foci of attention computed by a saliency operator for image matching is presented in [Fraundorfer and Bischof, 2003].

3.3.4 Image Segmentation

The automatic segmentation of images into regions usually deals with two major problems: first, setting the starting points for segmentation (seeds) and second, choosing the similarity criterion to segment regions (cf. appendix A.3). Ouerhani et al. present an approach that supports both aspects by visual attention [Ouerhani et al., 2002, Ouerhani and Hügli, 2003a]: the saliency spots of the attention system serve as natural candidates for the seeds and the homogeneity criterion is adapted according to the features that discriminate the region to be segmented from its surroundings.

3.3.5 Object Tracking

Tracking objects in dynamic environments is important in applications such as video surveillance or robotics. In [Ouerhani and Hügli, 2003b], the authors present an approach in which the salient spots are tracked over time; however, the tracking is only done by feature matching instead of using a proper tracking method as for example Kalman filters. In [Ouerhani and Hügli, 2004] the authors suggest to use this approach for robot localization. The localization itself has not yet been done.

3.3.6 Active Vision

Active vision represents the technical equivalent for overt attention by directing a camera to interesting scene regions and/or zooming these regions. The goal is to acquire data that is as suitable as possible to the current task and to reduce the processing complexity by actively guiding the sensors (usually the camera) to reasonable regions [Aloimonos et al., 1988]. In several cases, active vision is a subtask for applications like human-robot interaction and object manipulation, which will be discussed in the next sections.

In [Mertsching et al., 1999, Bollmann, 1999], the active vision system NAVIS is presented that uses an attention system to guide the gaze. It is evaluated on a fixed stereo camera head as well as on a mobile robot with a monocular camera head. In [Vijayakumar et al., 2001] an attention system is used to guide the gaze of a humanoid robot. The authors consider only one feature, visual flow, which enables the system to attend to moving objects. To simulate the different resolutions of the human eye, two cameras per eye are used: one wide-angle camera for peripheral vision and one narrow-angle camera for foveal vision. Other approaches which use attention systems to direct the gaze of an active vision system are described in [Clark and Ferrier, 1989] and [Driscoll et al., 1998].

3.3.7 Human-Robot Interaction

If robots shall interact with humans, it is important that both agree on a current object or region of interest. A computational attention system similar to the human one can help to focus on the same region. Breazeal introduces a robot that shall look at people or toys [Breazeal, 1999]. Although top-down information would be necessary to focus on an object relevant for a certain task, bottom-up information can be useful too if it is combined with other cues. For example, Heidemann et al. combine an attention system with a system that follows the direction of a pointing finger and so can adjust to the region that is pointed at [Heidemann et al., 2004]. In [Rae, 2000] this approach is used to guide a robot arm to an object and grasp it.

3.3.8 Object Manipulation in Robotics

A robot that has to grasp and manipulate objects first has to detect and possibly also to recognize the object. Attentional mechanisms can be used to support these tasks. For example, Tsotsos et al. present a robot for disabled children that detects toys by the help of attention, moves to a toy and grasps it [Tsotsos et al., 1998]. In another approach, Bollmann et al. present a robot that uses the active vision system NAVIS to play at dominoes [Bollmann et al., 1999]. The above mentioned approach of Rae in which a robot arm has to grasp an object a human has pointed at, falls also into this category [Rae, 2000].

3.3.9 Robot Navigation

In [Scheier and Egner, 1997] a mobile robot is presented that uses an attention system for navigation. The task was to approach large objects. Since larger objects have a higher saliency, only the regions with the highest saliency have to be approached. The task gives the impression to be rather artificially made up.

In [Baluja and Pomerleau, 1995,Baluja and Pomerleau, 1997], an attention system is used to support autonomous road following by highlighting relevant regions in a saliency map. These are obtained by computing the expectation of the contents of the inputs at the next time step.

3.3.10 Robot Localization

Another application scenario of an attention system in robotics is the detection of landmarks for localization. Especially in outdoor environments and open areas, the standard methods for localization like matching 2D laser range and sonar scans are likely to fail. Instead, localization by detection of visual landmarks with a known position can be used. Attentional mechanisms can facilitate the search of landmarks during operation by selecting interesting regions in the sensor data. By focusing on these regions and comparing the candidates with trained landmarks, the most probable location can be determined. A project that follows this approach is the ARK project [Nickerson et al., 1998]. It relies on hand-coded maps, including the locations of known static obstacles as well as the locations of natural visual landmarks.

As already mentioned, [Ouerhani and Hügli, 2004] suggest to use matching and tracking of salient regions for robot localization but a realization of the localization itself has not yet been done.

3.4 Discussion

In this chapter, we have introduced several of the best known computational systems of visual attention in the field of computer vision. Their objective is to profit from findings on human perception to improve technical computer vision systems. We first presented some of the most influential systems in detail; after we discussed several characteristics of current systems, for example the kind of features that are computed. Finally, we presented several application scenarios in computer vision and robotics in which attention systems are applied.

The modeling of visual attention is a wide field and it is hardly possible for one group to address all of the issues that arise. Therefore, each system emphasizes and specializes on a different aspect. However, there are aspects that are hardly considered due to costly realization or to missing evidence from the field of human perception. Let us summarize some of the limitations of current computational attention systems and some issues that are seldomly addressed.

First, features like depth and motion are seldomly considered in computational attention system. When changing from static 2D images to dynamical 3D applications, both provide useful information in natural environments. Second, there are few systems which integrate top-down influences and enable visual search. The few systems that do show hardly any evaluation of their approach and usually present only some isolated examples of the functionality of their system. A robust, well-evaluated approach does not yet exist. Third, since most systems focus on bottom-up computations, the evaluation of the systems is hard because there is usually no ground truth. The decision whether a computed focus of attention is reasonable, is usually left to the observer. Fourth, the computations usually focus on camera data although human attention operates for all senses. Especially in robotics, the consideration of additional sensors would be desirable. Finally, although there are several approaches that combine their attention system with object recognition, these approaches usually do not evaluate this combination and do not show its advantage. Neither the improvement in time performance nor a change in detection quality is discussed. Furthermore, since most systems operate merely in a bottom-up mode, the combination of top-down attention with object recognition has not yet been done. This results in recognition systems that are only able to recognize the most salient regions in a scene but not a target of current interest.

In the following chapters, we will present the computational attention system VOCUS that overcomes most of the discussed limitations of existing approaches.

4

The Visual Attention System VOCUS: Bottom-Up Part

In the previous chapter, we introduced several computational attention systems of the current state of the art and discussed their characteristics and limitations. In this and the following chapters, we present the new visual attention system VOCUS (Visual Object detection with a CompUtational attention System) which extends and outperforms the current approaches in several aspects, yielding an innovative, efficient, and robust system for detecting regions of interest. We start by introducing the bottom-up part of VOCUS that detects saliencies based merely on the image data in this chapter before we consider top-down influences in chapter 5.

The architecture of VOCUS shares the main concepts with the standard models of visual attention, especially with the model of [Koch and Ullman, 1985]. The implementation is roughly based on the *Neuromorphic Vision Toolkit (NVT)* [Itti et al., 1998], one of the best known attention systems currently (cf. section 3.1.3). However, there are several differences concerning implementation details as well as structural design components that yielded considerable improvements in performance.

We start in section 4.1 with the description of the system, emphasizing the differences to existing systems. In section 4.2, we continue with the presentation of our experiments and discuss several evaluation methods with reference to VOCUS. Finally, we discuss strengths and limitations of the approach in section 4.3.

4.1 System Description

The structure of the bottom-up model of visual attention is shown in Fig. 4.1. Before we go into the details of the system, we present a rough overview of VOCUS' structure. On the input image, three different *feature dimensions* (in the following simply called *features*) are computed: intensity, orientation, and color. For each dimension, the saliencies are computed on different scales and for different *feature types* (also called *feature characteristics*), e.g. red, green,

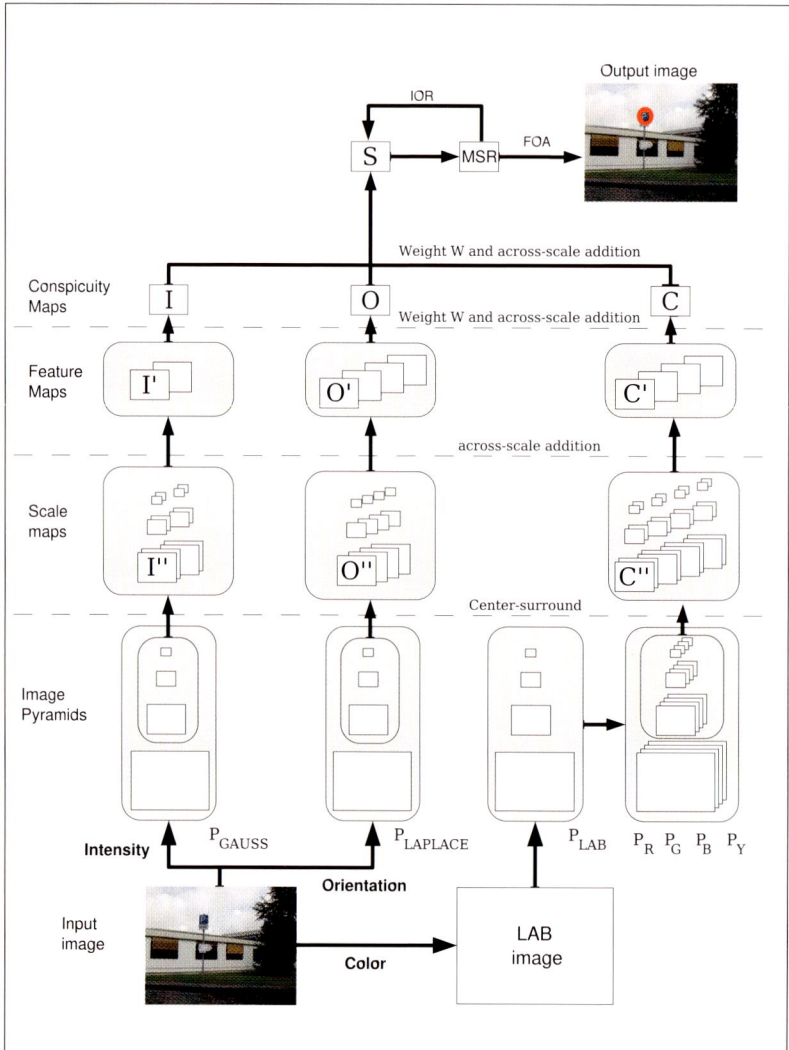

Fig. 4.1. The bottom-up attention system VOCUS. Saliencies according to the features intensity, orientation, and color are computed independently. First, *image pyramids* are computed. To create the color pyramids P_R, P_G, P_B, and P_Y, the input image is converted into the color space LAB and a color pyramid P_{LAB} is created. Second, *scale maps* I'', O'', and C'' are computed, representing saliencies on different scales and for different feature types. These maps are fused into the *feature maps* I', O', and C' which represent different feature types and these are combined to the *conspicuity maps* I, O, and C. Finally, the conspicuity maps are fused to a single *saliency map* S, with the degree of brightness proportional to the degree of saliency. From this map, the most salient region (MSR) is extracted and the focus of attention (FOA) is directed there (red ellipse). To enable the computation of the next FOA, inhibition of return (IOR) resets the selected region in the saliency map

blue, and yellow for the feature color. Thereafter, the maps are fused step by step, thereby strengthening important aspects and ignoring others.

For each feature, we first compute an *image pyramid* from which we compute *scale maps*. These represent saliencies on different scales for different feature types. The scale maps are fused into *feature maps* representing different feature types and these again are combined to *conspicuity maps*, one for each feature. Finally, the conspicuity maps are fused to a single *saliency map*, with the degree of brightness proportional to the degree of saliency. Altogether, 100 maps are computed (28 image pyramid maps, 48 scale maps, 10 feature maps, 3 conspicuity maps and 1 saliency map). From the saliency map, the most salient region (MSR) is extracted and the focus of attention (FOA) is directed there. If more than one FOA shall be computed, inhibition of return (IOR) resets the selected region in the saliency map and the next MSR is determined. These steps are repeated iteratively until enough foci are found. Usually, we stop the computation after 1, 5, 10, or 20 FOAs.

According to the standard attention model of [Koch and Ullman, 1985], we concentrate on the three features mentioned above since they belong to the basic features of human perception and are rather easy to compute. Of course, this can only approximate human behavior where many other features attract attention, e.g., size, curvature, and motion ([Treisman and Gormican, 1988], cf. chapter 2.3). Considering more features improves the quality but also slows down the system since the parallel organization of the model is usually implemented in a serial way. Nevertheless, the architecture of the system allows an easy extension to more features (cf. section 3.2.2).

The system architecture is presented as follows: we start in section 4.1.1 with the description of the feature computations. In section 4.1.2, we introduce a weighting function that enables the amplification of important maps and describe how the maps are fused. In 4.1.3, we finally show how the most salient region is computed and visualized. We illustrate the intermediate steps of the system consecutively using the example image of the foosball table of Fig. 4.2.

4.1.1 Feature Computations

VOCUS computes saliencies according to the features intensity, orientation, and color. To enable the detection of salient regions of different sizes, saliencies in the visual attention system are computed on several scales. Instead of rescaling the filters resulting in extremely time-consuming computations for large filters, the images are rescaled. This results in a so-called *image pyramid*, a standard method in computer vision (cf. appendix A.1.5). We compute an adapted image pyramid for each of the feature channels. In the following, we discuss the computation of the three feature dimensions successively.

The Feature Intensity

The channel for the feature intensity extracts regions with strong intensity contrasts from the input image. First, the color input image is converted into

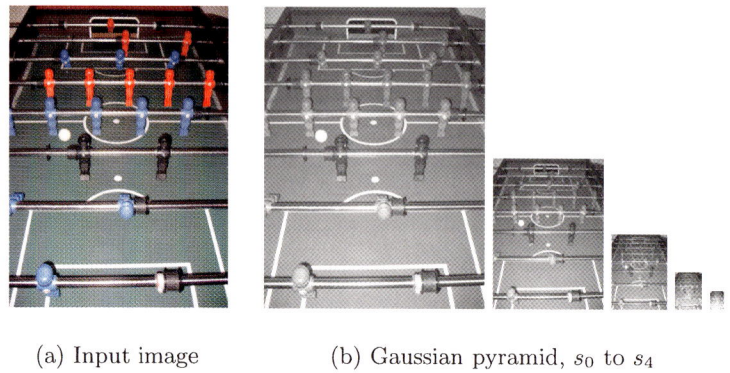

(a) Input image   (b) Gaussian pyramid, s_0 to s_4

Fig. 4.2. (a) the input image of a foosball table image, which serves as demonstration example throughout this chapter; **(b)** the derived Gaussian image pyramid

gray-scale. From the gray-scale image, a *Gaussian image pyramid* P_{Gauss} is computed by firstly applying a 3×3 Gaussian filter to the image resulting in a smoothed image (cf. appendix A.1.2). Secondly, the image is sub-sampled, i.e., every second pixel is taken. This results in an image of half the width and height of the original one. This strategy is repeated four times, resulting in an image pyramid with five different scales s_0 to s_4 (see Fig. 4.2, right). The following computations are all performed on the scales s_2 to s_4, i.e., on images smoothed at least two times. This makes the system robust to noise since no noise pixels occur in the smoothed images. The robustness to noise is shown in [Itti et al., 1998].

The intensity feature maps are created by *center-surround mechanisms*. These mechanisms are inspired by the ganglion cells in the visual receptive fields of the human visual system, which respond to intensity contrasts between a center region and its surround (cf. chapter 2.2). The cells are divided into two types: on-center cells respond excitatorily to light at the center and inhibitorily to light at the surround, whereas off-center cells respond inhibitorily to light at the center and excitatorily to light at the surround [Palmer, 1999].

In VOCUS, the center c is given by a pixel in one of the scales s_2 to s_4, the surround σ is determined by computing the average of the surrounding pixels for two different sizes of surrounds with a radius of 3 respectively 7 pixels. According to the human system, we determine two feature types for intensity: the on-center difference responding strongly to bright regions on a dark background, and the off-center difference responding strongly to dark regions on a bright background. This yields 12 intensity scale maps $I''_{i,s,\sigma}$ with $i \in \{(\text{on}), (\text{off})\}, s \in \{s_2, s_3, s_4\}, \sigma \in \{3, 7\}$. The center-surround algorithm for the computation of the intensity scale maps I'' is shown in Fig. 4.3, the intensity

> **center-surround(modus i, scale s, surround σ)**
> For each pixel $p_{x,y}$ of s with value $v(x,y)$
>   center $= v(x,y)$
>   For pixels with value v within image borders:
>   surround $=$ mean$(v(x-\sigma,y-\sigma),...,v(x+\sigma,y+\sigma))$
> $I''_{i,s,\sigma}(x,y) =$ center - surround;
>   If $(I'_{i,s,\sigma}(x,y) \leq 0)$
> $I'_{i,s,\sigma}(x,y) = 0$;

Fig. 4.3. The *center-surround algorithm* for computing the Intensity Scale Maps $I''_{i,s_c,\sigma}$, with $i \in \{(\text{on}), (\text{off})\}, s \in \{s_2, s_3, s_4\}, \sigma \in \{3, 7\}$

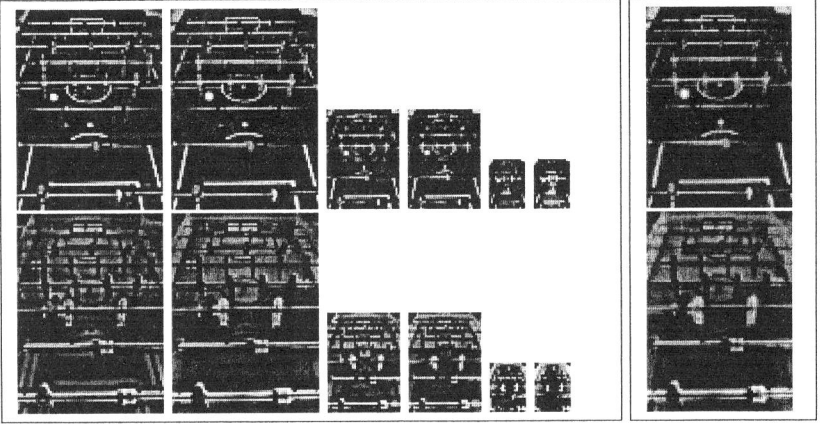

Fig. 4.4. Left: the 12 intensity scale maps $I''_{i,s,\sigma}$. First row: the *on-maps*. Second row: the *off-maps*. Right: the two intensity feature maps $I'_{(\text{on})}$ and $I'_{(\text{off})}$ resulting from the sum of the corresponding six scale maps on the left

scale maps I'' are depicted in Fig. 4.4. It remains to be said that we consider a rectangular surround whereas the surrounding region of the ganglion cells is circular. This was done for simplicity, more accurate results should be achieved with a circular region.

The six maps for each center-surround variation are summed up by *across-scale addition*: first, all maps are resized to scale s_2 whereby resizing scale s_i to scale s_{i-1} is done by duplicating each pixel. After resizing, the maps are added up pixel by pixel. This yields the intensity feature maps I':

$$I'_i = \bigoplus_{s,\sigma} I''_{i,s,\sigma}, \tag{4.1}$$

with $i \in \{(\text{on}), (\text{off})\}, s \in \{s_2, s_3, s_4\}, \sigma \in \{3, 7\}$, and $\bigoplus$ denoting the across-scale addition. In the NVT, the maps are reduced to s_4 before summing up; instead,

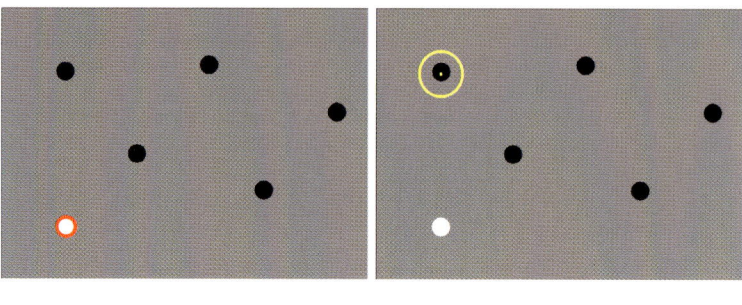

(a) First FOA by VOCUS   (b) First FOA by NVT

Fig. 4.5. The white pop-out is detected by VOCUS **(a)** but not by the NVT [Itti et al., 1998]**(b)**. Only separating the on-center difference from the off-center difference enables the detection of the pop-out (for an explanation see also Fig. 4.11). In the NVT, the six dots are all equally salient

we use the largest scale s_2 to prevent loosing information. The two intensity feature maps are shown in Fig. 4.4 on the right.

The computations in VOCUS differ from those in the NVT since we compute on-center and off-center differences separately. In the NVT, these computations are combined by taking the absolute value of the difference |center − surround|. This approach is a faster approximation of the above solution but yields some problems. Firstly, a correct intensity pop-out is not warranted: imagine an image with a gray background and white and black dots on it, both having the same intensity contrast to the background (Fig. 4.5). If there is only one white dot but several black ones, the white one pops out in human perception. One condition for this pop-out is the separation of on-center from the off-center mechanism: the on-center cells respond to the white dot, the off-center cells to the black ones. The same is true for the intensity feature maps in VOCUS (see section 4.1.2 and Fig. 4.11 for a detailed explanation of how the pop-out is enabled in VOCUS). The combination of on-center and off-center in one map in NVT does not enable the pop-out since there is only one intensity channel, showing six equally strong peaks. The detection results of VOCUS and NVT on the pop-out example are depicted in Fig. 4.5.

The second advantage of two separate intensity channels occurs if top-down influences are integrated into the system: a bias for dark-on-bright or bright-on-dark is not possible in the combined approach but in the separated one. This is for instance an important aspect if the robot searches for an open door, visible as a dark region in depth images (cf. chapter 6, e.g., Fig. 6.9).

VOCUS and the NVT vary also in the computation of the differences themselves. In the NVT, the differences are determined by subtracting two scales at a time, e.g., $I_6 = s_4 − s_8$. The problem with this approach is that it yields sort of "square-textured" feature maps and uneven transitions at the

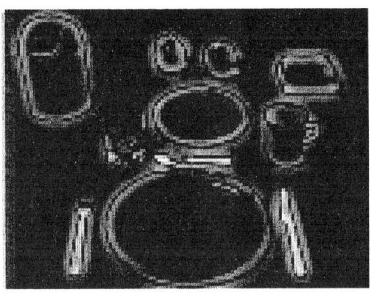 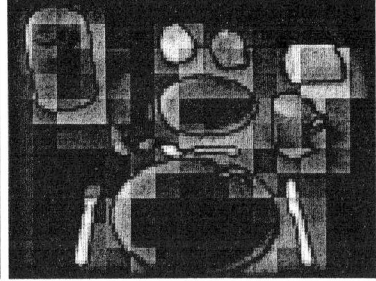

(a) Intensity map VOCUS   (b) Intensity map NVT

Fig. 4.6. Two intensity maps of a breakfast table scene, computed by VOCUS **(a)** and by the NVT [Itti et al., 1998] **(b)**. The square-textured structure in the right image resulting from taking the difference between two scales can be seen clearly, the left image shows a much more accurate solution

borders of the coarser scale (cf. Fig. 4.6, right). Our approach results in a slightly slower computation but is much more accurate (cf. Fig. 4.6, left) and needs fewer scales. VOCUS uses only five scales $(s_0, ..., s_4)$, the NVT uses nine scales, since Itti et al. need the four coarsest scales $(s_5, ..., s_8)$ to represent the surround.

The Feature Orientation

The orientation maps are computed from *oriented pyramids* built according to a method described in [Greenspan et al., 1994] (see appendix A for details). The oriented pyramid in fact consists of four pyramids, one for each of the orientations $0°, 45°, 90°, 135°$. The pyramid for each orientation highlights the edges having this orientation on different scales. The orientations are computed by *Gabor filters* detecting bar-like features according to a specified orientation (see appendix A.1.3). Gabor filters, which are the product of a symmetric Gaussian with an oriented sinusoid, simulate the receptive field structure of orientation-selective neurons in primary visual cortex [Palmer, 1999].

In contrast to the NVT, we do not use the center-surround technique explicitly for computing the orientation maps. The oriented center-surround difference that is determined by cells in the human cortex is already determined implicitly by the Gabor filters. So we take the orientation maps as are, yielding $3 \times 4 = 12$ orientation scale maps $O''_{\theta,s}$, for orientations $\theta \in \{0°, 45°, 90°, 135°\}$ and scales $s \in \{s_2, s_3, s_4\}$. These maps correspond to the maps O_{ij} in the appendix (Fig. A.5). The orientation scale maps $O''_{\theta,s}$ are summed up by across-scale addition for each orientation, yielding four orientation feature maps O'_θ of scale s_2, one for each orientation:

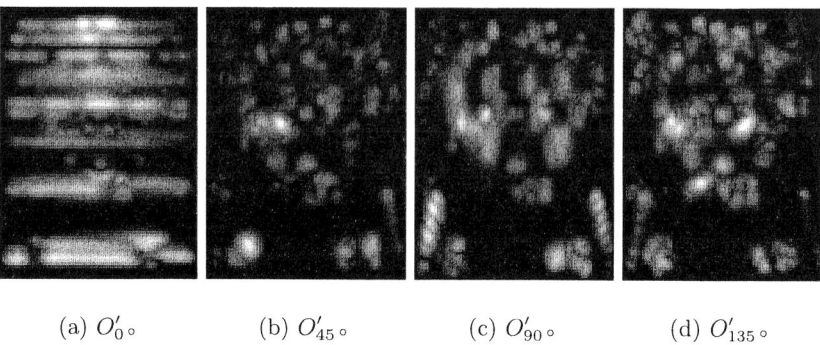

(a) $O'_{0°}$ (b) $O'_{45°}$ (c) $O'_{90°}$ (d) $O'_{135°}$

Fig. 4.7. The four orientation feature maps

$$O'_\theta = \bigoplus_s O''_{\theta,s},$$ (4.2)

with $\theta \in \{0°, 45°, 90°, 135°\}$, and $s \in \{s_2, s_3, s_4\}$. The orientation feature maps are depicted in Fig. 4.7.

The Feature Color

To compute the color feature maps, the color image is firstly converted into an LAB-image (cf. appendix A.2). The CIE LAB color space is currently one of the most popular uniform color spaces [Forsyth and Ponce, 2003]. In uniform color spaces, "the distance in coordinate space is a fair guide to the significance of the difference between two colors as perceived by a human observer" [Forsyth and Ponce, 2003]. This is especially important in our application because VOCUS imitates human perception. Earlier, we used the HSV color space (cf. appendix A.2), but this yielded some unintuitive results since this space treats the distances between colors not the same way as in human perception. The LAB space yielded considerable improvements.

From the LAB image, an LAB image pyramid P_{LAB} is generated by applying a Gaussian filter to the LAB image. From the pyramid P_{LAB}, four color pyramids P_R, P_G, P_B, and P_Y are generated for the distinct colors red, green, blue, and yellow. Note that P_{LAB} is a pyramid of color images, thus a pixel of a layer in the pyramid is a vector (p_l, p_a, p_b), whereas P_R, P_G, P_B, and P_Y are pyramids of gray-scale images, thus a pixel of a layer in these pyramids is a scalar.

The chosen four colors represent the color space well since they are the colors at the ends of the axes of the color space (the LAB color space is spanned by the parameters L (luminance), A (red-green), and B (blue-yellow) (cf. appendix A.2)). Luminance is already considered in the intensity maps, so we ignore this channel here (this means, we only consider the disk in the middle

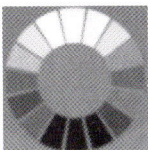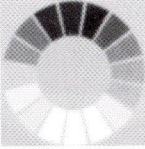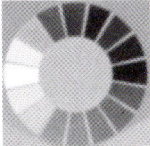

Fig. 4.8. A color wheel (left) and one layer of the color pyramids P_R, P_G, P_B, and P_Y representing the colors red, green, blue, and yellow. The color map for red has its brightest values at red regions and its darkest values at green region, since green is the opponent of red and has the largest distance to red in the color space

of Fig. A.7, right, in the appendix). Note that also three parameters suffice to represent the color space and even more, if luminance is ignored two parameters are enough. Choosing four parameters corresponds to human vision: in the human visual cortex, color is perceived by a color double-opponent system with the color opponent cells red-green, green-red, blue-yellow and yellow-blue. Red-green cells are excited by red light and inhibited by green and so on (cf. chapter 2.2). The representation of red and green as well as of blue and yellow in separate maps enables color specific pop-outs (cf. Fig. 4.22) and top-down search for specific color types. In contrast, in combined computations of one red-green and one blue-yellow map as in the NVT some color pop-outs are not possible and a top-down search is only feasible for "red or green" and "blue or yellow" but not for one specific color type. This is analog to the computation of two separated feature intensity maps (cf. page 60).

The maps of these color pyramids show to which degree a color is represented in an image, i.e., the maps in the pyramid P_R show how "red" the image regions are: the brightest values are at red regions and the darkest values at green regions (since green has the largest distance to red in the color space). The pixel value $P_{R,s}(x,y)$ in map s of the "red" pyramid P_R is obtained by the distance between the corresponding pixel $P_{\text{LAB}}(x,y)$ and the prototype for red $r = (r_a, r_b) = (255, 127)$ for a maximal value of 255 in the color space. Since $P_{\text{LAB}}(x,y)$ is of the form (p_a, p_b), this yields:

$$P_{R,s}(x,y) = d(P_{\text{LAB}}(x,y), r) \tag{4.3}$$

$$= ||P_{\text{LAB}}(x,y) - r|| \tag{4.4}$$

$$= ||(p_A, p_b) - (r_A, r_B)|| \tag{4.5}$$

$$= \sqrt{(p_A - r_A)^2 + (p_B - r_B)^2}. \tag{4.6}$$

where $d(a,b)$ is the distance between a and b. The maps of one layer of the color pyramids for a color wheel image are shown in Figure 4.8. The maps for the foosball table are shown in Fig. 4.9, top. On these pyramids, the color contrast is computed by on-center differences as described in the algorithm of Fig. 4.3, yielding $4 * 3 * 2 = 24$ color scale maps:

$$C''_{\gamma,s,\sigma} = \text{center} - \text{surround(on,s,}\sigma), \qquad (4.7)$$

with $\gamma \in \{(\text{red}), (\text{green}), (\text{blue}), (\text{yellow})\}$, $s \in \{s_2, s_3, s_4\}$, and $\sigma \in \{3, 7\}$. The off-center-on-surround difference is not needed, because these values are represented in the opponent color pyramid. The maps of each color are rescaled to the scale s_2 and summed up into 4 color feature maps C'_γ:

$$C'_\gamma = \bigoplus_{s,\sigma} C''_{\gamma,s,\sigma}, \qquad (4.8)$$

$\gamma \in \{(\text{red}), (\text{green}), (\text{blue}), (\text{yellow})\}$, $s \in \{s_2, s_3, s_4\}$, and $\sigma \in \{3, 7\}$. The color feature maps for the foosball table image are shown in Fig. 4.9, second row. Note that the scale maps in the first row show bright regions where the color of the map occurs whereas the feature maps only show the regions where blobs of the color occur because of the center-surround mechanisms.

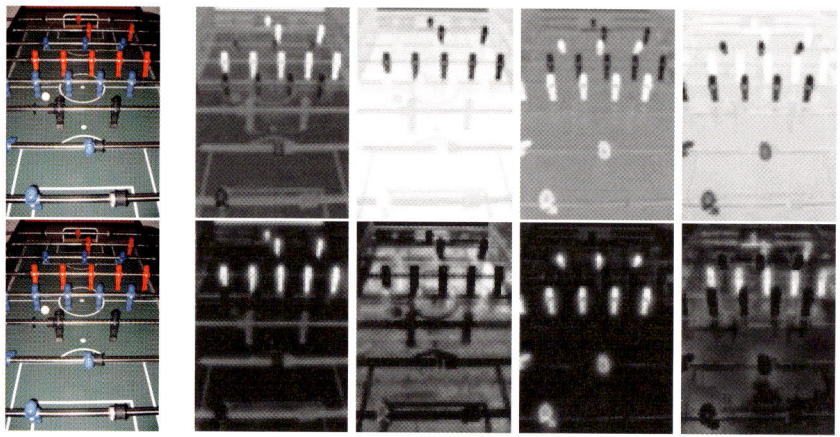

Fig. 4.9. Left: the input image. Right: first row: the maps of scale s_2 from the color pyramids P_R, P_G, P_B, and P_Y (red, green, blue, yellow). Second row: the color feature maps which result after applying the center-surround difference

4.1.2 Fusing Saliencies

The fusion of different maps is done by a weighted average: the maps are first weighted by a *uniqueness weight function*, then they are summed up, and finally normalized.

The Uniqueness Weight

If the maps were merely summed up in a straightforward manner, all maps had the same influence. This implies that if there are many maps, the influence

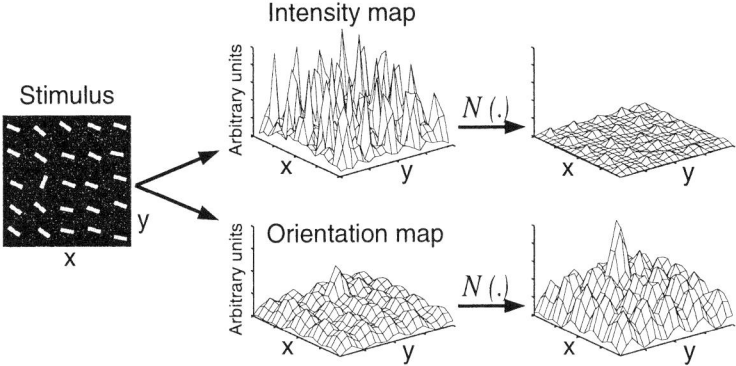

Fig. 4.10. Weighting for uniqueness: suppressing maps with many peaks and promoting maps with few peaks. This enables the detection of pop-outs (Fig. reprinted with permission from [Itti et al., 1998]. ©1998 IEEE)

of each map is very small and its values do not contribute much to the resulting map. To prevent this effect, we have to determine the most important maps and raise their influence. This can be achieved by an operator like the normalization operator presented in [Itti et al., 1998]: $N(X) = X * (M - \bar{m})^2$, for map X, the global maximum M and the average of the local maxima $\bar{m}$. It emphasizes maps with one strong peak and suppresses those which contain many almost equivalent peaks (cf. Fig. 4.10). This operator works by normalizing the maps to a fixed range and multiplying each map by the squared difference of the global maximum M and the average of the local maxima $\bar{m}$.

There are two problems with this approach. One concerns the normalization and will be discussed later. The other one was already pointed out in [Itti and Koch, 2001b]: taking the difference of the global and the local maxima only yields the desired result if there is just one strong maximum. If there are two equally high maxima, the difference yields zero, ignoring the map completely, while humans would consider both maxima as salient (imagine the eyes of a wolf in the dark, completely ignored by the attention system! Species with this attention system were probably not favored by evolution). The same article proposes a sophisticated complex iterative scheme to overcome this problem by local competition between neighboring salient locations. For simplicity reasons, we chose an alternative approach: we divide each map by the square root of the number of local maxima in a pre-specified range from the global maximum:

$$\mathcal{W}(X) = X/\sqrt{m}, \tag{4.9}$$

for map X and m the number of local maxima above a certain threshold. There are different ways to determine the threshold. In our experiments, we chose the simplest method of determining the threshold by trial and error, resulting in

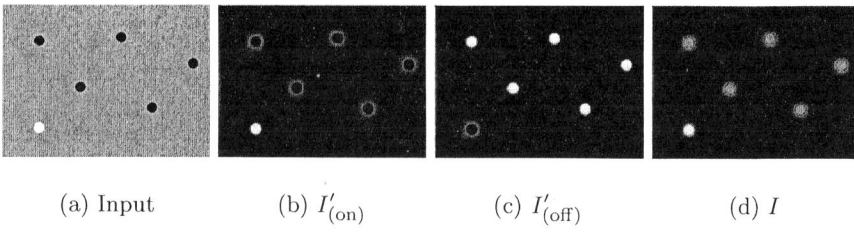

(a) Input   (b) $I'_{(on)}$ (c) $I'_{(off)}$ (d) I

Fig. 4.11. The effect of the uniqueness weight function $\mathcal{W}()$ (eq. 4.9). (a) input image, (b) on-center intensity feature map $I'_{(on)}$, (c) off-center intensity feature map $I'_{(off)}$, (d) conspicuity intensity map I. $I'_{(on)}$ has a higher weight $\mathcal{W}$ than $I'_{(off)}$ because it contains only one strong peak. So this map has a higher influence and the white dot pops out in the conspicuity map I

a threshold of 50% of the global maximum. More general methods determine the threshold automatically according to the distribution of the maximum values, e.g., they choose the median of the maxima as threshold. We leave the evaluation of such approaches to future work.

The effect of the uniqueness weight $\mathcal{W}$ is shown in Fig. 4.11: the map $I'_{(on)}$ with the single peak is weighted higher than the map $I'_{(off)}$ with five peaks. This enables the pop-out (cf. Fig. 4.6). The method yielded good results in our experiments, but it does not claim to be an optimal solution. This is also a problem with other existing methods, including the one by Itti mentioned above. However, a comparison with Itti's method would be interesting.

The fusion of different feature and conspicuity maps is a general problem in computational attention systems. The features represent a priori incommensurable modalities. How strong must a color cue be to appear equally salient as an orientation cue? Some of the problems arising here were solved by the later proposed normalization method and good results support this approach, however, this is still a difficult topic that should be examined further.

In human perception, the interaction of different features is much more interactive than a system based on classical filter mechanisms could possibly be. The interaction is adapted automatically and also depends on the environment and life conditions. Put in a gray world, the influence of the color feature channel will probably decrease more and more. More biologically motivated systems like the one by Tsotsos [Tsotsos et al., 1995] claim to have a more plausible basis for such feature bindings, however, at the moment in Tsotsos's system the binding only affects the fusion of feature types and not the fusion across feature dimensions like color and orientation.

The Conspicuity Maps

The next step in the saliency computation is the generation of the *conspicuity maps*. This notation was introduced by [Milanese, 1993] to denote the saliency of a feature dimension. To obtain the maps, all feature maps of one feature dimension are weighted by the uniqueness weight $\mathcal{W}$ and combined into one conspicuity map, yielding map I for intensity, O for orientation, and C for color:

$$
\begin{aligned}
I &= \textstyle\sum_i \mathcal{W}(I_i') & i &\in \{\text{on,off}\} \\
O &= \textstyle\sum_\theta \mathcal{W}(O_\theta'), & \theta &\in \{0^\circ, 45^\circ, 90^\circ, 135^\circ\} \\
C &= \textstyle\sum_\gamma \mathcal{W}(C_\gamma') & \gamma &\in \{\text{red, green, blue, yellow}\}
\end{aligned}
\tag{4.10}
$$

The conspicuity maps are illustrated in Fig. 4.12.

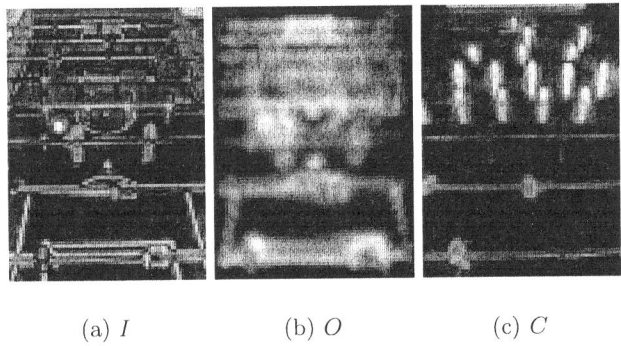

(a) I (b) O (c) C

Fig. 4.12. The conspicuity maps for intensity (**a**), orientation (**b**), and color (**c**)

Normalization

After summing up the weighted feature maps, some normalization has to be done to make the maps comparable. This is necessary since some channels have more maps than others. The function $N(\ )$ proposed by Itti et al. normalizes the maps to a fixed range. This method goes along with a problem: normalizing maps to a fixed range removes important information about the magnitude of the maps. Assume that one intensity and one orientation map belonging to an image with high intensity but low orientation contrasts are to be fused into one saliency map. The intensity map will contain very bright regions, but the orientation map will show only some moderately bright regions. Normalizing both maps to a fixed range forces the values of the orientation maps to the same range as the intensity values, ignoring that orientation is not an important feature in this case.

Since some normalization has to be done to make the maps comparable after they were summed up and weighted at least once, we propose the following normalization technique: if the maps X_1 to X_k have to be fused, we determine the maximal value $\hat{m}$ of these maps: $\hat{m} = \max(X_i)$, $i \in \{1,..,k\}$. Then, X_1 to X_k are summed up to X and this map is normalized between 0 and $\hat{m}$, expressed by the term $n_{(0,\hat{m})}(X)$. For example, the intensity feature maps I'_i, $i \in \{$on,off$\}$ are determined by:

get maximum $\hat{m}_{I'}$ of intensity feature maps: $\hat{m}_{I'} = \max(I'_i)$
add feature types: $I = \sum_i \mathcal{W}(I'_i)$
normalize I: $I = n_{(0,\hat{m}_{I'})}(I)$

This technique yielded much better results in our experiments than the normalization to a fixed range.

The Saliency Map

Finally, the conspicuity maps I, O, and C are weighted again with the weighting function $\mathcal{W}()$ and summed up to the global saliency map S:

$$S = \mathcal{W}(I) + \mathcal{W}(O) + \mathcal{W}(C) \tag{4.11}$$

The saliency map for our example is illustrated in Fig. 4.13 (a).

4.1.3 The Focus of Attention

To determine the *most salient region (MSR)* in S, first the most salient point is determined and, starting from there, the MSR. Then, the *focus of attention (FOA)* is directed to the MSR (cf. Fig. 4.13). This terminates the computations if only a single focus of attention has to be determined. If several FOAs are of interest, the MSR is inhibited with *inhibition of return (IOR)* and the next salient region is computed. Let us now consider these computations in more detail.

The computation of a region-shaped FOA instead of a point is contrary to most other systems which determine only the most salient point and draw a circular fixed-sized focus. We determine the most salient point straightforward by checking every value in S instead of using a WTA network as proposed by [Koch and Ullman, 1985] and the NVT. Although biologically less plausible, equivalent results are achieved with less computational resources. Starting from the most salient point (the *seed*), we extract the surrounding salient region with *seeded region growing*. This method recursively finds all neighbors with similar values within a certain range (see appendix A.3). We accept all values that differ at most 25% from the maximum value; the percentage was

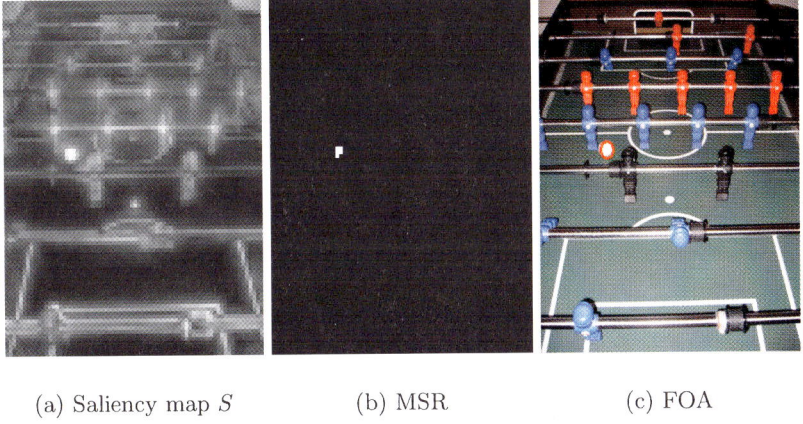

(a) Saliency map S (b) MSR   (c) FOA

Fig. 4.13. To obtain the focus of attention (FOA), the most salient region (MSR) is determined in the saliency map S by region growing starting from the brightest point in S

achieved experimentally. Another approach to find the maximum region is to apply the watershed algorithm as proposed in [Draper and Lionelle, 2003]. The watershed algorithm is a segmentation method that, when applied to a gray-scale image, detects and uniquely labels connected areas automatically. This makes the method independent of the threshold parameter. For simplicity reasons, we chose the simpler region growing approach.

To visualize the focus region, we use two different methods (cf. Fig. 4.14): first, the width and height of the most salient region yield an elliptic FOA, approximating size and shape of the salient region. Alternatively, we directly visualize the contour of the extracted region. The second method is more accurate since an ellipse is not able to show the form of arbitrary regions. Nevertheless, the ellipse looks more like a focus of attention simulating human eye movements, so we often use this kind of visualization when the position of the focus is more important than its shape. In both cases, notice that the region is not the result of an object segmentation but of a saliency segmentation.

In [Walther et al., 2002], a more sophisticated method for the segmentation of the salient region is proposed: starting from the most salient point in the saliency map, they investigate the corresponding point in the feature maps and determine the feature map with the highest activation. The segmentation step, performed by a flooding algorithm with adaptive thresholding, is then accomplished on this feature map. Fig. 4.15 depicts the result of this method on an example image and for comparison the result with VOCUS. However, since the segmentation in the saliency map already yielded good results and since we are more interested in the position of the focus than in the shape of the region, we adhere to our simpler method.

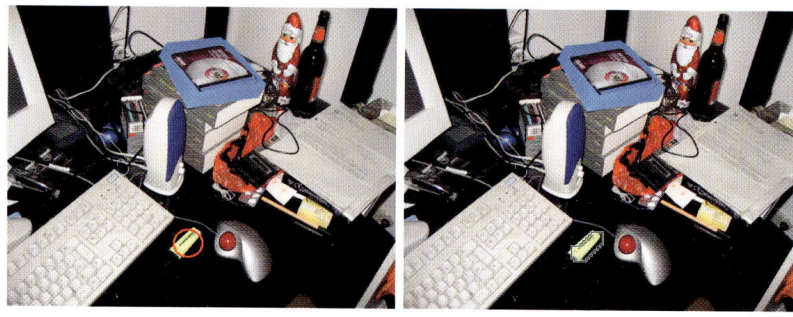

(a) Focus depicted as ellipse   (b) Focus depicted as contour

Fig. 4.14. The two different methods for visualization: (a) the focus of attention is approximated by an ellipse; (b) the contour of the salient region is shown. Both methods have its advantages; we will use both kinds in the following

Fig. 4.15. Left: salient region extracted by the method of Walther [Walther et al., 2002] (Image from [URL, 06]). Right: salient region extracted by VOCUS. In both examples, the uniqueness of the color blue makes the runner's dress the most salient image region

In a final step, IOR is applied to the FOA region in the saliency map. In our approach, this is done by first *dilating* the most salient region (cf. appendix A.1.4) and, second, zeroing the values of this region in the saliency map. The dilation yields an extended region and avoids sharp illumination transitions at the border of the region. This prevents the next focus from immediately returning to these borders. In more biologically oriented systems, the region should be inhibited only temporary with decreasing intensity over time, so that the focus may jump back to a salient region after some fixations.

In a system with technical purpose like ours, this is not desired. We want to sort regions according to their saliency, hence cycling is of no use.

Note that the problem is more difficult for dynamic systems that operate on a sequence of image frames over time. Here, the inhibition of return has to be extended to several images: a region focused in the first frame should be inhibited thereafter not only in this frame but also in following ones, preventing the system from sticking to the same region all the time. Since switching the focus at every frame results in too fast changes, it would be useful to stick to a fixated region for some time but after a while switch to another. In other cases, a tracking of the most salient region may be wanted or even a tracking of not only the first but the first n foci of attention, so the behavior should be adapted to the task. Backer gives in his work an excellent discussion of this topic [Backer et al., 2001, Backer, 2004]: he describes the tracking of up to 4 salient regions over time.

4.2 Experiments and Evaluation

The evaluation of a pure bottom-up system of visual attention is difficult because usually there is no ground truth. What is the "right" focus of attention on a natural scene? In the literature, there are few discussions on this topic, although or because the evaluation is not trivial. We propose several evaluation methods some of which were already discussed by Backer in his dissertation [Backer, 2004]:

- A comparison with human perception (cf. section 4.2.1).
- A comparison with other attention systems (cf. section 4.2.2).
- The repeatability of the results under image transformations (cf. section 4.2.3).
- The performance in an application (cf. section 4.2.4).

In the following, we will discuss the different approaches and evaluate VOCUS according to some of them. Much easier than the evaluation of a bottom-up attention system is the evaluation of an attention system regarding top-down influences that enable goal-directed search; this will be the topic of chapter 5.

4.2.1 Comparison with Human Perception

The comparison with human perception means comparing the FOAs with human eye movements. This is a suggestive solution, although one encounters some problems when doing so: is there an intersubjective scan-path of human eye movements on a scene? Usually, the answer is no. Mannan et al. show on examples of complex natural scenes that there is no evidence for repetitive scan-paths [Mannan et al., 1997]. Most scenes contain many objects competing for saliency and it is not clear in which order they are focused: each individual fixates different parts of a scene according to preferences, emotions, and motivations. One might focus the plate on a breakfast table, another the coffee cup, and a third one the flowers in the vase. This makes the comparison of the system's output with a human scan-path difficult. However, the comparison is easier for the first few fixations: these are more stable since it takes some time until top-down cues influence the processing. But also these fixations may differ according to changing viewing conditions and individual differences in perception.

Although the comparison with human perception is not trivial, it is possible. There are mainly two approaches. The first is what we call here "subjective analysis", that means "looking at the results and decide whether the foci of attention make sense". This method is intuitive, suggesting and easy to perform but also subjective and not scientifically sound. Despite the weaknesses of this approach, it gives a good impression of how the system performs. Since everyone has her or his own "built-in attention system", everybody has an intuitive understanding of what a "reasonable" focus of attention is. The subjective analysis is the main approach with which many systems are evaluated but because of its weaknesses it should not be the only one.

The second method to compare the system behavior with human perception is more objective and scientifically sound: the comparison with psychological data obtained from viewing experiments. The difficulty with this approach is that the data for the experiments is harder to obtain, especially for real-world scenes. In the following, we show several experiments concerning the two approaches.

Subjective Analysis

Usually, in subjective analysis just some real-world images are provided to the system and the evaluation of whether the results are sensible is left to the user. Although an objective evaluation is hardly possible with this method for most real-world scenes, there are special scenes in which it is intuitively clear which regions are most salient. Such scenes are for example those which contain objects that were explicitly designed to attract attention. Many of such objects are found in traffic scenes: traffic signs, traffic lights, brake lights, and signaling lights are all designed with strong colors, strong intensities, or flashing lights. Also other security relevant objects are designed salient, e.g., fire extinguishers, emergency exit signs, and police sirens. More examples are found in sports: the balls in many games are designed with colors that distinguish them well from their background, first of all the balls in the robot soccer game RoboCup (cf. chapter 7). Some examples of such objects and some FOAs computed by VOCUS are shown in Fig. 4.16.

Another example in which it is intuitively clear which region is the most salient is the detection of defects on different materials, e.g., in textiles, wood, or metal. If humans have the task to detect such defects in industrial applications they immediately know which is the region of interest. J. Pannekamp

Fig. 4.16. Foci of attention (FOAs) depicted as red ellipses on objects that were explicitly designed to attract attention. 1st row: saliency in traffic. 2nd/3rd row: saliency in security relevant areas. 4th row: saliency in sports: balls in many sports are designed to attract attention, e.g., in foosball, tennis, and especially in the robot soccer game RoboCup. The visual attention system focuses the balls immediately. Note that all results were generated with the same system and identical parameter settings, there were no image specific adaptations

from the Fraunhofer Institute IPA[1] kindly provided us with some images showing defects on different materials. The results are depicted in Fig 4.17. It showed that VOCUS was able to detect the defects in most of these images successfully. Only if not merely the material itself is presented but also

---

[1] Fraunhofer Institut für Produktionstechnik und Automatisierung (IPA), Stuttgart, Germany

its borders the system favors the borders instead of the defect (see Fig 4.17, second row left).

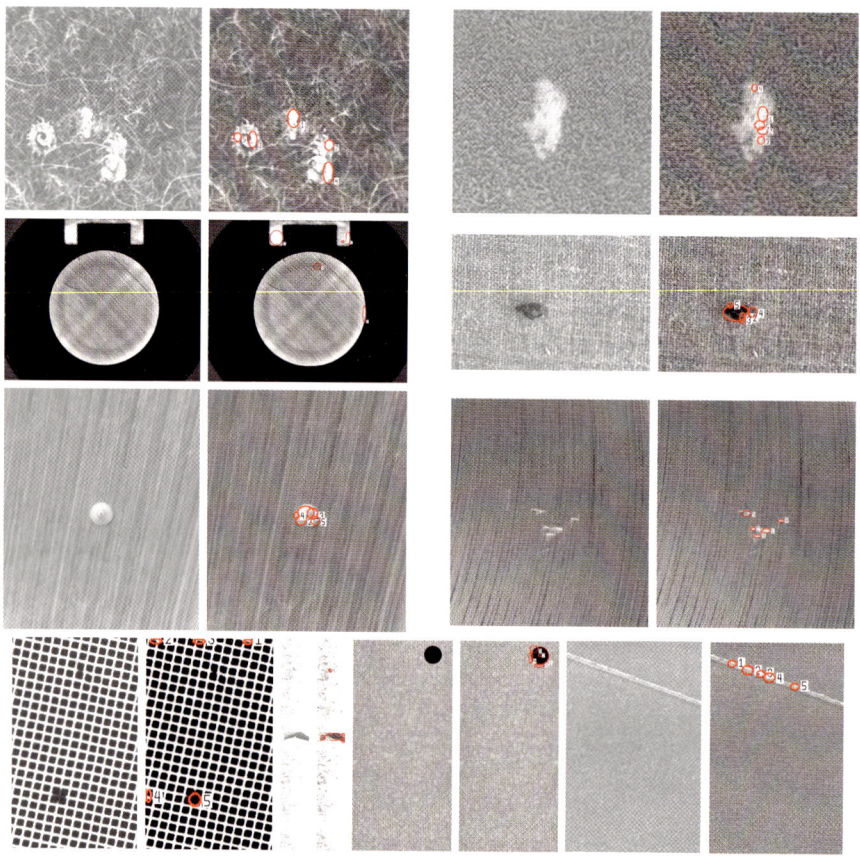

Fig. 4.17. FOAs on some images showing defects on different materials. The original image (left) and the detected FOAs on the image as red ellipses (right). Except one case (2nd row, left), all defects are detected by VOCUS (images kindly provided by J. Pannekamp from the Fraunhofer Institute IPA)

Comparison with Psychophysical Data

Although a general scan-path on complex scenes does not exist, there is a general viewing behavior on simple scenes. Examples of such simple scenes are the *pop-out scenes* often used in psychophysics (cf. section 2.1.4) in which one item differs in one feature from all the other regions in a scene. Psychologists often work with artificial pop-out images because they offer the possibility to gradually change feature values and set sizes. The attentional behavior on

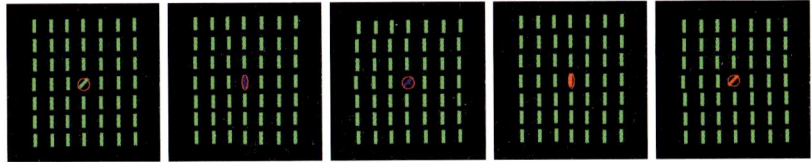

Fig. 4.18. FOAs (red ellipses) on some psychological pop-out data. Each image shows a target in the middle that is immediately focused by humans who watch the scene. The target is also immediately detected by VOCUS (images kindly provided by B. Schönwälder, psychological institute of the university of Munich)

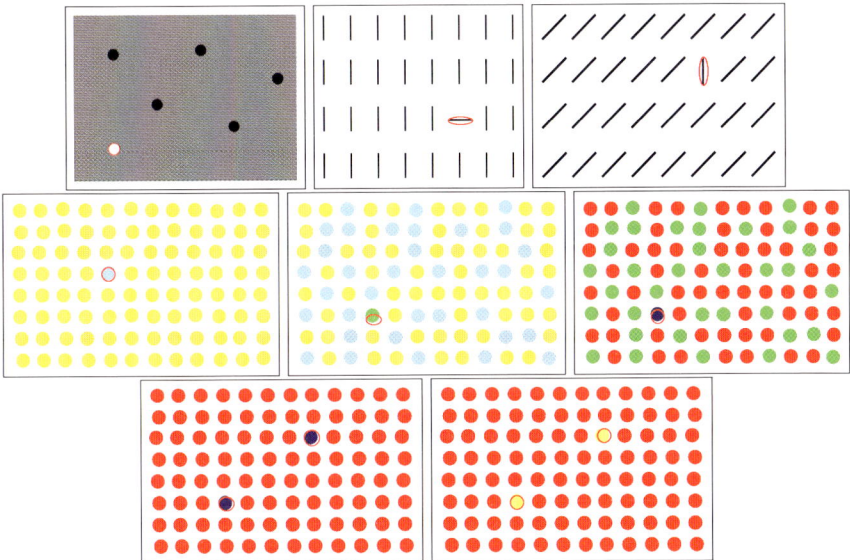

Fig. 4.19. FOAs (red ellipses) on some pop-out data containing one or two targets. Each of the targets is detected immediately

these data is well investigated, so they fit perfectly for comparative experiments. In Fig. 4.18, we see results on some psychological data provided by B. Schönwälder from the psychological institute of the university of Munich. The popping out item in the middle is immediately focused in all cases. These data show rather simple examples since the target is always in the middle and the variation of targets is rather small, so we present in Fig. 4.19 some more pop-out experiments, specially constructed to test the behavior of the system. The one or two popping out items are focused successfully in all of the examples.

In the following, we test the system behavior on pop-out scenes in more detail. Not only the uniqueness of a feature, but also the strength of the feature value has an influence on the pop-out effect: in human vision as well

as in VOCUS, a feature has to have a certain strength to pop out of a scene,
e.g., an oriented bar has to differ by certain degrees from its distractors. Here,
we examine these limits. In Fig. 4.20, we vary the background intensity of
the image with one white and five black dots. Usually, the white dot pops out
because of its uniqueness, but with a bright background, it does no longer pop
out: the intensity contrast of the black dots is so high that these attract the
focus of attention. The border between pop-out and no pop-out has shown to
be between 30% and 40% intensity of the background.

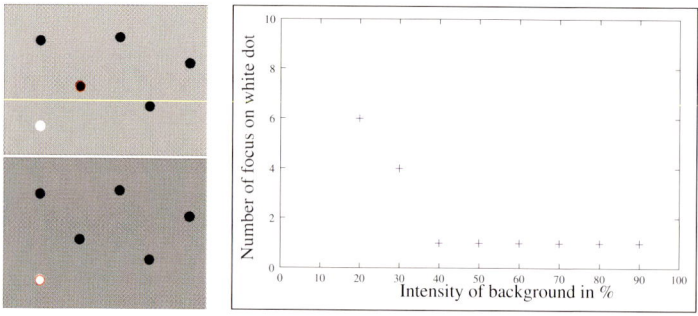

Fig. 4.20. How strong has the intensity contrast of an outlier to be to pop out?
We vary the background intensity of the presented image from 0% (white) to 100%
(black). Left, top: background intensity of 30% , no pop-out occurs. Left, bottom:
background intensity of 40%, the pop-out occurs. Right: the number of the focus on
the white dot for different background intensities. For 10%, none of the first 10 foci
is on the white dot, for at least 40% the white dot is focused immediately with the
first FOA, i.e., it *pops out*

In Fig. 4.21 we test how strong an oriented bar has to differ in orientation
to pop out from the distractors. On the left, we see that already a 5° oriented target pops out among vertical distractors (0°). When we exchange the
orientations of target and distractors, an effect occurs that seems strange at
first sight: the vertical target between distractors of 5° does not pop out and
even among distractors of 20° there is no pop-out (Fig. 4.21, middle). It is not
before 25° orientation of the distractors that the pop-out occurs (Fig. 4.21,
right). This effect can be explained by the activation in the feature maps: in
the first case, the 5° tilted bar shows activation in the 45° orientation map
whereas the 0° distractors do not. The single activation peak in the 45° map
leads to a high uniqueness weight and the pop-out occurs. In the second case,
the vertical target shows activation in the 0° orientation map but the 20°
oriented distractors also do. So, there is no map showing only target features
and no pop-out occurs. If the distractors are oriented by at least 25°, their
main activation occurs in the 45° maps and the target activation in the 0°
map is stronger than the one of the distractors.

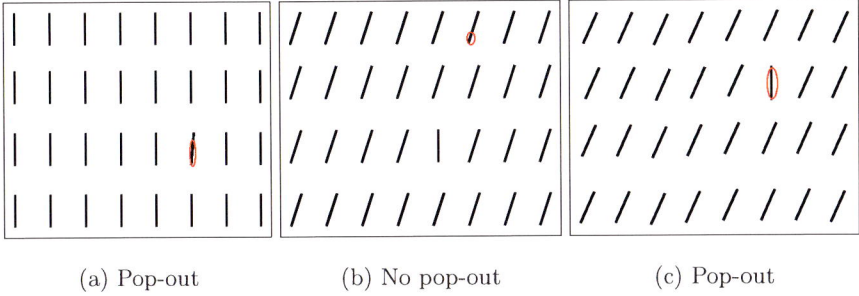

(a) Pop-out   (b) No pop-out   (c) Pop-out

Fig. 4.21. How strong must the orientation of an outlier differ to pop out? **(a)** target of 5° pops out among vertical distractors; **(b)** vertical target between distractors of 20° does not pop out; **(c)** vertical target between distractors of 25° pops out. That means, the required orientation for pop-out differs: in one case, 5° deviation is sufficient, whereas in the other 25° deviation is necessary. The effect is called *search asymmetry* and is consistent with psychophysical experiments [Treisman and Gormican, 1988]. For further explanations see text

This effect corresponds to the *search asymmetries* in human perception that were discussed in chapter 2.1.4: a search for target x among distracting y's does not yield the same result as a search for y among x's. The view of [Treisman and Gormican, 1988], in which prototypes exist for each feature and it is easier to search for a deviation among prototype distractors than for a prototype among deviations, fits well to our model since each feature map may be regarded as a prototype.

Since the evaluation of human viewing behavior is rather easy to evaluate on such simple artificial data, most experiments in psychophysics are performed on such data. But also the scan-paths on natural scenes have been investigated and although there is no general scan-path, there are accumulation points at which humans look more often than at others. The behavior of a computational system can be compared with this data. We do not have access to such data, but evaluations of similar systems can be found in [Parkhurst et al., 2002] and [Ouerhani et al., 2004]. Since a computational system can only approximate human behavior, these results show of course no exact congruence; however, they show that there is some correlation in the data.

4.2.2 Comparison with Other Attention Systems

In this section, we compare VOCUS with one of the most famous computational attention systems: the Neuromorphic Vision Toolkit (NVT) [Itti et al., 1998] (cf. page 37). This system was chosen for the comparison since it is one of the systems most similar to VOCUS, since it is one of the most cited systems and since it is online available [URL, 05] and thus can be easily used for comparative experiments. The comparison of the bottom-up part of VOCUS with other systems does not enable to evaluate the quality of the attention system but it shows the differences between the models. The most difficult aspect in such a comparison is that in most examples it is not possible to say which results are better. This is only possible if ground truth is available, as for example for psychophysical image data. We perform some tests on such psychophysical data and additionally some tests on real world scenes. Although on the latter an evaluation is not possible, we think that such a comparison is still interesting to get an impression on the differences of the systems.

To take fair conditions for our experiments, we chose two experimental sets. In the first, we took the images which were used in our previous experiments, i.e., the artificial pop-out images and the real-world images with salient objects. Since these images represent a subjective choice of images, we chose a second test set: we chose an image set with natural traffic scenes of Itti's data (downloaded from [URL, 07]).

In Fig. 4.22, we show the results of the first test set. It reveals that many of the FOAs are the same, especially in the artificial images. Exceptions are the red pop-out among green distractors and the white pop-out among black distractors. In these examples, the pop-out is detected by VOCUS but not by the NVT. The reason is, as discussed before, the combination of red and green in one channel and of on-off and off-on intensity in one channel in the NVT (cf. page 60). In the natural images, an objective evaluation is not possible so have a look yourself. The same is true for the results on the second test set; a selection of these results is depicted in Fig 4.23.

4.2.3 Image Transformations

In their evaluation of *interest point detectors*, Schmid et al. propose to evaluate a system with respect to the repeatability of the results under geometric image transformations like translation, rotation, scale, variation of illumination, and 3D viewpoint [Schmid et al., 2000]. These qualities are desired in technical systems, especially for robots acting in a dynamic environment.

Nevertheless, even in human perception, there is no invariance concerning scan-paths: there is the tendency of humans to scan a scene in reading direction, i.e., in Europe from upper left to lower right. This yields different scan-paths for rotated images. Furthermore, humans tend to prefer the center of a scene, yielding variances on translated images [Enoch, 1959]. Even more difficulties arise under illumination variations as well as changing of scale and 3D viewpoint: Different illuminations may highlight other parts of a scene; zooming a scene draws attention to small objects or object parts whereas zooming out draws attention to larger objects or groups of objects (cf. Fig. 4.26). This is similar under changes in 3D viewpoint: some objects are closer than others, what has effects on the saliency.

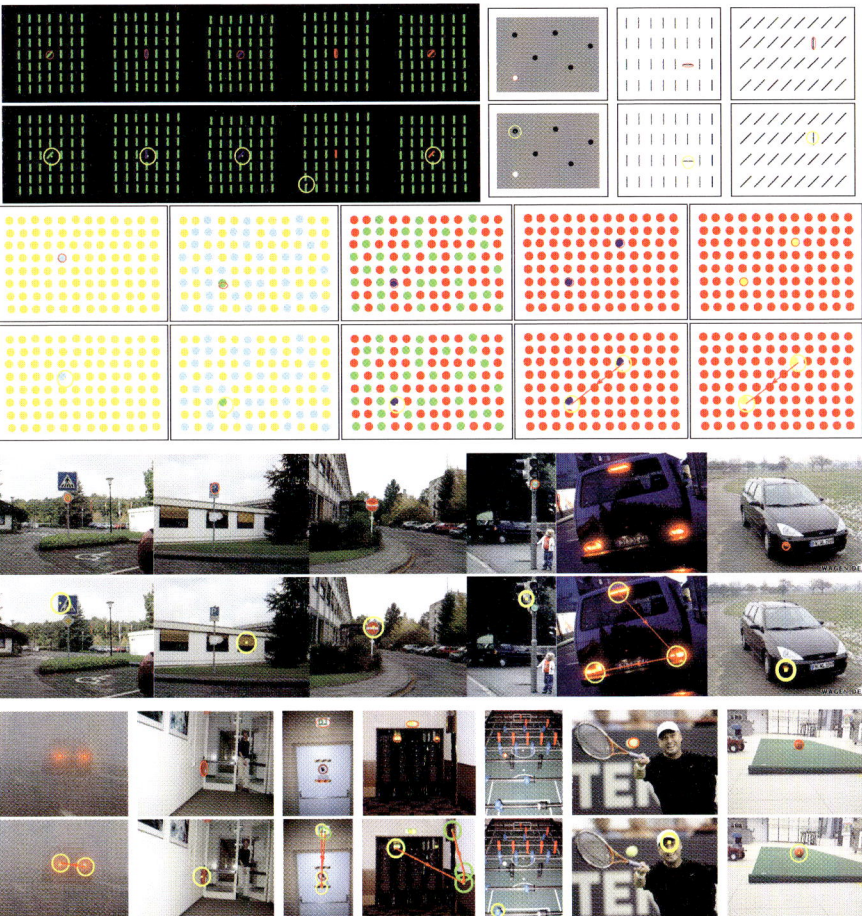

Fig. 4.22. Comparison of VOCUS with the NVT [Itti et al., 1998]. The FOAs of VOCUS are depicted as red ellipses, the FOAs of the NVT as yellow circles. On the artificial images, VOCUS detects two of the pop-outs which are not detected by the NVT (first row, 4th and 6th example); see text for explanation. On the natural images, an objective evaluation is not possible, they are just displayed to get an impression of the differences

Despite these effects in human perception, it might be useful to design a computational attention system for technical purposes that shows largely invariance at least for special transformations, i.e., for 2D similarity transformations like translation, rotation, and reflection. Draper and Lionelle [Draper and Lionelle, 2003] stressed the importance of invariances to such transformations when attentional systems shall be used as front ends for object recognition. They also showed that the *Neuromorphic Vision Toolkit* [Itti et al., 1998]

Fig. 4.23. Comparison of VOCUS with the NVT [Itti et al., 1998] on a test set of Laurent Itti ([URL, 07]). The FOAs of VOCUS are depicted as red ellipses, the FOAs of the NVT as yellow circles. On these images, an objective evaluation is not possible, they are just displayed to get an impression of the differences

is highly sensitive to these transformations due to implementation details. One of such details is the computation of the center-surround mechanism by the difference of two pyramid scales. This makes the system highly sensitive to rotations and translations. This disadvantage was eliminated by Draper in his system $SAFE$ and is also eliminated in VOCUS. However, Draper's system as well as ours still contains aspects that yield different results under transformations, for example, the approximation of the circular center-surround with a rectangle in VOCUS (cf. page 59).

We evaluated VOCUS concerning these transformations. Some of the results concerning flipped images and scale transformations are shown in Fig. 4.24 – 4.25. In these experiments as well as in the experiments concerning the other transformations, we found the following: The invariance of the foci depends mainly on the difference between the saliency values. As long as these differences were large enough, the foci proved to be stable. One ex-

Fig. 4.24. Foci in flipped images. First row: the 1st focus on the traffic sign is stable because its saliency value differs clearly from the value of the 2nd focus. Second row: the first 10 FOAs on a breakfast table image. Similar saliency values result in slight changes of position and order of the FOAs

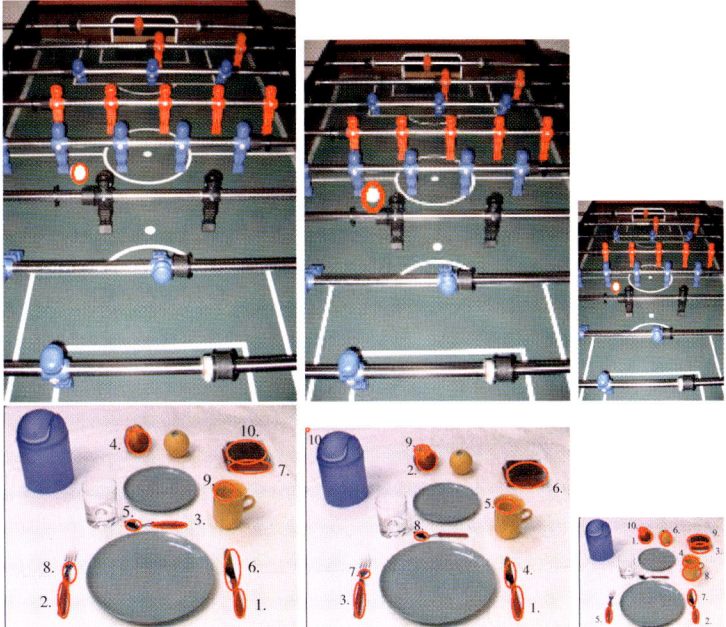

Fig. 4.25. Scale transformations. Saliencies are not always size independent: in the first row, the 1st FOA is stable in all three scales, in the second row, the same image presented with different sizes yields slightly different results. The image was presented with size 485×363 (left) as well as with width and height reduced by 10% (middle) and 50% (right)

ample is the image in the top row of Fig. 4.24: the saliency value of the first focus is 22 whereas the next salient region has only a saliency value of 14. In all of the flipped images, the first focus is on the traffic sign. If the saliency values in the image are more equally distributed, i.e., there are several nearly equally salient regions in the image, the focus may be diverted when the image is transformed. This is shown in the bottom row of Fig. 4.24: although roughly the same objects are focused within the first 10 foci, there are small differences in position and order of the foci. The first focus is stable on the knife, it only slightly changes its size, but the 2nd focus is sometimes on the knife and sometimes on the fork.

The same applies to scale transformations: the foci are stable as long as the difference between the saliency values is high enough. This is shown in Fig. 4.25 on two example scenes presented at three different sizes: 100%, 90%, and 50%. On the foosball table scene, the first FOA is stable, it is the same in all three scales. In contrast, on the breakfast table scene you can see that the foci of attention differ slightly in size and order. For example, in the original image, the knife is focused with the first FOA, in the half-size image it is focused with the second one. This results from the high similarity of the saliency values of the objects. Note, however, that even if the order changes, the same objects are focused.

However, this applies only to scale changes of a certain extent. If the scale changes are very large, the fixation behavior changes. Furthermore, the flexibility concerning size is restricted to some fixed sizes since the image pyramids are limited to 5 scales. This results in a preference for saliencies of particular sizes. Usually, FOAs do not exceed a size of about 40×40 pixels (the size of the focus is constrained since the bright regions in the saliency map are blob-like resulting from the center-surround mechanisms). If an object is zoomed, i.e., it occupies a large part of the image, not the whole object is considered as salient but only smaller parts of it, usually the borders. This is similar to human perception: looking at a large close object, one focuses on details of the object whereas a small object in some distance is considered as a whole. This is shown in Fig. 4.26: on the left, we see a small highlighter on a desk. The focus spans the whole object. On the right, the highlighter is zoomed. Here, the foci cover smaller parts of the highlighter. Note that not the relative size of the object with reference to the image size is considered, but the absolute size of the object.

This behavior has of course an effect on how the system performs on differently sized input images. Usually, VOCUS shows the best performance on images of a width and height of 80 to 500 pixels. In smaller images, not all scales of the image pyramids can be computed (the smallest map that is computed has a size of 5×5 pixels). In larger images, the regions that are focused are very small relative to the image. If in some scenes the regions of interest are large in the images (larger than 40×40 pixels), it might be useful to shrink the images in advance. This was done for example in the experiments of

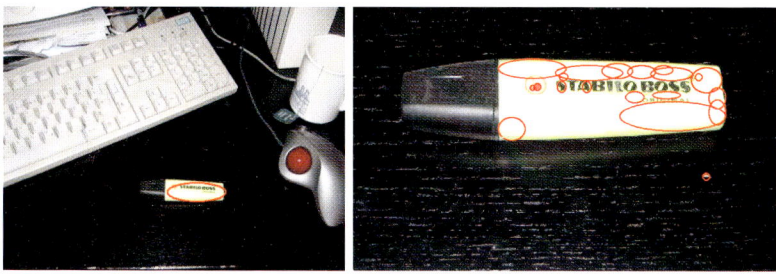

(a) Focus on whole object   (b) Foci on object parts

Fig. 4.26. Scale transformations. As in human vision, saliencies are not size independent: on a small object the focus is on the whole object (**a**), on a large object the FOAs are on smaller object parts (**b**)

chapter 7.3.2 in which VOCUS searched for balls. The performance improved when the input images were reduced to size 320×240.

4.2.4 Performance in an Application

A good approach to evaluate a system is to embed it in an application and show that this enables a performance not achieved with other approaches. The performance gain by an attention system may be a time saving, a reduction of false detections, or the filtering-out of irrelevant objects. As we mentioned in chapter 3.3, there are several approaches which use a computational attention system in the area of computer vision and robotics. In this kind of applications it depends on the environment and the objects whether the bottom-up method of attention is sufficient. If the objects of interest are salient by themselves and pop out of their environment, the bottom-up method yields good results. The toy bricks in Tsotsos' PLAYBOT scenario are a good example of such objects [Tsotsos et al., 1998]. It saves time to use attention as a front-end for object recognition (assumed that the implementation is fast enough) and helps to focus on salient objects and ignore non-salient ones. However, if the environment is crowded and the objects to be detected are not extremely salient by themselves, top-down information is needed to enable the system to focus on the desired objects (cf. chapter 5). The combination of VOCUS with an object classifier will be demonstrated in chapter 7.

4.3 Discussion

In this chapter, we introduced the bottom-up component of our computational attention system VOCUS. The system finds salient regions in images by computing different features in parallel, weighting them with a uniqueness weight, and finally fusing them into a single saliency map. Our work is influenced by existing attention models, mainly by the *Neuromorphic Vision Toolkit* [Itti et al., 1998], but we presented several enhancements concerning implementation details as well as structural design components that yielded considerable improvements in performance. Examples are the computation of two instead of one intensity channels, of four instead of two color channels, and the use of the color space LAB that is adapted to human perception.

One of the strengths of a bottom-up system attention system is its generality. It is not tuned to certain scenes or applications, it may be applied to any image from any context. All examples in this chapter were performed with the same set of parameters, there was no image-specific adaptation. In every scene, the system detects autonomously what is most salient, i.e., which parts differ from the rest of the scene.

However, although there was no parameter tuning and most computations are independent of parameters, there are still some parameters in the system. These include the number of features, the number of scales in the image pyramid, the size of the surround in the center-surround algorithm, the threshold in the uniqueness weighting function $\mathcal{W}$, and the threshold for region growing. Some of these were adopted from other systems, e.g., the number of features, some were set experimentally.

It is possible to reduce the number of required parameters for example by using the watershed algorithm instead of region growing as proposed on page 69. Other parameters represent a trade-off between time performance and implementation effort on the one hand, and accuracy and biological plausibility on the other hand. For example, it is not absolutely clear which are the early features of visual perception, but there are certainly more than three [Wolfe, 1998a]. The restriction to three features is clearly a trade-off that enables researchers to achieve a reasonable approximation of human behavior without getting stuck in implementing feature channels and without slowing down the system too much. Inevitably, this yields some problems. Since the system is not able to regard other features than the implemented ones, there are for example no pop-outs possible for these features, e.g., curvature. However, the quality of the results with the given features implies that these features already yield a good approximation of human behavior. Especially objects explicitly designed to attract attention seem to rely strongly on color, as was shown in section 4.2.1.

A special role as a feature concerns the size of objects: although size seems to be no real feature [Treisman and Gormican, 1988], there is a pop-out effect concerning size (the reader may verify this in a "self-test" in Fig. 4.27, (a)). The image pyramids in VOCUS enable the computation of saliencies of several sizes but a uniqueness weighting concerning size is not implemented, thus no pop-out concerning size is possible: in Fig. 4.27 (a) the system focus is on one of the small dots (bottom-left), not on the single big one.

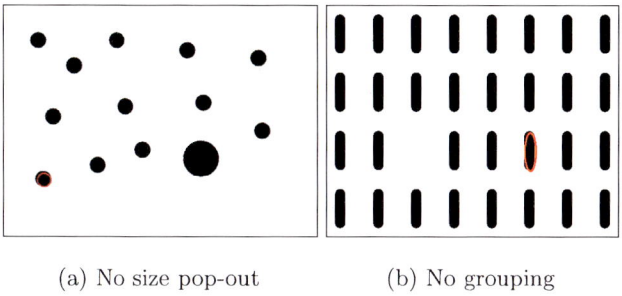

(a) No size pop-out   (b) No grouping

Fig. 4.27. And humans are still different: the size popout (a) and the missing item (b) are not focused by VOCUS although they pop out in human perception

Other differences to human behavior concern grouping effects. If there is one missing item in a systematically ordered field, humans immediately notice this absence. Imagine how fast your reaction is if someone has pilfered one of the chocolate candies out of your new chocolate box: you do not have to count them first to detect the gap! Since no grouping effects are included into the system, such effects cannot be detected (Fig. 4.27, (b)).

One drawback of current attention systems is that their implementation is usually too slow to yield substantial time savings in object recognition tasks (VOCUS requires 1.7 sec on a 300×300 pixel image on a 1,7 GHz Pentium IV). This has mainly two reasons. First, the structure of the system is highly parallel but the implementation is usually serial. Anyway, this is no conceptual drawback because the realization might be parallelized with help of several CPU's that share computation [Itti, 2002] or with a dedicated hardware [Ouerhani and Hügli, 2003c]. Second, accepting the overhead of an attentional front-end only makes sense if the recognition backend is a complex, time-consuming task. This is certainly true for general object recognizers able to cope with objects of different shapes, poses, scales, and illuminations. However, good general object recognizers do not yet exist. Existing approaches usually fit special kinds of recognition tasks. Since some of these specializations have a fast implementation, as for example the classifier of [Viola and Jones, 2004], the overhead of an attentional front-end might not pay off in a specialized recognition task as, for example, face detection. This changes if more than one object class is considered and if more complex recognition tasks have to be fulfilled [Frintrop et al., 2004b]. A detailed discussion on this topic will be found in chapter 7.

The full benefit of a computational bottom-up system of visual attention will be obtained when there are complex vision systems that have several tasks at the same time and have to decide what to do first according to the perception of the environment. The concentration on salient scene regions enables an efficient processing and prevents the system from getting lost in the bulk of details. Especially in robotics applications, it is important to recognize many object classes to achieve a robust and flexible behavior; attentional pre-selection of regions of interest is a highly promising approach to cope with complex sensor input.

5

The Visual Attention System VOCUS: Top-Down Extension

Detecting regions of interest with visual attention is an important mechanism in human visual perception. However, what is of interest depends on the situation. In the previous chapter, we focused on simulating bottom-up mechanisms of visual attention. These define regions as interesting which have a high contrast to their surroundings and are unique in the setting. As mentioned in chapter 2, top-down influences also play an important role in human visual attention: knowledge, motivations, emotions, and goals define what is of interest in a certain situation. For example, hungry people focus on food, architects consider buildings in detail and if looking for a fire extinguisher, red items attract the view more easily than other parts of the view [Vickery et al., 2005, Wolfe et al., 2004]. While the influences of motivations and emotions are beyond the scope of this work, the topic of this chapter will be the goal-directed search for target objects.

In human behavior, bottom-up and top-down attention are always intertwined and may not be considered separately, although one part may outweigh the other in certain situations. Even in a pure exploration mode, each person has own preferences resulting in individual scan-paths for the same scene. On the other hand, even if searching highly concentrated for a target, the bottom-up pop-out effect is not suppressible, an effect called *attentional capture* [Theeuwes, 2004]. Despite its importance in the human visual system, top-down influences are rarely considered in computational attention systems (cf. chapter 3.2.4 for a discussion of the state of the art). One of the reasons is that the neuro-biological foundations are not yet completely understood. Nevertheless, the extension of an attention system with top-down mechanisms is unavoidable if regions of interest shall be detected depending on a task. Moreover, the evaluation of the system is much easier with this extension since ground truth is available.

In this chapter, we present an extension of VOCUS that is able to regard top-down cues. In a learning phase, the system learns target-relevant features from a training image considering the properties of the target as well as of the surrounding (section 5.1). In search mode, the system considers this information to excite or inhibit features and computes a target-dependent top-down saliency map (section 5.2). An overview of the complete algorithm is shown in Fig. 5.1. In section 5.3, we discuss how several training images improve the performance before finally presenting detailed results proving the efficiency of the system in section 5.4 and concluding with a discussion in section 5.5.

Learning mode:
    mark region of interest (ROI) manually or provide coordinates
    compute bottom-up saliency map S_{bu}
    determine most salient region (MSR) in ROI of S_{bu}
    for each feature and conspicuity map X_i
        compute mean value $m_{i,(MSR)}$ of MSR in map X_i
        compute mean value $m_{i,(image-MSR)}$ in map X_i
        compute weight $w_i = m_{i,(MSR)}/m_{i,(image-MSR)}$
Search mode:
    compute bottom-up saliency map S_{bu}
    compute top-down saliency map S_{td}:
        compute excitation map $E = \sum_i (w_i * X_i)$ $\forall i : w_i > 1$
        compute inhibition map $I = \sum_i ((1/w_i) * X_i)$ $\forall i : w_i < 1$
        compute top-down saliency map $S_{td} = E - I$
        saturate values < 0 in S_{td}
    compute saliency map $S = t * S_{td} + (1 - t) * S_{bu}$ with $t \in [0..1]$
    determine most salient region in S

Fig. 5.1. The algorithm for goal-directed search

5.1 Learning Mode

Learning in our application means learning the object properties of a specified target. In learning mode, the system is provided with a region of interest containing the target object and learns which features distinguish the target best from the rest of the image. For each feature, a weight is determined that specifies to what amount the feature distinguishes the target from its background. This yields a weights vector **w** which is used in search mode to weight the feature maps according to the search task (cf. Fig. 5.2).

5.1.1 Computing Most Salient Region (MSR)

The input to VOCUS in learning mode is a training image and a *region of interest (ROI)*. The ROI is provided as a rectangle which is usually determined manually by the user but might also be the output of a classifier that specifies the target. Inside the ROI, the *most salient region (MSR)* is determined.

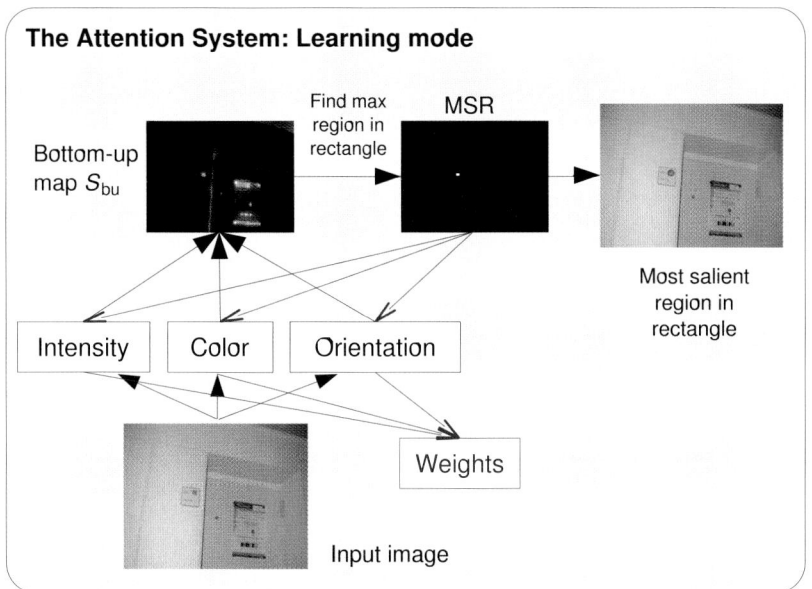

Fig. 5.2. In learning mode, VOCUS determines the *most salient region (MSR)* within the *region of interest (ROI)* (yellow rectangle in input image). Feature weights are determined for each feature and conspicuity map by the quotient of the mean target saliency (within MSR) and the mean background saliency (outside of MSR)

This is done by first computing the bottom-up saliency map, as described in chapter 4. Second, instead of determining the most salient region in the whole saliency map, the search is restricted to the ROI, i.e., the system determines which region is most salient in the specified rectangle. This makes the system stable: usually, VOCUS computes the same MSR, regardless of the exact coordinates of the rectangle. So the system is independent of variations the user makes when determining the rectangle manually and it is not necessary to mark the target exactly; the resulting weights vector will be the same for different sizes of the rectangle. The only problem occurs if a region more salient than the target is included in the rectangle; then, this region is extracted. This case is discussed in section 5.1.4. Furthermore, this method enables VOCUS to determine autonomously what is important in a specified region. It concentrates on parts that are most salient according to the features that it is able to compute and disregards the background or less salient parts. Figure 5.3 (left) shows a region of interest ROI detected by a classifier containing a name plate as target (yellow rectangle) and the most salient region MSR in this rectangle (red ellipse).

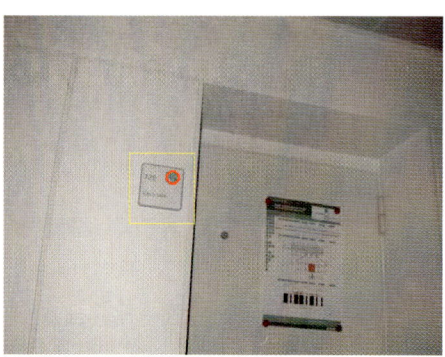

Feature	weights
intensity on/off	0.001
intensity off/on	9.616
orientation $0°$	4.839
orientation $45°$	9.226
orientation $90°$	2.986
orientation $135°$	8.374
color green	76.572
color blue	4.709
color red	0.009
color yellow	0.040
conspicuity I	6.038
conspicuity O	5.350
conspicuity C	12.312

Fig. 5.3. Learning the target "name plate". Left: a region of interest (ROI) detected by a classifier (yellow rectangle) and the most salient region (MSR) inside the rectangle (red ellipse). Right: the weights for 10 feature and 3 conspicuity maps learned from the MSR. The green color feature map has the highest weights value

5.1.2 Determining Weights

Next, weights are determined for each feature and each conspicuity map. The weights indicate how important a map is for detecting the target. They are computed as the ratio of the mean target saliency and the mean background saliency: the weight w_i of map X_i is computed by

$$w_i = m_{i,(MSR)}/m_{i,(image-MSR)}, \qquad i \in \{1, ..., 13\},$$

where $m_{i,(MSR)}$ denotes the mean intensity value of the pixels in the MSR in map X_i, showing how strong this map contributes to the saliency of the region of interest, and $m_{i,(image-MSR)}$ is the mean of the rest of the image in map X_i, showing how strong the feature is present in the surroundings. The weights are computed for 10 feature and 3 conspicuity maps, together they form the *weights vector* $\mathbf{w} = (w_1, ..., w_{13})$.

In Fig. 5.3, the weights for the MSR of a name plate are shown. The values imply that the learned region is dark on a bright background (intensity values), that the diagonal filters yield stronger values than the vertical and horizontal ones (orientation values) and that the most important color is green, followed by blue, whereas red and yellow with values smaller than 1 are less present than in the rest of the image and are used for inhibition. Furthermore, the weights of the conspicuity maps indicate that color is the most important feature dimension for this object.

5.1.3 The Role of the Environment

Learning the features of the target is important to enable goal-directed search but if these features also occur in the environment they might be of not much use. For example, if a red target is placed among red distractors it is not sensible to consider color for visual search, although red might be the strongest feature of the target. In VOCUS, not only the target's features but also the features of the background are considered and used for inhibition. This method is supported by psychophysical experiments, showing that both excitation and inhibition of features are important in visual search [Navalpakkam et al., 2004].

We show in Fig. 5.4 an example that reveals the advantage of considering background information additionally. A red horizontal bar is searched in different contexts. In the first one, it is surrounded by black distractors (top) and in the second image by red ones (bottom). Surrounded by black distractors, red is the most important feature and the weights of the color conspicuity map are higher than the other ones (left column). Note that this kind of red has a high portion of yellow, so the yellow feature map has also high values. Surrounded by red distractors, red no longer discriminates the target from the distractors, but the horizontal orientation does. This is expressed in the weight values: red has still a high value but it diminished significantly in comparison to the first case. In opposite, the value for horizontal orientation increased, showing now the highest feature weight and the most important conspicuity map is here the one for orientation.

The consideration of background information is one of the characteristics of VOCUS that distinguishes it from most existing approaches: for example, the system of Hamker [Hamker, 2004] also considers the features of the target for visual search but does not regard the surroundings of the targets and so it is not able to extract the best features in a given setting.

5.1.4 Choosing Training Images

When choosing a training image, there are several points to consider. First, from the above example we see that it is important to choose representative training images in which the object occurs in a similar environment as in the test images. Simple training images containing only the target on a uniform background work less well because they do not necessarily consider the most discriminating features.

Second, there are some images that are not suitable for training because the region extracted for learning is not suitable. An algorithm to test the suitability of a training image will be given later in Fig. 5.6, here we will deal with an informal description: a training image is suitable if the weights learned from it enable an efficient visual search in other images (efficient search means the target is detected with one of the first fixations).

Feature	weights (top)	weights (bottom)
intensity on/off	0.01	0.01
intensity off/on	9.13	13.17
orientation 0°	20.64	**29.84**
orientation 45°	1.65	1.96
orientation 90°	0.31	0.31
orientation 135°	1.65	1.96
color green	0.00	0.00
color blue	0.00	0.01
color red	**47.60**	10.29
color yellow	**36.25**	9.43
conspicuity I	4.83	6.12
conspicuity O	7.90	**11.31**
conspicuity C	**17.06**	2.44

Fig. 5.4. Effect of background information on the weight values. Left: the same target (red horizontal bar, 2nd in 2nd row) in different environments: all vertical bars are black (top) resp. red (bottom).[1] Right: the learned weights; the values which are most important for distinguishing the examples are printed in bold face. In the upper image, the red color is the most important feature. In the lower image, surrounded by red distractors, red is no longer the prime feature to detect the bar but orientation is

If a training image is unsuitable this might have several reasons. First, not the target itself might be extracted by VOCUS, but a region close to it. This happens if there is a region inside the marked ROI that is more salient than the target (cf. Fig. 5.5, (b)). This is easily recognized by the user and is usually prevented by drawing the rectangle tight around the object and not including other image regions. If this is not possible, another training image should be chosen.

The second case of a non-suitable training image occurs if a region is extracted that is not representative for the target. This happens for example, if a part of the target is extracted that is not visible in all test images. This might be a writing or a label on the object or just a light reflection (cf. Fig. 5.5, (c)). In this case, the image should not be used for training. An example of a "suitable" and two "non-suitable" ones is shown in Fig. 5.5. On the left, nearly the whole fire extinguisher is extracted for learning, resulting in representative weights. In the middle, the extracted region is beneath the target and on the right, a white imprint on the fire extinguisher is extracted which is not visible in all images and therefore unsuitable for learning.

There might be cases in which no reasonable learning is possible because always regions are extracted that are not representative for the target. This

---

[1] If you have a gray-scale print-out or you have problems to recognize the colors, have a look at the bold printed and labeled images in Fig. C.1 top and middle on page 199.

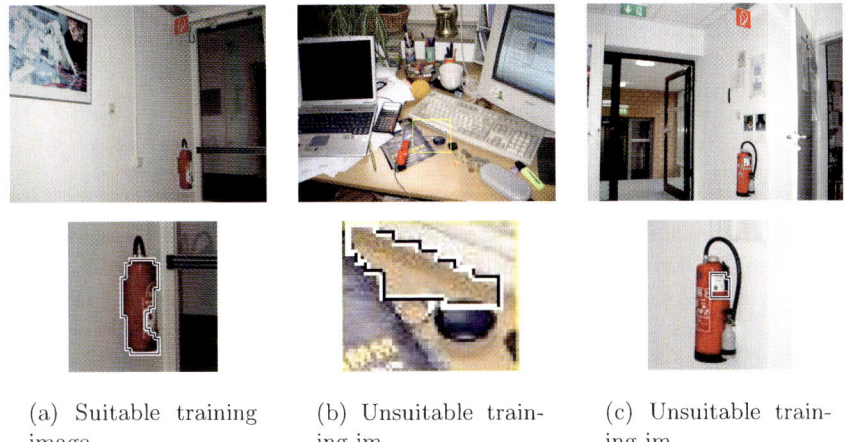

(a) Suitable training image

(b) Unsuitable training im.

(c) Unsuitable training im.

Fig. 5.5. Some suitable and unsuitable training images (top) with the extracted MSR (black-white contour). Below, the target with the MSR enlarged. In **(a)**, the extracted region is representative for the target (fire extinguisher); the image is suitable. In **(b)**, the extracted region is inside the marked rectangle but beneath the target (key fob); the image is not suitable. In **(c)**, the extracted region is not representative because the white imprint on the target (fire extinguisher) is not visible in all test images

might happen if the shape of the target deviates significantly from a rectangular shape, so that inevitably a significant amount of background regions is included in the ROI and if, additionally, the target is so inconspicuous that always unsuitable regions are extracted. However, in all of our experiments this happened only rarely for individual cases and was easily overcome by drawing the rectangle closer to the object or exchanging the training image. If this problem might not be eliminated by these methods, it is possible to use a binary mask to determine the region to be learned [Navalpakkam et al., 2005]. However, we do not recommend this procedure since it firstly takes away a lot of flexibility and usability from the system and, secondly, does not enable the system to automatically concentrate on features suitable for learning.

Usually, the decision whether a training image is suitable is easily made by the user with common sense as the examples in Fig. 5.5 imply. However, it might require some experience with the system to do so, therefore it is reasonable to provide a method how to determine the suitability of a training image automatically. To achieve this, we first introduce some definitions:

Definition 1 (Hit number). *The **hit number** on image I for target t is the rank of the focus that hits the target in order of saliency.*

For example, if the 2nd focus is on the target, the hit number is 2. The lower the hit number, the better the search performance. If the hit number is 1, the target is immediately detected. In pop-out experiments, the hit number is 1 by definition.

Definition 2 (Average hit number). *The* **average hit number** *for an image set is the arithmetic mean of the hit numbers of all images.*

Note that usually only a determinate number of fixations is considered so that images with undetected targets are not included in the average. To indicate this, we show in our experimental results the percentage of detected targets additionally.

Definition 3 (Self-test, self-test hit number). *A* **self-test** *on image I for a target t means: first, learn the weights* **w** *for t from image I. Second, apply* **w** *to I itself. The resulting hit number is the* **self-test hit number.**

The self-test hit number is a good base for comparisons, since the weights of an image itself yield a good chance to discriminate the target from its surrounding. A self-test hit number of 1 indicates that the weights are sufficient to detect the target in similar environments. A greater self-test hit number indicates that there are distractors in the scene that are very similar to the target and that the features of the system are incapable to distinguish between target and distractors. This test is not suitable for deciding whether a training image is useful or not, because if there are distractors in a scene which are too similar according to the given features, there is nothing we can do about it. It might be useful to train on such scenes anyway, because the extracted weights are the best possible solution for these kinds of scenes. Note that a hit number of 2, 3, or even 10 is often still useful since the regions to be investigated by an object classifier are still considerably reduced.

Although the self-test is not sufficient to decide on the suitability of a training image, it is useful in combination with a second image: it provides a ground truth with which the performance of a second image can be evaluated. This brings us to the announced **suitability test**: A training image I_1 is **suitable** iff its hit number on a second image I_2 is equal or smaller than the self-test hit number on I_2. The algorithm for this test is shown in Fig. 5.6.

---

choose training image I_1 and compute its weights w_1
choose test image I_2 and determine self-test hit number n_2
determine hit number n_1 of w_1 on I_2
If $(n_1 \leq n_2)$ then I_1 is suitable

Fig. 5.6. Suitability test

More stable detection results are achieved if several training images are used. This is especially true if the environment differs between test images, e.g., if the target object occurs on different backgrounds. Since this will be better understood after explaining the search mode, we will first concentrate on this before describing the use of several training images in section 5.3.

5.2 Search Mode

In search mode, we search for a target with help of the previously learned weights. The weights are used to excite or inhibit the feature and conspicuity maps according to the search task. The weighted maps contribute to a top-down saliency map highlighting those regions that are salient with respect to the target and inhibiting others. The top-down saliency competes for global saliency with the bottom-up saliency map. Fig 5.7 illustrates this procedure.

5.2.1 Excitation and Inhibition Map

The excitation map E is the weighted sum of all feature and conspicuity maps X_i that are important for the target, namely the features with weights greater than 1:

$$E = \sum_{i:\, w_i > 1} (w_i * X_i). \tag{5.1}$$

The inhibition map I collects the maps that are not present in the target region, namely the features with weights smaller than 1:

$$I = \sum_{i:\, w_i < 1} ((1/w_i) * X_i). \tag{5.2}$$

Weights with value 1 are ignored since they indicate that the mean saliency of the target region is exactly the same as the mean saliency of the surrounding; such a feature is completely useless for detecting the target. However, in practice this usually does not occur unless a feature is not present at all, e.g., color is not present in a gray-scale image and the color weights are set to 1. The excitation and inhibition map are not normalized to the same range since we want to preserve the differences among the maps.

5.2.2 The Top-Down Map

The top-down map is obtained by subtracting the inhibition map from the excitation map:

$$S_{td} = E - I \tag{5.3}$$

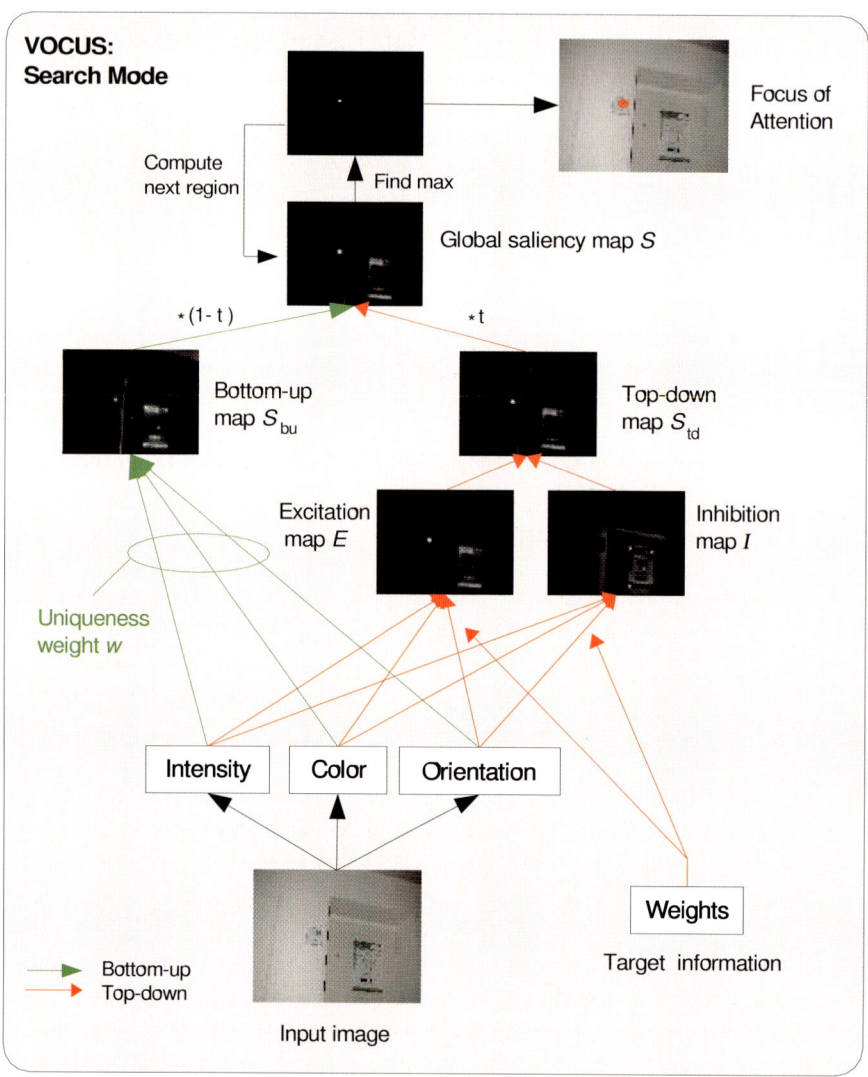

Fig. 5.7. The search mode of the visual attention system. The bottom-up saliency map S_{bu} competes for saliency with a top-down saliency map S_{td} which results from an excitation map E and an inhibition map I. These maps result from the weighted sum of the feature and conspicuity maps, using the learned weights vector. When creating the global saliency map S, the influence of bottom-up and top-down is adjustable by the top-down factor t. The images in this figure were produced with t=1

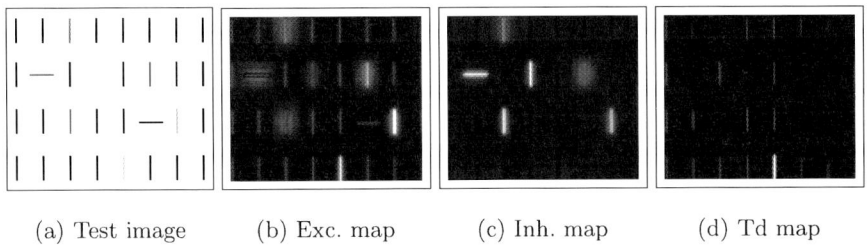

(a) Test image   (b) Exc. map   (c) Inh. map   (d) Td map

Fig. 5.8. Some maps of the search for the cyan vertical bar (5th in last row).[2] The bar region is highlighted in the excitation map **(b)** but the green bar (7th in 3rd row) shows even more activation. Only the inhibition **(c)** of the green bar enables the highest activation of cyan in the top-down map **(d)**

After subtraction, negative values are clipped to 0. An example of the excitation and inhibition of regions is shown in Fig. 5.8 when searching for the cyan vertical bar. Here, we see that not only the excitation map but also the inhibition map has an important influence. The excitation map shows bright values for the cyan bar but the brightest region occurs at the green bar. The inhibition map shows activation at the green bar but no activation at the cyan bar, so in the resulting top-down map, only the cyan bar is represented.

5.2.3 The Global Saliency Map

The global saliency map is the weighted sum of the bottom-up and the top-down map; combining bottom-up and top-down cues by a weighted sum is also suggested in the psychological Guided Search model in [Wolfe, 2001b]. Both maps compete for saliency: the bottom-up map showing regions that are salient because of scene-specific conspicuities, the top-down map emphasizing the features of the learned target. To make the maps comparable, S_{td} is normalized in advance to the same range as S_{bu}. When fusing the maps, it is possible to determine the degree to which each map contributes to the sum. This is done by weighting the maps with a top-down factor $t \in [0..1]$:

$$S = (1 - t) * S_{bu} + t * S_{td}. \tag{5.4}$$

After the computation of the global saliency map, the most salient region is determined as before and the focus of attention is directed there.

The fusion of bottom-up and top-down map might be a problematic step: in human perception, it is not clear how bottom-up and top-down cues work together. It is clear, however, that it depends on your degree of concentration

---

[2] If you have a gray-scale print-out or you have problems to recognize the colors, have a look at the bold printed and labeled image in Fig. C.1 (top) on page 199.

how easily your attention will be diverted from your task by bottom-up cues. If you are highly concentrated on your task, you will be less sensitive for diverting cues. Imagine, for example, reading a thrilling novel and forgetting everything around you. But even if you are highly concentrated, strongly salient cues are able to divert your attention, e.g., a person suddenly entering a room or an emergency bell. This was shown by [Theeuwes, 2004] in psychological experiments: he has shown that colored cues divert the search for objects although the task is searching for objects defined by shape. This phenomenon is called *attentional capture* (cf. chapter 2.1.3).

The dependency of bottom-up and top-down influence on concentration motivated us to introduce the top-down factor t representing a kind of "concentration factor". This enables the system to regulate the influence according to the system's state. In a high concentration mode, the system looks only for top-down cues and may not be diverted ($t = 1$). In a lower concentration mode, e.g., in an exploration phase, also bottom-up cues have an influence and may divert the focus of attention ($t < 1$). Theeuwes has also shown that in humans this *attentional capture* can not be overridden by top-down search strategies [Theeuwes, 2004]. That means, for a severely biologically motivated system a top-down factor of 1 should not be allowed. Nevertheless, for a technical system that usually has to solve only one clearly defined task at a time, also a top-down factor of 1 is often useful. The use of the top-down factor made the previous normalization of both maps a sensible step since it equates the maps and leaves the regulation to the choice of this factor.

Although it is beyond the scope of this work and subject of future work to investigate how the top-down factor has to be chosen, it shall be noted that this might be a difficult task that has to be carefully examined. Various tests have to reveal how strong the top-down factor has to be to enable the system to fulfill its task and yet be sensitive to salient regions and/or events and to determine which task requires which top-down factor. It might also be useful to not leave the complete control to this factor but to first weight both the bottom-up and the top-down saliency map with the uniqueness weight $\mathcal{W}$. Notice however that if this weighting and the top-down factor are used simultaneously, it is not obvious how they work together.

5.3 Several Training Images

Learning weights from one single training image yields good results when the target object occurs in all test images in a similar way, i.e., the background color is similar and the object occurs always in a similar orientation. Although this sounds like an unacceptable constraint, in fact these conditions often occur if the objects are fixed elements of the environment. For example, name plates or fire extinguishers usually are placed on the same kind of wall, so the background has always a similar color and intensity. Furthermore, since the object is fixed, its orientation does not vary and it is sensible to learn that fire extinguishers have usually a vertical orientation.

Although the search is already quite successful with weights from a single training image, the results differ slightly depending on the choice of the training image. This is shown in Tab. 5.1: a highlighter was searched in a test set of 60 images using the weights from a single training image. The table shows the different results for several training images; the detection rate differs between 95 and 100%.

Table 5.1. The search for a highligher with different single training images on a test set of 60 images (examples of training and test images in Fig. 5.13 and 5.14). The first 10 foci were determined. The performance is shown as the average hit number and, in parentheses, the percentage of targets detected within the first 10 foci. The performance differs slightly depending on the training image

Target	# test im	average hit number (and detection rate [%])				
		w_1	w_2	w_3	w_4	w_5
Highlighter	60	1.83 (99%)	1.70 (97%)	1.43 (100%)	1.93 (95%)	1.78 (97%)

Furthermore, the results usually differ slightly depending on the test set the weights are applied to. One training image might fit better to a special image set than to another. To weed out these special cases, it is sensible to take the average weight of at least two training images to enable a more stable performance on arbitrary test sets. For movable objects it is even more important to compute average weights. A highlighter may lie on a dark or on a bright desk and it may have any orientation. Here, it is necessary to learn from several training images which features are stable and which are not.

5.3.1 Average Weights

To achieve a robust target detection even in changing environments, it is necessary to learn the target properties from several training images. This is done by computing the average weight vector from n training images with the *geometric mean* of the weights for each feature, i.e., the average weight vector $\mathbf{w}_{(1,..,n)}$ from n training images is determined by:

$$\mathbf{w}_{(1,..,n)} = \sqrt[n]{\prod_{j=1}^{n} \mathbf{w}_j}. \tag{5.5}$$

If one feature is present in some training images but absent in others, the average values will be close to 1 leading to only a low activation in the top-down map. In Tab. 5.2 this is shown on the example of searching for red bars: the target occurs in horizontal or vertical orientations and on a dark or bright

Table 5.2. Left: four training examples to learn red bars of horizontal and vertical orientation and on different backgrounds.[3] The target is marked by the yellow rectangle. Right: The learned weights. Column 2–5: the weights for a single training image (vertical bar on bright background (v,b), horizontal on bright (h,b), vertical on dark (v,d), horizontal on dark (h,d)). The highest values are highlighted in bold face. Column 6: average weights. Color is the only stable feature

Feature	\multicolumn{5}{c}{weights for red bar}				
	v,b	h,b	v,d	h,d	average
int on/off	0.00	0.01	**8.34**	**9.71**	0.14
int off/on	**14.08**	**10.56**	0.01	0.04	0.42
ori 0°	1.53	**21.43**	0.49	**10.52**	3.61
ori 45°	2.66	1.89	1.99	2.10	2.14
ori 90°	**6.62**	0.36	**5.82**	0.32	1.45
ori 135°	2.66	1.89	1.99	2.10	2.14
col green	0.00	0.00	0.00	0.00	0.00
col blue	0.00	0.00	0.01	0.01	0.00
col red	**18.87**	**17.01**	**24.13**	**24.56**	**20.88**
col yellow	**16.95**	**14.87**	**21.21**	**21.66**	**18.45**
consp I	7.45	5.56	3.93	4.59	5.23
consp O	4.34	7.99	2.87	5.25	4.78
consp C	4.58	4.08	5.74	5.84	5.00

background; the only stable feature is the red color. This is reflected in the rightmost column of the table which shows the average weights: the weights for intensity and orientation feature maps are almost equal, only weights for the color feature maps show high values. This enables the search for red bars, regardless of the background and the orientation.

5.3.2 An Algorithm to Choose the Training Images

In the previous example in Tab. 5.2, four training images were chosen that were claimed to represent the test data. In practice, the problem is: how do we find suitable training images? We could think about the test application and reason about suitable training data or we could just use a bunch of training images that cover many possible contexts presenting the target at different orientations and on different backgrounds. However, this does not guarantee a good training set and, moreover, it depends heavily on the user's experiences and skills. In this section, we introduce a method how several training images should be chosen.

Let us first think about how an optimal weight vector could be achieved. Since the average weights do not always improve when more training images

---

[3] If you have a gray-scale print-out or you have problems to recognize the colors, have a look at the bold printed and labeled image in Fig. C.1 (bottom) on page 199. The images in the bottom row are the same with a black background.

are considered, the best performance is usually not achieved by considering all images of a training set T_1. The reason is that training on too similar images results in *overfitting*, e.g., generating too specialized weights. Instead, there exists a subset of T_1, the average weights of which yield the best performance on another image set T_2. The only possibility to find this subset is to test all possible combinations, an effort costing to check 2^n combinations for n training images. Since these computations are too costly even for rather small n, we propose an approximation algorithm that yields a local optimum in performance.

First notice that since the test data is not known during training, it is only possible to tune the weights to the training set. Although this does not guarantee a local optimum in performance on a test set, we show in section 5.4.2 that the difference in performance is usually small as long as the training set is representative. To achieve this, a good strategy is to divide the image set into two parts and use one part for training and one for testing.

The overall idea of the approximation training algorithm is to first choose one arbitrary image I_1 from the training image set. Then, the weights from I_1 are applied to the whole training set T and the image I_2 is determined on which the hit number is worst. A bad hit number might mean that I_1 was not *suitable* for this image. Whether this assumption is true can be checked by comparing the hit number with the self-test hit number of I_2 (cf. the algorithm in Fig. 5.6). If the latter is better, the assumption was true: I_1 was unsuitable. In this case, I_2 is a good choice to improve the weights thus the average weights of I_1 and I_2 are determined. This procedure is continued as long as the average hit rate on the training set improves. A flowchart of the algorithm is shown in Fig. 5.9.

As we will show in our experiments in section 5.4.2, usually the local optimum in performance is already reached for two training images, only in rare cases several training images are useful. We also show that it is sensible to take at least two training images even if the performance is better with the first single image, because often a single image is too specific for the training image set. An average weights vector yields a more stable performance on arbitrary test sets.

5.4 Experiments and Results

In this section, we apply the described mechanisms of learning and visual search on several image sets and evaluate the search performance. We start in section 5.4.1 with experiments in which the weights are learned from a single training image. We first apply the system to artificial images that are specifically well-suited to vary certain aspects of the images and investigate the system behavior according to these aspects. We then continue with applying the system to real-world images including arranged scenes as well as natural ones. In section 5.4.2, we show how the use of several training images

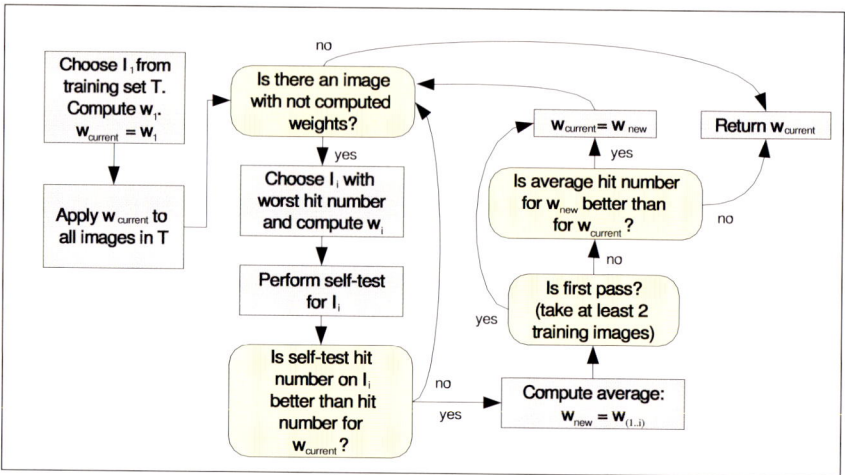

Fig. 5.9. The algorithm to find the most suitable training images out of an image set. Output is the average weights vector of the selected images. With this vector, a local optimum in detection quality on the training set is achieved

improves the performance and investigate how many training images yield the best performance in different cases. The competition between bottom-up and top-down cues is examined in section 5.4.3 by varying the top-down factor t and the robustness for viewpoint and illumination changes is analyzed in section 5.4.4. Finally, we compare VOCUS with two of the closest related systems for top-down attention in section 5.4.5.

5.4.1 Experiments: Search with One Training Image

In the experiments of this section, the weight vector was determined in the learning phase from a single training image. We first show several experiments with artificial images before we continue with real-world data.

Artificial Images

In this section, we examine the visual search on artificial images since these are especially well suited for evaluation. It is possible to choose the exact feature values for intensities, orientations, and colors of target and distractors and it is possible to disregard noise and pose changes and so concentrate on the investigated items.

The images used for our first experiment are depicted in Fig. 5.10. On top, we see the training image, below the test image that is the same image flipped horizontally. As targets, we considered several of the bars in the image. We computed the weights vector of a target from the training image, applied it to

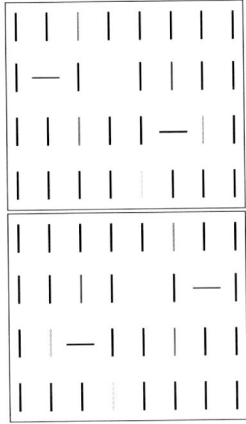

Target	Hit number		
	$t = 0$	$t = 0.5$	$t = 1$
red horiz	1 (24)	1	1
blue vert	2 (23)	1	1
black horiz	3 (21)	1	1
magenta vert	4 (18)	2	2
red vert	5 (17)	2	1
black vert	6 (15)	1	1
green vert	- (12)	1	1
cyan vert	- (8)	1	1
yellow vert	- (7)	1	1

Fig. 5.10. Search performance of VOCUS on artificial data. Left: training image (top) and horizontally flipped test image (bottom).[4] Right: search results for different top-down factors t regarding the first 10 foci. $t = 0$ is pure bottom-up search, $t = 1$ pure top-down search, and $t = 0.5$ a mixture of both. The hit number denotes the number of the focus on the target. The numbers in parentheses show the saliency value at the target region. In pure top-down mode, all targets are detected with the first focus except of one detection with the 2nd focus. For further explanations see text

the test image, and determined the *hit number* (Def. 3). The table in Fig. 5.10 shows the *hit number* for different top-down factors t. The first column shows the results obtained with $t = 0$, i.e., it illustrates the bottom-up saliency of the bars. The targets are named in the order of bottom-up detection, i.e., the red horizontal bar is focused first, then the blue vertical bar and so on. The green, cyan, and yellow bar are not focused within the first 10 foci of attention, since their saliency value is lower than the one of the black vertical bars. The saliency value in the target region is shown in parentheses.

The last column shows the hit numbers for pure top-down search ($t = 1$). Except in one case, the searched object is always focused immediately. The exception is the magenta vertical bar that is only detected with the second focus. Magenta has significant blue portions, so the blue regions are also enhanced during search for magenta. This leads to the focusing of blue before detecting the magenta bar. Note that also black objects are found, regarding the lack of color by inhibiting colored objects.

The middle column shows the results obtained with a top-down factor $t = 0.5$, i.e., bottom-up and top-down cues are both equally regarded. It shows that in most cases the number of the focus on the target is the same as for $t = 1$, except for the red vertical bar. Here, the bottom-up saliency

---

[4] If you have a gray-scale print-out or you have problems to recognize the colors, have a look at the bold printed and labeled image in Fig. C.1 (top) on page 199.

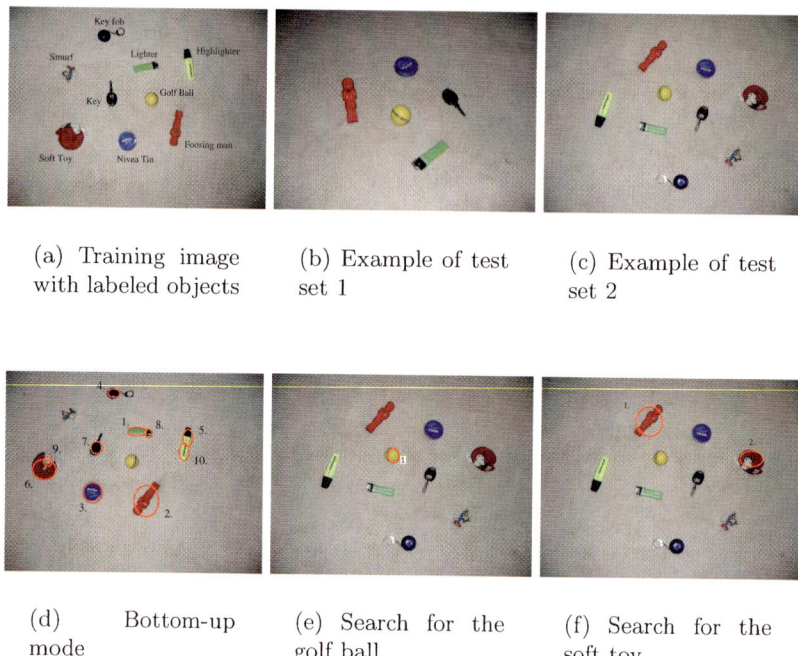

(a) Training image with labeled objects

(b) Example of test set 1

(c) Example of test set 2

(d)   Bottom-up mode

(e) Search for the golf ball

(f) Search for the soft toy

Fig. 5.11. The real-world objects which were used for the experiments of Tab. 5.3. First row: the training image (**a**) and two example images of the two utilized test sets (**b,c**). Test set 1 contains 20 images each with 5 objects taken from different viewpoints; test set 2 contains 9 images each with 9 objects. Second row: foci of attention in bottom-up mode (**d**) and top-down mode (**e,f**). When similar objects are present, the focus might be diverted (**f**)

of the red horizontal bar diverts the focus. Although it might look as if the bottom-up cues have less influence than the top-down cues, this is not true. Note that the saliency values in the bottom-up saliency map do not differ much, so a small top-down influence is enough to change the order of the foci. For a pop-out experiment, the difference between target and distractor values is much bigger, e.g. 29 for the horizontal target and 15 for the vertical distractors of Fig. 4.19. A detailed examination of the influences of bottom-up and top-down is presented in section 5.4.3.

Real-World Images

In this section, we apply VOCUS to real-world objects (Fig. 5.11). We chose two test sets with objects from different viewpoints varying up to 180°, one set containing 5 objects, the other 9 objects. This enables to show how the

Table 5.3. Search performance of VOCUS for different top-down factors t on the objects of Fig. 5.11. $t = 0$ is pure bottom-up search, $t = 1$ pure top-down search, and $t = 0.5$ a mixture of both. Weights were learned from a single training image. The numbers denote the number of the focus on the target. The numbers in parentheses show the percentage of targets that were detected within the first 10 foci. When no percentage is given, this means all targets have been detected (100%)

Test set	# test im.	Target	Av. hit number (and detection rate [%])		
			$t=0$	$t=0.5$	$t=1.0$
1	20	golf ball	4.40	1.00	1.00
		lighter	3.15	1.15	1.10
		foosing man	2.35	1.00	1.00
		nivea tin	2.80	1.00	1.00
		key	4.35 (80%)	1.50	1.25
2	9	golf ball	2.60 (46%)	1.00	1.00
		lighter	4.69 (78%)	1.13	1.00
		foosing man	3.90	1.10	1.20
		nivea tin	5.00	1.50	1.20
		key	2.70 (33%)	2.90	2.10
		key fob	3.70	1.30	1.20
		highlighter	2.00	1.90	2.10
		soft toy	5.30	2.00	1.80
		smurf	- (0%)	2.8 (22%)	6.4 (78%)

complexity of a scene changes the performance: of course, a visual search is more difficult in more complex scenes and similar objects may mislead the focus of attention. This is shown in the example results in the second row of Fig. 5.11: the golf ball is immediately detected, whereas it takes two fixations to detect the red soft toy. The equally red foosing man misleads the focus.

This can also be seen in Table 5.3. For some objects, e.g., the foosing man, the Nivea tin, and especially the key, the results are worse in the more complex test set 2, since similar objects mislead the focus. Nevertheless, search is successful in nearly all examples, since in test set 1 the target is usually detected with the first focus and in test set 2 with the first or second focus. In contrast, if one of the objects was chosen randomly, the hit number would be on average 2.5 in the first and 4.5 in the second test set. Even this would only be achieved if there was always only one focus on an object, which is usually not true because the segmentation is based on saliency rather than on objects (e.g., in Fig. 5.11 (d) there are 2 FOAs on the highlighter).

Note that even the black key is detected, what is enabled by inhibiting color cues. The only exception is the smurf, which is too small and not salient enough to enable a fast visual search. The examples show also convincingly how stable the system is with respect to viewpoint changes. Although the pictures were taken from completely different viewpoints, the detection results are stable and usually the targets are detected with the first or second focus.

(a) Search for red books

(b) Search for white books

(c) Search for yellow books

Fig. 5.12. The 20 most salient regions (black-white contour) when VOCUS was trained to detect differently colored books. Weights were always learned from a single training image

Only in the presence of similar objects with similar saliency values, viewpoint changes lead occasionally to a changed order of fixations.

An example of a real-world application in a not specially arranged scene is shown in Fig. 5.12. We trained VOCUS on books of a special color in a bookshelf and illustrate the 20 most salient regions as contours. Most difficult is the search for white books, since the white wall diverts the focus of attention. But even here, 14 of the 20 foci point to white books.

5.4.2 Experiments: Search with Several Training Images

In the previous experiments, the weights vectors were always computed from a single training image. In this section, we show how the system performance is improved if several training images are considered and demonstrate the search performance on various real-world scenes. As targets, we used four kinds of objects: two objects which are fixed in our office environment (fire extinguishers and name plates) and two movable objects (a key fob and a highlighter). The highlighter was presented on two different desks, a dark (black) and a bright (wooden) one. For each target, we used a training set of 10 to 54 images and chose suitable training images from the set with the training algorithm in Fig. 5.9. In Fig. 5.13, we depict one of the training images for each target as well as the most salient region that VOCUS extracted for learning.

In the following, we present four experiments that illustrate different aspects of the system performance. First, we show the search performance on four test sets and illustrate the performance for different numbers of training images. Second, we test VOCUS on a search task in which the environment of the target differs. Third, we investigate the system's ability to generalize to environments disjoint from the training environment and, fourth, we give an

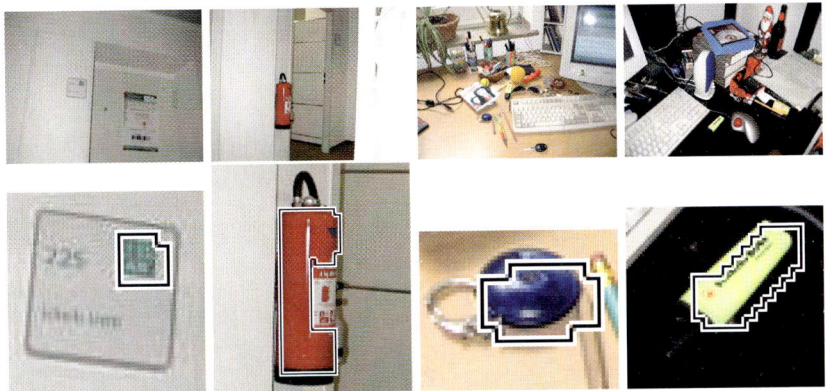

Fig. 5.13. Top: some training images with targets (name plate, fire extinguisher, key fob, and a highlighter on the dark desk). Bottom: The part of the image that was marked for learning (region of interest (ROI)) and the contour of the region that was extracted for learning (most salient region (MSR))

overview of the search performance for different test sets, different top-down factors, and different numbers of FOAs considered for the detection.

Experiment 1

In the first experiment, we demonstrate with different image sets how the search quality depends on the number of training images considered for learning. We determine the weights vector with the training algorithm of Fig. 5.9 and show the search results with the computed vectors first on the training set itself (training phase) and then on a test set (test phase). Some example results are depicted in Fig. 5.14.

The image sets used for this experiment consisted of images with similar backgrounds for each set: the walls behind the fire extinguisher and the name plate were always white and the key fob and the highlighter lay on the same desk within a set. Although the backgrounds in these examples were roughly the same for each image set, the images were highly complex and include a highly structured surrounding with many distracting regions.

To compute the weight vectors, we chose the most suitable training images from the training set with the algorithm of Fig. 5.9. Remember that the algorithm chooses the first image at random and then the images with the worst detection results on the training set; it stops when a local optimum in performance is reached. We document this by presenting the detection results (average hit number and detection rate) for each weight vector that is computed during the iterations of the algorithm (Tab. 5.4 (a)). This corresponds to visualizing the intermediate steps of the algorithm.

Target: name plate

Target: fire extinguisher

Target: highlighter

Target: key fob

Fig. 5.14. Some of the results from searching the targets of Fig. 5.13. Quantitative results are shown in Tab. 5.4 – 5.7. The FOAs are depicted by red ellipses. After the target was focused, the search was canceled so the number of depicted foci is equal to the number of required fixations. The hardest example is the one in the upper right corner: the poster shows colors similar to the logo of the name plate and diverts the focus so the target is only detected by the 6th focus. In all other depicted examples the target is found with the first or second focus

Table 5.4. Experiment 1: Search performance of VOCUS on training sets **(a)** and test sets **(b)** with weight vectors from 1, 2, and 3 training images which were obtained with the algorithm in Fig. 5.9. The performance is presented as the average hit number on the training set and, in parentheses, the percentage of detected targets within the first 10 foci. The best value is highlighted in bold face. Already two training images yield the local optimum in performance and the algorithm stops. Note that in the test set the best performance is not always reached for the same number of training images

Target	# train im.	av. hit number (and detection rate [%])		
		$\mathbf{w}_1$	$\mathbf{w}_{(1,2)}$	$\mathbf{w}_{(1,..,3)}$
Fire extinguisher	10	1.10 (100%)	**1.00 (100%)**	1.00 (100%)
Key fob	10	1.33 (100%)	**1.00 (100%)**	1.00 (100%)
Name plate	54	1.61 (87%)	**2.04 (94%)**	1.97 (93%)
Highlighter (dark)	10	1.50 (100%)	**1.50 (100%)**	1.50 (100%)
Highlighter (bright)	10	3.40 (100%)	**2.10 (100%)**	2.40 (100%)

(a) Search results on training sets

Target	# train im.	# test im.	av. hit number (and detection rate [%])		
			$\mathbf{w}_1$	$\mathbf{w}_{(1,2)}$	$\mathbf{w}_{(1,..,3)}$
Fire extinguisher	10	46	1.14 (100%)	**1.09 (100%)**	1.09 (100%)
Key fob	10	30	1.40 (100%)	**1.23 (100%)**	1.40 (100%)
Name plate	54	238	2.31 (79%)	**2.55 (86%)**	2.28 (86%)
Highlighter (dark)	10	30	**1.30 (100%)**	1.37 (100%)	1.37 (100%)
Highlighter (bright)	10	30	2.43 (100%)	1.97 (97%)	**2.13 (100%)**

(b) Search results on test sets

It turned out that the search performance is in most cases better with the average of two training images than with a single one. Most obvious is this for the name plate: the detection rate within the first 10 foci increased from 87% to 94% (the detection rate is more important for evaluating the performance than the average focus, because a single image that is additionally detected increases the detection rate slightly but decreases the average hit number. That means, a performance of average hit number 2.04 and detection rate of 94% is better than a performance of average hit number 1.97 and detection rate of 93%). Only for the highlighter on the dark desk the detection remains the same. If the first training image yields an equal or better performance than the average of the first two images, we recommend still using the average because this usually yields a better performance on test sets, since the solution is less specialized to the test set. For three images, the performance does not improve any more, on the contrary, the results are worse for some of the examples (name plate, highlighter bright). Therefore, the algorithm stops with the weights vectors $\mathbf{w}_{(1,2)}$ as local optima.

In a second step, we apply these weight vectors to test image sets that were disjoint from the training data (Tab. 5.4 (b)). This shows how the system generalizes on unknown data. It revealed that the performance is in most cases slightly worse than on the training set; this is evident since the weights were chosen to fit best on the training set. However, the detection quality is still very high: fire extinguisher, key fob, and the highlighter on the dark desk are detected in all images (detection rate 100%) and the highlighter on the bright desk is missed only in 3% of the images ($\mathbf{w}_{(1,2)}$). In the successful cases, the target is detected on average with the first or second focus. The most difficult example is the name plate; here, the target is missed in 13% of the images.

It also revealed that the best performance is not always achieved with the same weights as on the training data: For the highlighter on the dark desk, the best performance is already achieved with the first training image, and for the highlighter on the bright desk, three training images yield the best performance. This is inevitable since every test set is slightly different and has another combination of weights that fits best for it. Nevertheless, the performance results differ only slightly and the proposed approach yields a good approximation of the optimal performance.

Experiment 2

In the previous experiment, the background within each image set was similar. Here we show what happens if a target appears on different backgrounds. To achieve this, we combined the image sets of the highlighter on the dark and on the bright desk into one image set. We expected that here more training images are required to yield a local optimum in performance since the training set is inhomogeneous. It turned out that this is usually true but even here the local optimum is sometimes achieved with two images (cf. Tab. 5.5 (a)). We found that it depends on the starting image how many training images are required until the algorithm stops: when the first image was from the bright desk only two images were needed to yield the local optimum. For the starting image of the dark desk it took longer until the optimum was reached: the best performance was achieved when the weights vector was computed from the average of four training images. The performance was then better than the performance achieved with two images with a bright-desk starting image.

This results from the fact that the search on the dark desk is considerably easier than on the bright one due to the high contrast of the yellow highlighter to the dark desk. Therefore, weights obtained from the bright desk applied to the dark one yield a good performance but not vice versa. If the starting image is that of the bright desk, the images that perform badly are also of the bright desk. After taking the average of two training images, the performance does not improve anymore. In contrast, if the starting image is that of the dark desk, the bad-performing images are of the bright set and $\mathbf{w}_{(1,2)}$ is the average of dark and bright. This is repeated and the average of dark and bright yields a performance that excels the former performance after 4 iterations.

In Tab. 5.5 (b), the computed weights are applied to a test set of 60 images disjoint from the training set. The detection quality is very high: although the

Table 5.5. Experiment 2: Search performance for target *highligher* on a training set (20 images) with different backgrounds: the target lay on a dark and on a bright desk. The weight vectors are obtained with the algorithm in Fig. 5.9. The performance is presented as the average hit number on the training set and, in parentheses, the percentage of detected targets within the first 10 foci. The best value is highlighted in bold face. The performance depends on the start image: if the start image is one of a bright desk (b), the local optimum is reached for 2 training images. If it is one of a dark desk (d), 4 images yield the best performance. Note that the application to test data gives slightly different results

Target	start im.	average hit number (and detection rate [%])				
		$\mathbf{w}_{i,1}$	$\mathbf{w}_{i,(1,2)}$	$\mathbf{w}_{i,(1,..,3)}$	$\mathbf{w}_{i,(1,..,4)}$	$\mathbf{w}_{i,(1,..,5)}$
Highl.	b	2.45 (100%)	**1.70 (100%)**	1.85 (100%)		
Highl.	d	2.50 (95%)	1.95 (100%)	1.75 (100%)	**1.55 (100%)**	1.75 (100%)

(a) Search for highlighter on training sets

Target	start im.	average hit number (and detection rate [%])				
		$\mathbf{w}_{i,1}$	$\mathbf{w}_{i,(1,2)}$	$\mathbf{w}_{i,(1,..,3)}$	$\mathbf{w}_{i,(1,..,4)}$	$\mathbf{w}_{i,(1,..,5)}$
Highl.	b	1.80 (100%)	1.53 (99%)	**1.62 (100%)**		
Highl.	d	1.83 (99%)	1.58 (100%)	1.55 (100%)	**1.48 (100%)**	1.60 (100%)

(b) Search for highlighter on test sets

target lay on different backgrounds, it is found in all images and on average with the first or second focus. Again, it showed that the optimal performance is not always reached for the same weights as the optimal performance on the training set, but the training results yield a good approximation of the optimum. Interestingly, with both kinds of weight vectors (bright and dark starting image) the performance on the test set is better than on the training set. Probably this results from a few difficult example images in the training set which decline the average hit number. Note that despite the different results depending on the start image it is not necessary to attach great importance to the choice of this image since the average hit numbers for both cases are very similar. A randomly chosen image will usually suffice.

Experiment 3

In this experiment, we investigate whether the system is able to generalize and find the targets in unknown environments. Therefore, we trained the target in one environment and tested it in completely disjoint environments. Not only the test images are disjoint from the training images, the environment is physically different. To achieve this, we chose the target name plate and used four test sets from different corridors of our office environment: test sets 1 and 2 came from the same corridor as the training set; test sets 3 and 4 came from two different corridors. The results of the experiments are shown in Tab. 5.6.

Table 5.6. Experiment 3: Search performance of VOCUS for test sets with name plates from different corridors. The search was done with the weight vectors $\mathbf{w}_1$ and $\mathbf{w}_{(1,2)}$ obtained from the training set of 54 images (cf. Tab. 5.4). The performance is presented as the average hit number on the test sets and, in parentheses, the percentage of detected targets within the first 10 foci. The results differ depending on the test set and the average weight $\mathbf{w}_{(1,2)}$ from 2 training images yields a significantly better result on all test sets than the weight $\mathbf{w}_1$ from a single training image

Test set	# test im.	av. hit number (det. rate [%])	
		$\mathbf{w}_1$	$\mathbf{w}_{(1,2)}$
name plate set 1	238	2.31 (79%)	2.55 (86%)
name plate set 2	124	1.86 (78%)	2.62 (87%)
name plate set 3	301	1.66 (81%)	1.84 (85%)
name plate set 4	243	1.80 (97%)	1.56 (97%)
all together	958	1.78 (85%)	2.05 (89%)

The search was done with the weight vectors $\mathbf{w}_1$ and $\mathbf{w}_{(1,2)}$ obtained in experiment 1 from the training set of 54 images (cf. Tab. 5.4). As to be expected, the search performance for test sets 1 and 2 are very similar: the detection rate for $\mathbf{w}_{(1,2)}$ is 86% and 87% and the average hit numbers are 2.55 and 2.62. Although from a different corridor, the results on test set 3 are similar too (detection rate 85% and average hit number 1.84). Interestingly, the results on test set 4 are significantly better (detection rate 97% and average hit number 1.56). This results from the fact that in this corridor there are much less posters on the walls that divert the focus of attention.

These experiments show that the system is able to generalize and might be applied to scenes physically disjoint from the training environment. Furthermore, it revealed again that the average weight $\mathbf{w}_{(1,2)}$ yields significantly better results on all test sets than the weight $\mathbf{w}_1$ from a single training image.

Experiment 4

In this experiment, we show a complete overview of the performance of the previous test sets (see Tab. 5.7). In addition to the previous examples, here we show the performance for different top-down factors ($t = 0, t = 0.5, t = 1$) and we show how the average hit numbers and detection rates differ according to the number of foci that are considered; we consider 5, 10, and 20 foci. If less foci are considered, the detection rate is worse but the average hit number is better and vice versa.

The experiments with the highlighter reveal again that it is useful to train on a representative image set to prevent overfitting: training merely on the dark desk as well as training merely on the bright desk yields worse results than training on a mixture of both.

Row 4 of Tab. 5.7) a) and b) exhibits an effect that seems strange at the first view: while having the same detection rate, the average hit number is

Table 5.7. Experiment 4: Search performance of VOCUS on real world data. The number of training images is the local optimum computed with the algorithm of Fig. 5.9. The table shows the average hit number (number of the focus on the target) for different top-down factors t. The percentage of detected targets is shown in parentheses. The highlighter is learned on a dark background (d), on a bright one (b), and on both (d+b), but it is tested always on the mixed set

Target	# train im.	# test im.	Average hit number and detection rate		
			$t= 0$	$t = 0.5$	$t = 1$
fire extinguisher	2	46	1.94 (78%)	1.09 (100%)	1.09 (100%)
key fob	2	28	3.06 (53%)	1.27 (100%)	1.23 (100%)
name plate	2	906	2.30 (33%)	1.71 (74%)	1.54 (81%)
highlighter	2 (d)	60	2.37 (86%)	1.67 (96%)	1.74 (96%)
highlighter	2 (b)	60	2.37 (86%)	1.55 (93%)	1.56 (98%)
highlighter	4 (d+b)	60	2.37 (86%)	1.48 (93%)	1.41 (98%)

a) Regard first 5 foci of attention.

Target	# train im.	# test im.	Average hit number and detection rate		
			$t= 0$	$t = 0.5$	$t = 1$
fire extinguisher	2	46	2.69 (94%)	1.09 (100%)	1.09 (100%)
key fob	2	28	4.42 (80%)	1.27 (100%)	1.23 (100%)
name plate	2	906	3.94 (48%)	2.48 (85%)	2.05 (89%)
highlighter	2 (d)	60	2.54 (90%)	1.78 (98%)	1.86 (98%)
highlighter	2 (b)	60	2.54 (90%)	1.76 (96%)	1.56 (98%)
highlighter	4 (d+b)	60	2.54 (90%)	1.73 (98%)	1.48 (100%)

b) Regard first 10 foci of attention.

Target	# train im.	# test im.	Average hit number and detection rate		
			$t= 0$	$t = 0.5$	$t = 1$
fire extinguisher	2	46	3.61 (100%)	1.09 (100%)	1.09 (100%)
key fob	2	28	5.08 (86%)	1.27 (100%)	1.23 (100%)
name plate	2	906	6.91 (65%)	3.50 (92%)	2.74 (94%)
highlighter	2 (d)	60	2.93 (93%)	2.03 (100%)	2.03 (100%)
highlighter	2 (b)	60	2.93 (93%)	1.93 (98%)	1.73 (100%)
highlighter	4 (d+b)	60	2.93 (93%)	1.98 (100%)	1.48 (100%)

c) Regard first 20 foci of attention.

slightly better for $t = 0.5$ than for $t = 1$. Here, the question arises how a pure top-down search can be worse than the mixture of top-down and bottom-up. To understand this, it is necessary to regard the foci on the test data and the weight vector in detail: the yellow highlighter has a strong color and intensity contrast to the dark desk. Therefore, the weight vector shows not only high values for the feature yellow but also for the on-off feature (bright-on-dark). This means that in search mode not only yellow regions are extremely salient, but also white ones. Thus, for $t = 1$ the first FOA is sometimes on a white region with strong intensity contrast before it jumps to the target. But for $t = 0.5$, the bottom-up saliency increases the highlighter region because of its popping out color and leads the focus to the target. Notice that this happens especially if the training data is not representative: if there are few bright regions in the training data but many in the test images, the on-off feature gets a high value although yellow is more important. If the training data contains as many bright regions as the test data, yellow is the most important feature and the performance for $t = 1$ increases.

Here again it might look as if the bottom-up cues have less influence for $t = 0.5$ than the top-down cues for the same reasons as discussed for Fig. 5.10. That this is not the case is shown in the next section.

5.4.3 Varying the Influence of Bottom-Up and Top-Down

To test the influence of the top-down factor t systematically, we use an image with one white and 5 black dots on a grey background with different intensities. Usually, the white dot pops out due to its uniqueness, but this is dependent on the intensity of the background: on a very bright background there is no pop-out effect. Thus, the top-down factor required to override the pop-out and to focus on a black dot depends on the background intensity. Here, we vary the intensity of the background between 10% (nearly white) and 90% (nearly black) and determine the top-down factor required to override the white pop-out. The result is shown in Fig. 5.15: The pop-out occurs for background intensities over 30%. With increasing intensity, the value of t required to override the pop-out increases too, up to $t = 0.9$ for 80% intensity. For 90%, the pop-out is so strong that it cannot be overridden anymore.

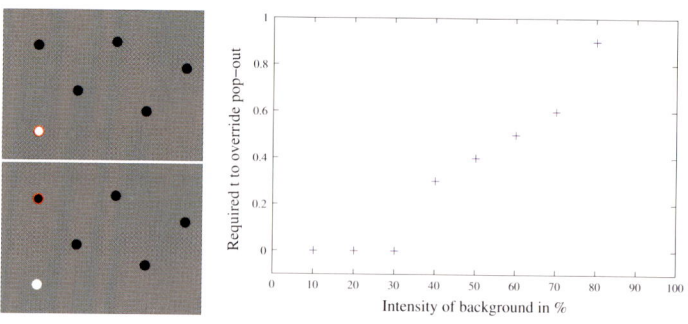

Fig. 5.15. Searching for black dots on varying background intensities of a test image. The value of the top-down factor required to override the pop-out increases with increasing background intensity. Left, top: intensity 50%, $t = 0.3$; the pop-out wins. Bottom: Intensity 50%, $t = 0.4$; the pop-out is overridden. Right: required t for differently strong pop-outs

5.4.4 Robustness

In this section, we discuss the robustness of VOCUS. Implicitly, this was already shown in the previous experiments since we tested a large amount of targets in different real-world environments. In contrast to artificial images, real-world data contain always noise, changing illumination conditions and different poses of objects. No two images ever have equal conditions. This means that a certain robustness is essential to enable a somehow stable system behavior at all. Nevertheless, in this section we consider this topic in more detail. We first discuss the robustness according to image transformations and second the system behavior under variations of illumination.

Image Transformations

As already mentioned in chapter 4, it is a very important property of a detection system to be robust against image transformations. What is the use of a system capable of detecting an object only if it is presented the same way as during learning? Here, we regard changes in viewpoint since this is the most difficult case of image transformations that includes other transformations like the Euclidian 2D transformations, and since this is the kind of transformations that really occurs in practical applications, at least if these have a certain complexity as it is the case for mobile robots.

Since in our previous experiments we presented the targets with different orientations, on different backgrounds and regarded from different viewpoints, the robustness of the system was implicitly already proven. Although the order of foci might slightly change if there are regions in the scene similar to the target, the target is in average still detected with one of the first three foci. To investigate this behavior in more detail, we rendered one scene of different viewpoints: a wall in our office environment was regarded from 9 viewpoints, each about 40 cm distant from the next so the farthermost perspectives had a distance of about 3.60 m. In these images, we searched for name plates. The result is shown in Fig. 5.16. It revealed that the name plate was always detected with the first focus, only in one image the hit number was 2. These results show convincingly that the system is able to detect a target in real-world applications from different viewpoints. This means that also tracking of the salient region in subsequent image frames is easily possible. More stable tracking results could be achieved if an image is biased in favor of the previously detected position. Furthermore, using Kalman or Particle filters helps in performing tracking while considering detections in previous frames [Forsyth and Ponce, 2003].

Variations in Illumination

Another important property of visual systems is the robustness under variations of illumination. This is a problem that frequently induces difficulties in

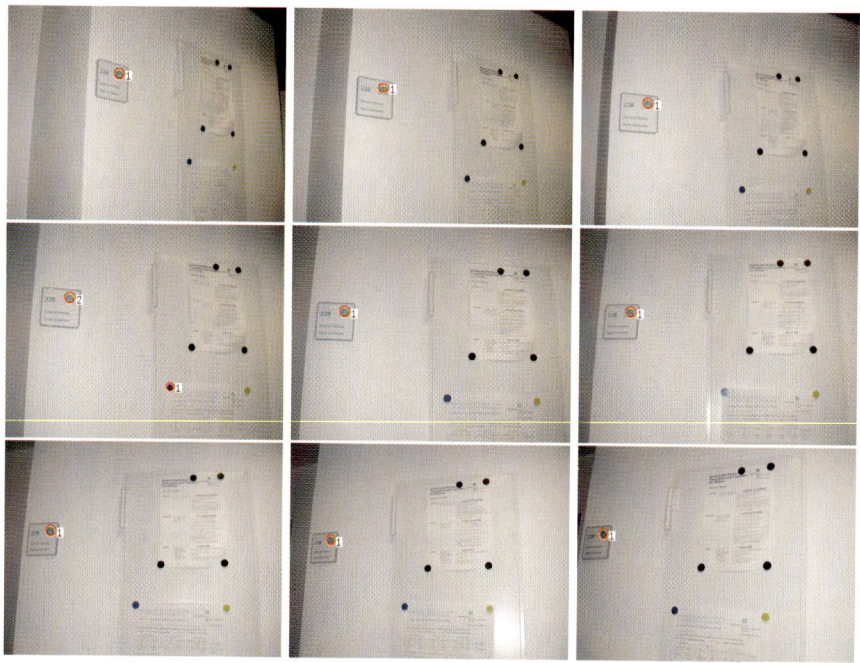

Fig. 5.16. Search for name plates under viewpoint changes. The same scene was regarded from 9 viewpoints, each about 40 cm distant from the next one. The hit number is always 1, only in one image it is 2 (middle row, left)

real-world applications since images often look very different if illumination changes. This is especially true for color images: the colors of one object in two differently illuminated images may differ significantly making object detection an extremely hard task. This is one of the reasons why many approaches in object recognition focus on gray-scale images and disregard color. We show that VOCUS is able to deal with illumination variances of a reasonable extent, i.e., of an extent occurring in real-world applications. Such variances include the changes between artificial and natural light as well as between sunny and cloudy weather. However, we remark that all experiments were performed inside of buildings. The illumination changes that occur outdoors are usually even stronger. It remains to be investigated how the system works under these conditions.

The previously presented results dealt already with normal changes in illumination resulting from changes of viewpoint. Moreover, several of the test images were taken at different days, inevitably resulting in changes of illumination due to daytime and weather conditions. In the following, we investigate the system behavior under controlled changes of illumination for two different scenes. In Fig. 5.17 we show the search for the highlighter on a desk.

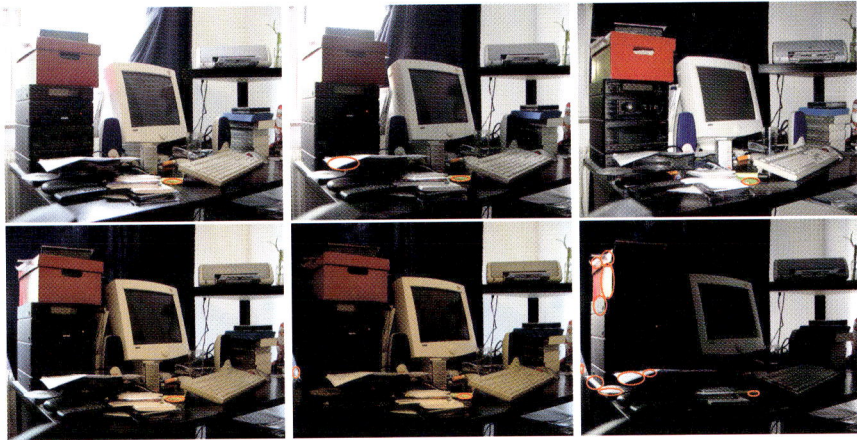

Fig. 5.17. Search for the highlighter under different illumination conditions. In reading direction, the hit number was 1,2,1,1,2,10

Fig. 5.18. Search for the blue key fob under different illumination conditions. In reading direction, the hit number was 1,1,1,1,3,2

Artificial illumination was switched on and off and the curtain was opened by different degrees resulting in different amounts of natural light coming in. In three of six cases, the target was detected with the first focus. In two images, strong light reflexes diverted the focus resulting in a hit number of 2. This happened, because when learning the highlighter on the dark desk, the bright-on-dark intensity has a strong weight. Only the image in the rightmost lower corner is too dark to enable a sufficient detection: the artificial illumination was turned off and the curtain was almost closed yielding an inadequate illumination of the scene. The few beams of light reached only the left image region, resulting in several false detections at bright spots. The target was only detected with the 10th focus. Notice that it is also very difficult for humans to detect the highlighter in such a scene and that knowledge about likely positions of the target ("the highlighter is probably on the desk") facilitates the search strongly.

In Fig. 5.18 we show a similar experiment: the blue key fob was searched on a wooden desk. The amount of natural light from the window was varied by successively closing the blinds. It showed that the target was successfully detected with the first focus in four out of the six images. Only with nearly completely closed blinds the hit number increased to 3 and 2 in the remaining two images.

The experiments reveal that the system is highly robust to illumination changes despite the use of color. This results firstly from the use of the uniform color space LAB that is adapted to human perception, but mainly from the definition of saliency: not the region is selected which has a special feature combination, but the region whose feature combination is closest to the specified one. Since under illumination changes the illumination of the whole image changes, there is a good chance that the target's feature combination is still closest to the learned weights. Notice however that this would fail under colored illumination: in disco light, color is no suitable feature for distinguishing targets from the background. When learning objects in disco light, the average weights for color would be close to 1 and it would be necessary to concentrate on other features. The above results could be probably improved if the feature vector was learned from several training images with different illuminations. We leave this examination to future work.

5.4.5 Comparison with Other Systems

In this section, we compare the search mode of VOCUS to related approaches in order to show similarities and differences. The two systems that are most similar to VOCUS and so are best suited for such a comparison are the system of Hamker [Hamker, 2005] and the derivative of the NVT [Navalpakkam et al., 2005]. Like VOCUS, they also enable the learning and redetection of a target by top-down influencing the attentional process. We start with a comparison with Hamker's system, followed by a comparison with the NVT.

Comparison with Hamker's System

The attention system of Fred Hamker was introduced in section 3.1.4. Here, we compare VOCUS with this system. The basis of the comparison were the results on natural images presented in Fig. 10 of [Hamker, 2005]. The images underlying these experiments were kindly provided to us by Fred Hamker. In these experiments, Hamker's system learns a target and tries to redetect it in a test scene. The target is cut out from the test scene and presented to the system on a black background. Note that therefore the viewpoint and appearance of the target is exactly the same in training and test image. The search was stopped manually when the target was hit or after 4 fixations. We tried to imitate the experimental setup as closely as possible, but since VOCUS considers additionally the background information for the learning of the target's features, it was not possible to learn the target from the training images with the black background. Due to the lack of additional training images, we learned the target features directly from the test scene. Since in Hamker's training images the target is cut from the test scene, the difference is not large.

In Fig. 5.19 and 5.20, we show the results of Hamker's system and VOCUS. On the left, the training image is presented that shows the target extracted from the image. In the middle, we see the results of Hamker's system and on the right our results. On Hamker's images, blue circles denote covert and red ones overt attention. Remember that the covert shifts correspond to the most salient regions in the perceptual map whereas the overt shifts are the result from the "match detection units" that compare the encoded pattern with the target template. This means that when searching, for example, for the green pencil on the table (Fig. 5.19, last row), the most salient location in Hamker's system was the glass, but the match detection units decided that this region does not correspond to all feature values (probably the green color led to the high saliency, but since the orientation is different, the object is said to be not detected). This leads to a covert shift of attention to the box. Here, the same procedure occurs leading to a covert shift to the pencil. Here finally the feature values are similar, leading to an overt shift of attention. This simple recognition method leads easily to false detections as can be seen in the images with red circles on other regions than the target, e.g., for the targets ashtray or cup. Note that usually the system stops after an eye movement and claims to have found the target but in these experiments the search was continued and stopped manually when the target really was found or else after 4 fixations.

In these examples, none of the once fixated targets were rejected by the match detection units, but note that this is only possible because the targets were always presented the same way in training and test images. If an object was shown, for example, with another orientation than during training, the units would reject the target even if the color cue was sufficiently salient to fixate it. To yield a higher robustness, it would be necessary to learn from several training images the stable features and use this information for the match detection. Despite some current weaknesses, the idea of an object recognition directly intertwined with the attentional process is an interesting idea and surely worth to be investigated further.

The comparison of the two systems shows that on these images rather similar results are achieved. In some images, the target is better detected with Hamker's system, in others better results are achieved with our approach; a clear favorite is not identifiable. Note however that these experiments do not touch at all the question of robustness. Neither the effects of illumination changes nor the ones of changes in orientation or even viewpoint are evaluated.

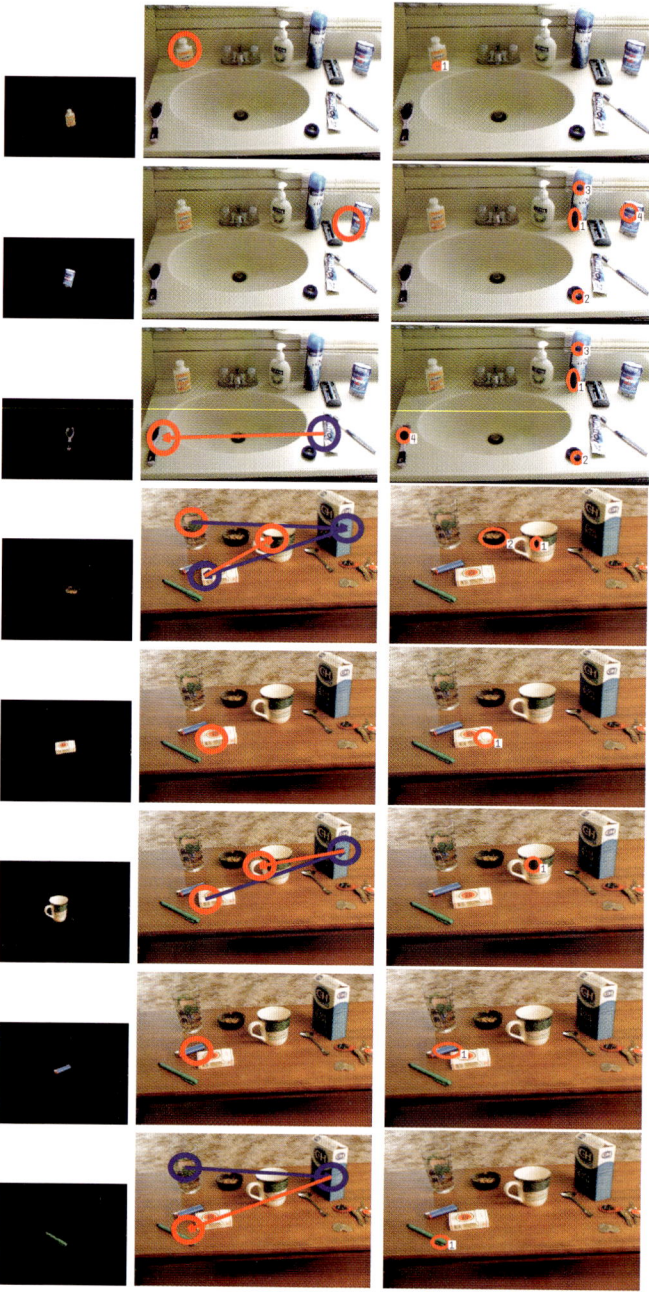

Fig. 5.19. Comparison of VOCUS with the system of Hamker [Hamker, 2005]. Left: the target image used for learning in Hamker's system. In VOCUS, the targets were learned directly from the scene. Middle: foci of Hamker's system; blue circles denote covert and red ones overt attention (see text). Right: foci of VOCUS

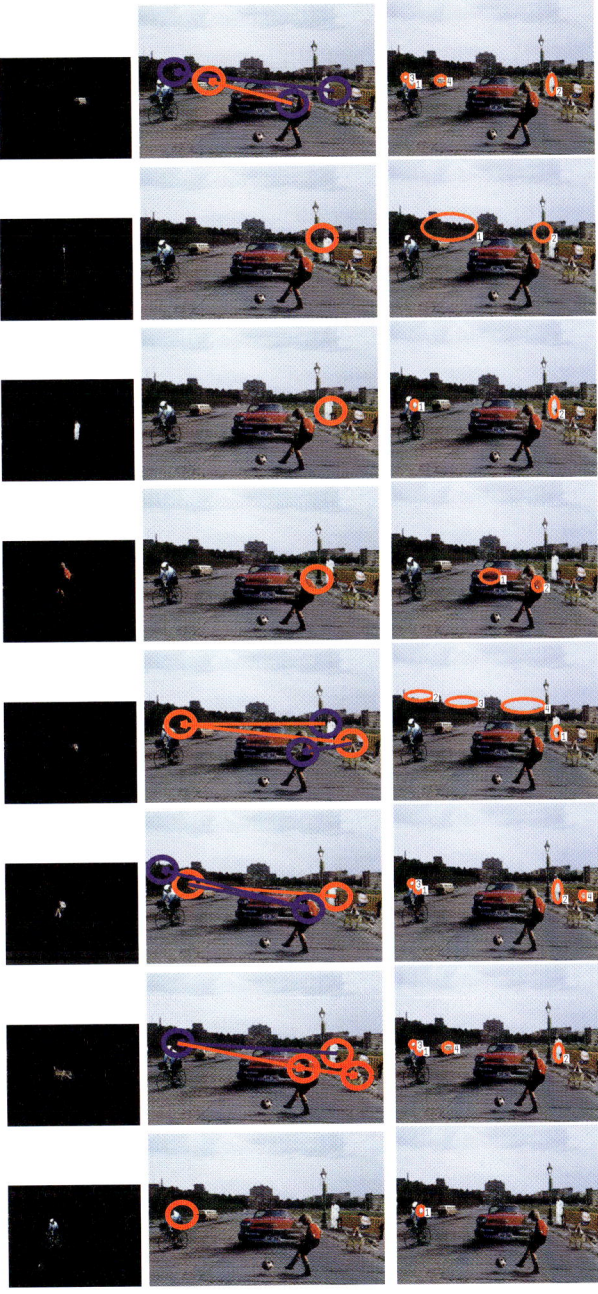

Fig. 5.20. Comparison of VOCUS with the system of Hamker [Hamker, 2005]. Left: the target image used for learning in Hamker's system. In VOCUS, the targets were learned directly from the scene. Middle: foci of Hamker's system; blue circles denote covert and red ones overt attention (see text). Right: foci of VOCUS

Therefore, some of the strengths of VOCUS concerning the robustness do not show off to its best advantage in Hamker's experiments.

Comparison with the NVT

The system with the most similar approach to VOCUS is the NVT [Itti et al., 1998] with its extension to top-down mechanisms [Navalpakkam et al., 2005], which was introduced in chapter 3. The differences between the systems were pointed out in this and the previous chapter, but let us summarize here the main points again. The differences fall into three categories, firstly the differences concerning the bottom-up system, secondly the differences concerning the top-down mechanisms and thirdly the choice of the training images.

First, there are several differences in the bottom-up system (cf. chapter 4). There is the exacter computation of center-surround in VOCUS, the separation of on-off and off-on intensity as well as of red, green, blue, and yellow and the use of different color spaces (RGB in NVT and LAB in VOCUS). Additionally, the computations of the weighting for uniqueness and the normalization differ as well as the computation of the most salient region.

Secondly, there are differences in the top-down mechanisms in both the learning and the search mode. In learning mode, NVT considers the whole region of the object, which is determined by a binary mask, whereas VOCUS computes the most salient region within the object region and learns merely the features in this region. The approach of VOCUS is more user-friendly, but which approach yields better results is not intuitively clear and should be examined further. Another difference is the choice of features that are learned. NVT learns the features depending on the scale, i.e., it learns 42 feature values (red/green, blue/yellow, intensity, and 4 orientations, each on 6 scales). In contrast, VOCUS learns the features after the scales have been summed up, yielding 13 feature values (2 intensity, 4 orientations, 4 colors, 3 conspicuity maps). We think that learning the scale of a target is not useful since in search mode the target should be detected at arbitrary scales, but this is just a supposition and should be investigated further.

Additionally, both systems consider target as well as background information for the learning of features but NVT considers 9 locations from a 3×3 grid of fixed size centered at the salient location whereas VOCUS regards the whole background. Probably, the approach of NVT is more biologically plausible since there is evidence that mainly the local neighborhood of the target influences its salience. How this difference influences the performance of a technical system should be investigated further. In search mode, VOCUS computes an excitation and an inhibition map separately before joining them in the top-down saliency map. Furthermore, the top-down saliency map is separated from the bottom-up saliency map and the influence of each map is adjustable. In contrast, NVT weights the features directly so that exciting and inhibiting as well as bottom-up and top-down cues are mixed and directly fused into the resulting saliency map. We favor our approach since we

Fig. 5.21. Some images from the four data sets that were used to compare VOCUS with the NVT of Navalpakkam and Itti. The targets are a campus information map (1st row), a handicap sign (2nd row), a fire hydrant (3rd row), and a coke can (4th row). The images were kindly provided by V. Navalpakkam and L. Itti and are the same that were used in [Navalpakkam et al., 2005]

think that for a technical system it is more sensible to separate the influences and make them adjustable according to the system state. Additionally, there is evidence that two distinct brain areas are associated with bottom-up and top-down mechanisms in human perception [Corbetta and Shulman, 2002] what suggests to separate the processing also in a computational system.

Finally, there is a difference in how several training images are learned. In VOCUS, the algorithm of Fig. 5.9 is used to choose the training images which are suitable and enable a good representation of the target. In NVT, all images are used for training.

In the following experiments, we compare the performance of VOCUS with the one of the NVT. For the comparison, we chose the real-world image data the NVT was tested on in the experiments in [Navalpakkam et al., 2005]. The targets were a campus map, a handicap sign, a fire hydrant and a coke can; some of the scenes are shown in Fig. 5.21. The handicap sign and the fire hydrant are easy-to-find targets because of their high saliency. The campus map is more difficult, especially because different instances of maps are involved, but in the few present examples the map is always a bright region on a darker background what facilitates the detection. The coke can has a strong color too but because of different viewpoints and lightings its appearance differs

Table 5.8. Comparison of the NVT with VOCUS. The measure for comparison (column 5 and 6) is the average hit number on the target, that means the average focus that hit the target. Training was in both cases performed solely on the training set. The training images for VOCUS were chosen from the training image set with the algorithm in Fig. 5.9. The resulting number of images used for computing the feature weights vector is shown in column 4

Target	# test im.	# train im.	# train im. VOCUS	av. hit number NVT	av. hit number VOCUS
campus map	9	9	2	1.2	1.0
handicapped sign	7	4	1	1.0	1.0
fire hydrant	8	8	2	1.0	1.0
coke	59	45	5	3.8	1.3

strongly and the detection is much more difficult. It may be noted that only the last test set enables a reasonable investigation because the other ones contain too few images (7 to 9 images per set).

Unfortunately, the results in [Navalpakkam et al., 2005] do not say anything about the actual performance of the NVT on these images but concentrate on pointing out the improvement of the top-down extensions over the previous bottom-up system. Therefore, a comparison based on the data in the paper was not possible. But, fortunately, Vidhya Navalpakkam kindly provided us with the performance values of NVT on these test sets as well as with the image data. The results of the comparison of NVT and of VOCUS are shown in Tab. 5.8.

The images had a size of 800×600; we first converted them to the size 400×300 since VOCUS performs better on this image size (cf. chapter 4.2.3). In learning mode, we used the training algorithm in Fig. 5.9 to select the best suitable training images from the training set. The number of images selected for training is shown in column 4 of Tab. 5.8. The experiment revealed that for the first three targets, only 1 or 2 training images were required to yield a good performance. This results firstly from the small size of the training set and secondly from the homogeneity of the data. For the coke can target with much higher variations in the image data, 5 training images were selected.

The quality of detection of both systems can be seen in the 5th and 6th column of Tab. 5.8, which shows the average hit number (cf. Def. 1) on the test set (the detection rate is not shown since the target was detected in all images: detection rate 100%). The performance of both systems is the same for the handicap sign and the fire hydrant: both systems detect the target with the first focus in all test images (average hit number = 1.0). For the campus map, VOCUS has slightly better results since it detects the target in all images with the first focus whereas the NVT has an average hit number of 1.2. For the coke can, VOCUS clearly outperforms NVT: whereas the NVT detects the target on average with focus number 3.8, VOCUS needs on average only 1.3 fixations. Looking closer at the coke can results reveals that the NVT detects the target in 21 of the 59 images with the first FOA whereas VOCUS finds the can in 52 images with the first focus.

5.5 Discussion

In this chapter, we introduced an extension of VOCUS to enable goal-directed search. The system is able to operate in a top-down mode in which it considers previously learned information about an image region. In a learning phase, one or several training images are presented to the system that learns the relevant features. In search mode, the system considers this information in the computation of saliencies and generates hypotheses about the location of the target.

We presented detailed experiments on artificial and real-world data showing that the system is able to detect different kinds of objects in complex environments. The target objects were presented from different viewpoints, in different environments, and with different distractors around. We showed that on average less than three fixations were necessary to detect the target. Furthermore, we investigated the performance of the system under illumination changes and showed that the system is robust to a large extent.

When using several training images, the performance of the system was stabilized and better results were reached, especially if the target occurred in different environments. We presented an algorithm that chooses suitable training images from a set of images and show that usually less than five training images are sufficient to yield a local optimum in performance; in most cases, already two images are enough.

Essential for a good performance of the system is the quality of the feature computations since these form the basis for the weights. It is important to choose features that are able to distinguish the targets the user wants to find. In our approach, we used the standard features intensity, orientation, and color since these are used in most attention systems and are important features in the human visual system. Therefore, they enable a good performance in many applications, similar to the human system. Although most systems are based on these features, there is a remarkable difference in VOCUS: we compute two separate intensity channels (on-off and off-on) and four color channels. In most other systems, only one intensity channel and two color channels (red-green and blue-yellow) are computed [Itti et al., 1998, Ouerhani and Hügli, 2004]. Although this design has also disadvantages in bottom-up mode (cf. chapter 4), its drawbacks outcrop especially for goal-directed search: in these systems, it is not possible to search for bright-on-dark or vice versa — an especially useful property in applications with gray-scale data, e.g., laser scanner data (cf. chapter 6) — and it is not possible to search for a certain color, only for a combination of colors, e.g., for "red or green". These additional feature dimensions that are influenced by the human visual system are the basis of the good performance of VOCUS. Although the given features provide a good basis for general applications, in special applications it might be useful to include additional features. If the targets contain, for example, textures like speckled or striated patterns, it could be useful to include filters able to detect these properties.

We tested VOCUS with objects of different sizes, textures, shapes, and poses. However, there are kinds of objects that are difficult to detect with such a system. First of all, inconspicuous objects have to be mentioned. If an object hardly differs from its environment, it is difficult to detect by a computational attention system as well as by the human system. An example is the famous needle in a haystack. Other objects that are difficult to detect are complex, inhomogeneous objects that are characteristic not by a single feature but by a combination, e.g., an object that is red and blue among objects that are red and those that are blue. VOCUS will concentrate on the most salient part of the object, e.g., the blue one, and so will have difficulties to distinguish the target from the blue distractors. Note that such a search task is also difficult for humans requiring several fixation until recognition verifies the object hypothesis.

In the previous chapter, we discussed the time performance of the bottom-up attention system. Since the bottleneck of the system are the feature computations, the time needed to perform visual search is about the same as the time to compute a bottom-up FOA. But in contrast to the bottom-up mode in which all features have to be computed since it is not known which ones will be the most important ones, in top-down mode it is possible to restrict the processing to the most important features: the more distant a weight is from 1, the more important is the corresponding feature. Depending on the available time, features with weights close to 1 may be omitted in the computations, yielding a considerable increase in performance. Implementing and testing this approach will be subject to future work.

Another task for future work is visual search depending on the environment. If a gray object is placed on a black background, the on-off feature weight has high values, whereas the off-on feature weight is high if the object is placed on a white background. A universally valid weight vector could not be achieved in this case but it is possible to make the weights vector dependent on the environment. This means that one weights vector is learned for one environment (black background) and another one for another environment (white background). In search mode, first the overall properties of the environment would be analyzed, e.g., the intensity and color histogram, the entropy, and the spatial frequency. Then the weights vector would be chosen that fits best to the environment. An example in which such an approach would be useful is the search for objects in an office environment with different corridors that have differently painted walls.

The extension of the system with top-down mechanisms is an important step towards more realistic and useful vision systems. It joins the advantages of attention and object recognition systems. Although an object recognizer is still necessary to verify the results, its task is much simplified by the preparatory work of VOCUS providing image regions with a high probability to contain the target. Finally it shall be noted that in human vision there are top-down mechanisms that are much more complex than visual search. The preference of an architect for buildings, of an ornithologist for birds, of a pregnant woman for children, or of a starving for food include much more than a bias for simple features. These effects are not yet completely understood in human perception and the conversion into computer vision systems will take considerable time in the future.

6

Sensor Fusion

In the previous chapters, we have dealt exclusively with the part of attention that is concerned with visual processing. This part is the best investigated one in human behavior, probably because vision is the sense using the most capacity in the human brain: the 32 representations of the retina occupy more than half of the whole cortex [Kandel et al., 1996] and the primary visual cortex V1 has the richest architecture of all cortical areas [Zeki, 1993]. Usually, computational attention systems simulate also only visual attention. One exception is the model of [van der Willigen and von Campenhausen, 2002] which models *audio-evoked orienting* — the orienting behavior in which eyes (and head) are turned to an unexpected sound — with an artificial neural network.

However, human eye movements are not only biased by vision but also by other senses, e.g., the gaze may be directed into the direction of a sound, a smell, or even a touch, [Watanabe and Shimojo, 2005] and the fusion of different cues competing for attention is an essential part of human attention. In robotics, attentional mechanisms might also profit from additional sensor modalities since they yield a richer set of data that enable the detection of more object properties, resulting in more useful foci of attention.

This chapter presents an extension of the attention system VOCUS which enables the fusion of saliencies from different sensor modes: the Bimodal, Laser-based Attention System (BILAS). This allows the detection of different object properties and the detection of a wider variety of saliencies than within a single sensor mode. The modes provided to the attention system are depth and reflection data acquired by a 3D laser scanner in a single scan pass. BILAS takes the data from both laser modes as input and searches both modes for saliencies according to principles described in chapter 4: saliencies of different features, here intensity and orientation, are computed in parallel and fused into one global saliency map on which a single FOA is determined. Most of this chapter was also published in [Frintrop et al., 2005c].

We apply BILAS to laser data of real-world indoor and outdoor scenes and elaborate on the different advantages of range and reflectance values. We show that these data modes complement each other: contrasts in range and in intensity need not necessarily correspond for one scene element, i.e., an object of similar texture as its background may not be detected in the reflection image, but in the range data. On the other hand, a flat object — e.g. a poster on a wall or a letter on a desk — that could be distinguished in the reflection image, will likely not be detected in the range data. The results indicate that the combination of different modes enables considering a larger variety of object properties. Additionally, we compare the performance of attentional mechanisms on laser data with that on camera data. The comparison reveals the respective advantages of the two kinds of sensors.

Typically, computational models of visual attention use features like intensity, color, and orientation. Depth is rarely considered although it plays a special role in deploying attention. It is not clear from the literature whether depth is simply a feature, like color or motion, or something else (cf. chapter 3.2.2). Definitely, depth is an important feature in human vision; in particular, range discontinuities at the borders of many objects can help to separate objects from each other and from their background and to compute object shapes.

Two approaches that include depth are presented in [Backer and Mertsching, 2000] and [Maki et al., 2000]. They obtain depth data from stereo vision and regard it as another feature. The data obtained from stereo vision is usually not very accurate and contains large regions without depth information. This may justify the integration of the depth values as a feature in the above mentioned models; in our approach the range data come from a special sensor and yield dense and accurate range information, so we regard depth as an additional sensor mode.

The remainder of this chapter is structured as follows: we start in section 6.1 with a description of the data acquisition including a specification of the bimodal 3D laser scanner. In section 6.2, we continue with introducing the extended attention system BILAS. The main part of this chapter are the experimental results in section 6.3 investigating in detail the respective advantages of the two laser modes and of camera data. We finish with a discussion on the presented approach.

6.1 Data Acquisition

The data for the experiments of this chapter were acquired with the AIS 3D Laser Scanner which will be introduced in section 6.1.1. It yields range and reflectance data that are rendered into images (section 6.1.2). In section 6.1.3, we discuss the differences of range data obtained from laser scanners and from stereo vision.

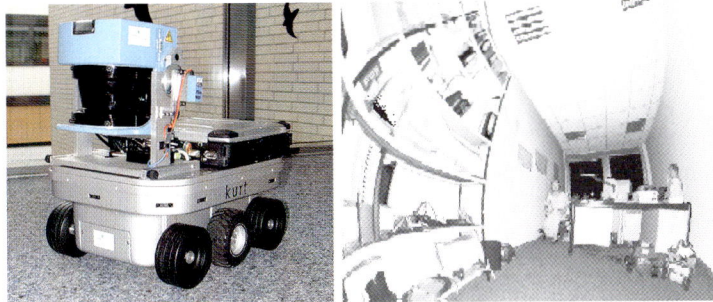

Fig. 6.1. Left: the custom 3D range finder mounted on top of the mobile robot Kurt3D. Right: an office scene imaged with the 3D scanner in reflection value mode, medium resolution (361 × 211 pixels, distortions not corrected)

6.1.1 The 3D Laser Scanner

For the data acquisition in our experiments, we used a custom 3D laser range finder which is mounted on the mobile robot Kurt3D (Fig. 6.1, left). The scanner is based on a commercial SICK 2D laser range finder. In [Surmann et al., 2001], the custom scanner setup is described in detail. The paper also describes reconstruction algorithms and their use for robot applications. Here, we provide only a brief overview of the device.

The scanner works according to the time-of-flight principle: it sends out a laser beam and measures the returning reflected light. This yields two kinds of data: the time the laser beam needs to come back gives the distance of the scanned object (range data) and the intensity of the reflected light provides information about the reflection properties of the object (reflection data). This reflectance measurement is the result of the light measurement by the receiver diode. It measures the amount of infrared light that is returned from the object to the scanner and thus describes the surface properties concerning non-human visible light.

The 2D scanner serially sends out laser beams in one horizontal slice using a rotating mirror (LIDAR: LIght Detection And Ranging). It is very fast and precise: the processing time is about 13 ms for a 180° scan with 181 measurements and the typical range error is about 1 cm. A 3D scan is performed by step-rotating the 2D scanner around a horizontal axis, i.e., the 3D scan is obtained by scanning one horizontal slice after the other. Usually, the area of 180°(h) × 120°(v) is scanned in 1°, 0.5°, or 0.25° steps resulting in the resolutions (181, 361, 721 pts) horizontal and (121, 241, 481 pts) vertical. By restricting the scan area to more narrow angles or by ignoring values at the borders, other resolutions may result. In the experiments in section 6.3, we used resolutions of 152 × 256 and 361 × 211.

Fig. 6.2. Visualized laser data. Left: scene from camera image, middle: visualized depth data, right: visualized reflection data. Depending on the sensor, the presented images have slightly different extensions, the laser scanner getting a wider angle than the camera in all directions

6.1.2 Rendering Images from Laser Data

The scanner is able to operate in two data modes. In the default mode, it returns only the range data in a predefined resolution. In an alternative mode, it is able to yield the range as well as the reflection data in a single scan pass. The reflection data can directly be converted into a gray scale intensity image as is depicted in Fig. 6.1, right. Here, it shows that the raw data from the scanner is spherically distorted. The distortion was removed in later experiments by rectifying the images as can be seen, e.g., in Fig. 7.12. The visualization of the depth values from the range data requires some transformation. The basic approach is to interpret the depth values as intensity values, representing small depth values as bright intensity values and large depth values as dark ones. Since close objects are considered more important for robot applications, we introduce an additional double proximity bias. Firstly, we consider only objects within a radius $r = 10\,m$ of the robot's location. Secondly, we code the depth values by using their square roots, so pixel p computes from depth value d by:

$$p = \begin{cases} I - (\sqrt{d/max} * I) & : \quad d \leq max \\ 0 & : \quad d > max, \end{cases} \tag{6.1}$$

with the maximal intensity value I and the maximal distance $max = 1000\,cm$. This measure leads to a finer distinction of range discontinuities in the vicinity of the robot and works better than a linear function. If the robot works outdoors and distant objects should be detected, the maximal distance can be increased. Fig. 6.2 shows an example of the visualized laser data.

Since the data from the different sensor modalities result from the same measurement, we know exactly which reflection value belongs to which range value. There is no need to establish correspondences and to perform costly calibration by complex algorithms. The laser data are illumination independent, i.e., the data is the same in sunshine as in complete darkness and no

reflection artifacts by external light occur. This yields a robust approach that
enables all day operation.

6.1.3 Laser Data Versus Stereo Vision

In current attention systems integrating depth information, the range data is
usually extracted from stereo vision. With today's available computing power
and advanced stereo algorithms, even real-time stereo vision at frame rate is
possible. A 3D scan pass (between 1.2 and 15 seconds, with typically 7.5 s)
is slow as compared to the frame rates of CCD cameras. However, for several target applications, for example automatic 3D map building, high frame
rates are not needed. In this application, 3D laser range scanning has some
considerable advantages over 3D stereo reconstruction.

Firstly, range scanning yields very dense depth information. On the other
hand, most 3D stereo vision algorithms rely on matching grey level values
for finding pixel correspondences. This is often not possible since, first, correspondences can only be found in textured parts of the stereo images, so
large image regions yield no depth data at all; second, ambiguous grey values
that cannot be disambiguated result in false matches and, third, shading may
prevent finding matches. Hence, the generated depth maps are sparse, often
containing large regions without depth information.

Secondly, the precision of the depth measurement of a laser range scanner
relies only on the tolerance that its construction foresees. Industry standard
scanners like the SICK scanner that we use have an average depth (Z axis)
error of 1 cm. The precision error of the Z axis measurement in 3D stereo
reconstruction is dependent on a number of parameters, namely the width
of the stereo base, the focal lengths of the lenses, the physical width of the
CCD pixel, the object distance and the precision of the matching algorithm.
The error increases by increased squared object distance, and decreases with
increasing focal length (narrowing the field of view). For small robots like
Kurt3D, the width of the stereo base is limited to small values ($\leq$ 20 cm),
resulting in a typical Z axis error of about 78 cm for objects at a ranging
distance of 8 m ($error = d * (d * w)/(b * f)$) with distance $d = 8000$ mm, pixel
width $w = 0,0098$ mm, stereo base $b = 200$ mm, $f = 4$ mm, precision 1
pixel).

And finally, our 3D laser scanner provides a very large field of view and the
data of the laser scanner are illumination independent. This enables all-day
operation and yields robust data. The named strengths make the 3D laser
scanner the sensor of choice in this application. An alternative may be 3D
cameras which are about to enter the market. The bimodal attention system
can equally be applied to their data as will be briefly discussed in section 6.4.

Fig. 6.3. Combining depth (2nd) and reflection (3rd) image into one colorized image (right). Range is coded as intensity, reflection as red-green transition

6.2 The Bimodal, Laser-Based Attention System BILAS

The first plan to build a system of visual attention able to process several sensor modes came from the idea to apply attentional mechanisms on data from a 3D laser scanner. This was a promising idea since the sensor yields dense and precise data and the availability of range and reflection data let us expect the possibility to detect new kinds of saliency. In section 6.3.1 we show that these expectations were fulfilled.

In first experiments, we applied the bottom-up system of visual attention — at that time the NVT [Itti et al., 1998] since our system didn't yet exist — to each sensor mode image separately. This enabled the investigation of saliencies in laser data and the comparison of the complementary effect of the modes. Nevertheless, it yielded two foci of attention for a single scene instead of one. It was suggesting to combine the results from both sensor modes to yield a single focus of attention especially since the data points directly correspond. Unfortunately, this was not possible with the NVT since this system is only able to process one input image at a time.

To overcome this problem we used a workaround in a first approach (see also [Frintrop et al., 2003b]): the laser data is gray-scale so the color feature channel in the NVT was not used. Utilizing this fact, we fused range and reflection image into one colorized image. To accomplish this, the range data were treated as intensity values of the new input image and the reflection values were coded as color (hue) information. High reflection values were coded in red hues, low ones in greens. This resulted in suitable color images because the color feature computations in the NVT take into account blue-yellow contrasts as well as red-green contrasts. An example scene with range and reflection image as well as the combined colorized image is depicted in Fig. 6.3. This colorized image was fed into the attention system, which computed a single focus of attention based on range and reflection data. In Fig. 6.4 we present this approach.

Although working quite well in our experiments, there were some problems with this approach. First, the approach is restricted to the processing of gray-scale images; the fusion of color images is not possible. Also the extension to more input images is difficult. A third gray-scale image might be coded as blue-yellow transition, but it is questionable whether the processing of

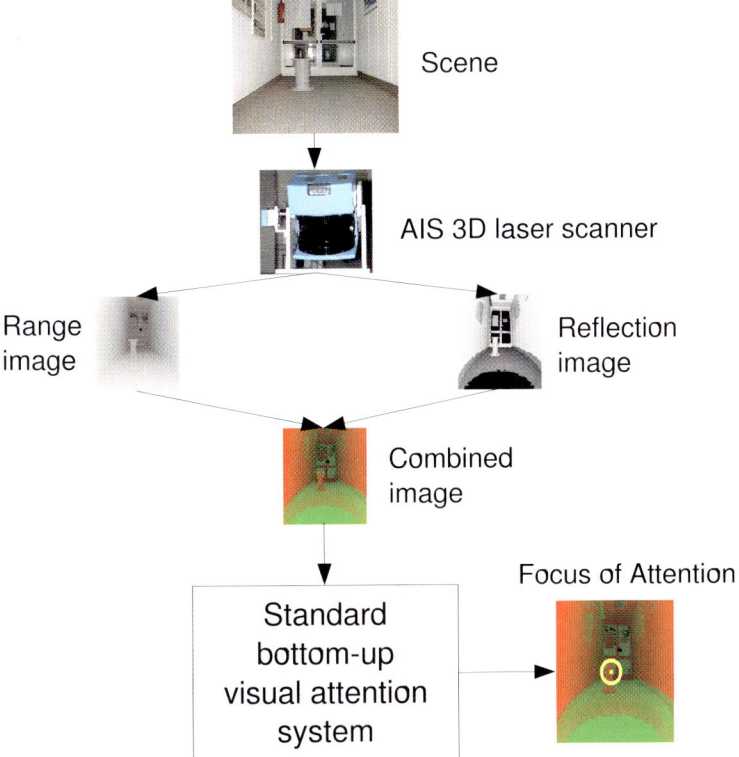

Fig. 6.4. First approach to compute a single focus of attention from range and reflection data: data from both modes is combined into a colorized image by coding range as intensity and reflection as color. On this image, a single focus of attention is computed by a bottom-up attention system (here the NVT [Itti et al., 1998]). A better solution is the new system BILAS which is shown in the following figures

blue-yellow and red-green is independent in the NVT. More than three input images could definitely not be processed with this approach. Second, since in the NVT the computation of the orientation maps works only on the gray-scale data, no orientations are computed for the reflection values. And finally, a new system that computes the saliencies for each mode separately is not only more intuitive but enables also the direct inspection of depth or reflectance saliencies as well as their tuning by top-down mechanisms. These thoughts were the first cause to build an own attention system that is able to process several modes. The single-mode version of the system was introduced in chapter 4, here we show the extension of the system to two modes: the Bimodal Laser-Based Attention System (BILAS) (see also [Frintrop et al., 2005c]).

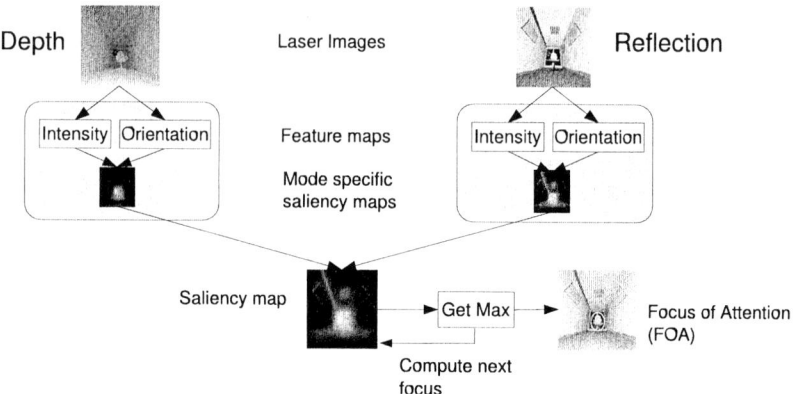

Fig. 6.5. Overview of the Bimodal Laser-Based Attention System (BILAS). The images from the two laser modes "depth" and "reflection" are computed independently. Saliencies according to intensity and orientations are determined and fused into a mode-specific saliency map. After combining both of those maps, the focus of attention is directed to the most salient region. A more detailed figure is shown in Fig. 6.6

BILAS computes regions of interest in the depth and reflection data independently and finally fuses their saliencies yielding a single focus of attention. In Fig. 6.5, we show an overview of this system, in Fig. 6.6 the system is shown in more detail. Since the laser scanner provides only gray-scale data, no color feature is computed and the processing is restricted to intensity and orientation. Notice that depth is not a feature in our approach but a separate sensor mode. Generally, also other sensor modalities may be regarded: all sensor data that are representable in a 2D map might be used as input to the system.

Base of the system is the bottom-up part of VOCUS (chapter 4). First, the images from each mode of the laser scanner are processed independently, i.e., intensities and orientations are computed for the depth as well as for the reflection image. These computations take place as described in chapter 4: the feature maps are computed with center-surround mechanisms and Gabor filters, the maps are weighted according to the uniqueness of the features, they are summed up to conspicuity maps and normalized. The conspicuity maps are weighted again and summed up to a mode-specific saliency map which contains the saliencies according to the specific sensor mode. Finally, the saliencies of each mode are weighted again and fused into a global saliency map.

The fusion of two different kinds of data allows to exploit the respective advantages of both modes: saliencies in one mode correspond not necessarily to saliencies in the other mode. Therefore, a larger variety of object properties is considered and it is possible to detect a pop-out — e.g., in depth — that

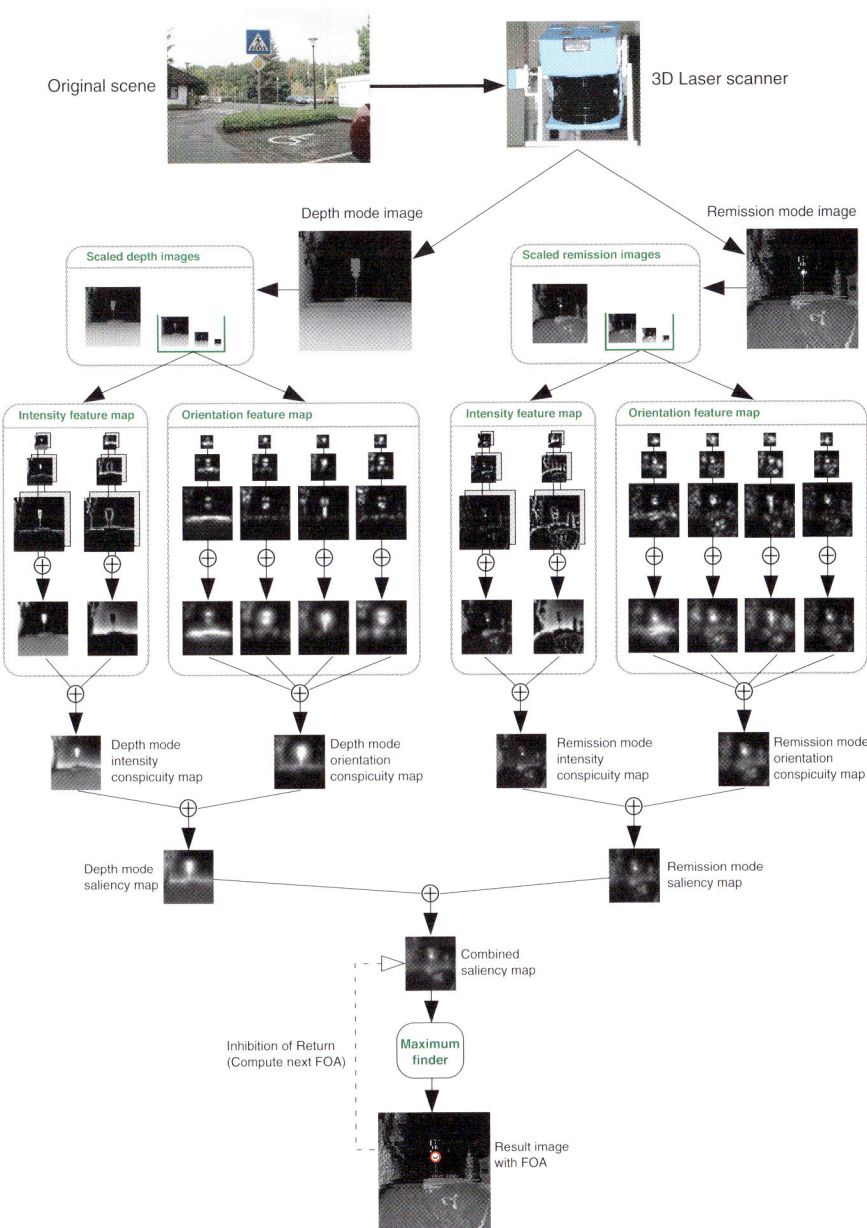

Fig. 6.6. The Bimodal Laser-Based Attention System (BILAS) in detail. The images from the two laser modes "depth" and "reflectance" are computed independently. Saliencies according to intensity and orientations are determined and fused into a mode-specific saliency map. After combining both of those maps, the focus of attention (FOA) is directed to the most salient region (shown as red ellipse)

would be missed otherwise. The saliencies of both modes compete with each other and the focus of attention is directed to the strongest cue.

Note that we do not claim that one sensor mode is better than the other or that laser is better than camera data. Each mode has its advantages and only the combination allows to use all of them.

6.3 Experiments and Results

We have tested our approach on scans of both indoor and outdoor scenes. The laser scans were taken at two different resolutions: 152×256 and 361×211 data points. From these points, images of sizes 244×256 and 288×211 were generated. The pixel dimensions do not match exactly the number of data points, since some of the border pixels in horizontal direction are ignored due to distortion effects and in the lower resolution mode the pixels in the horizontal direction were duplicated to yield adequately dimensioned images. The lower resolution proved to be sufficient for the application of attentional mechanisms. The computations of the first focus on both laser images took 230 ms on a Pentium IV with 2400 MHz. The computation of further foci was determined nearly at once (less than 10 ms).

The camera images depicted in this section represent the same scenes as the laser scans to facilitate the scene recognition for the reader and to enable comparison between the sensor modalities. It has to be remarked that camera and laser images do not show identical parts of the scene, since the apex angles and their fields of view are different.

In this section, we focus on three aspects. Firstly, we show the general performance of attentional mechanisms on laser data (section 6.3.1). Secondly, the different qualities of the two laser modes are shown (section 6.3.2), and finally, we compare the performance of attentional mechanisms on laser images with those on corresponding camera images (section 6.3.3).

6.3.1 Regions of Interest in Laser Data

Here, we briefly demonstrate the general performance of attentional mechanisms on laser data to indicate that it makes sense to determine salient regions in laser data with an attention system since the regions are of potential interest in robotic applications. Fig. 6.7 shows four scenes, a camera image as reference on the left and the laser image combined from both laser modes on the right.

In the first three laser images, the FOAs point to objects that also a human observer would consider as salient: a traffic sign, two flower pots and a statue with flowers. These objects are focused because they are highly salient in laser images: the traffic sign has strong reflection properties that yield high saliencies in the reflection image. Furthermore, it pops out in depth and shows a vertical orientation (cf. the maps in Fig. 6.5). Similar effects are true for

Fig. 6.7. The first two foci of attention computed by BILAS on laser scanner data. Left: the scene in a camera image. Right: foci on the combination of range and reflection data

the objects in the next two images. The last row shows an example of a scene in which the foci point to regions, the windows, that most human observers would not consider as conspicuous, since they are not useful to most tasks. However, in a pure bottom-up approach the window region is highly salient in the laser data, because the glass is transparent for the laser scanner, yielding black regions in both laser modes. Note that similar effects would arise in the processing of the camera image, which shows the window region much brighter than the rest of the image.

6.3.2 Fusing Two Laser Modes: Depth and Reflection

This section shows the different qualities of the two laser modes. For that purpose, we applied our system separately to range and reflection data. Additionally, we applied it to the simultaneous input of both modes, showing how their different properties influence the detection of salient regions. We start with the presentation of some scenes where certain saliencies are only detected in the range data and other saliencies only in the reflection data. The shown examples (Fig. 6.8–6.11) are presented in reading order as follows: depth image, reflection image, combined image, and camera image as a reference of the scene.

The advantages of the depth mode are illustrated in Fig. 6.8 and 6.9. The example in Fig. 6.8 shows a rubbish bin in a corridor. The rubbish bin is highly salient in the depth image, but not in the reflectance image. Here, the vertical line of the door attracts the attention. In the combined image, the influence of the depth focus is stronger, resulting in a focus on the rubbish bin. Remember that the influence of the maps is determined by the weighting function $\mathcal{W}$ that strengthens maps with few salient regions (cf. eq. 4.9). Of course, the focus in the combined image is not always on the desired object since this is a task-dependent evaluation. The region with the highest bottom-up saliency wins and attracts the FOA.

The example in Fig. 6.9 shows a hallway scene. The depth image shows a FOA on an open door — visible as dark region — which could be interesting for a robot as a passage. In the reflection image the foci point to other regions. Here again, the influence of the depth image is stronger, resulting in FOAs on the open door in the combined image, too.

Please note that the foci in the combined image are not a union of the foci of both modes. In the combined image, the first focus might point to a region that is the most salient region neither in the depth nor in the reflection image. This might happen for a simple reason: if the depth image has its most salient point at location a and the reflection image at location b, whereas both images have a point with lower saliency at location c, then the saliency of location c sums up to the highest saliency in the combined image, yielding the primary focus of attention.

The advantages of the reflection mode are shown in Fig. 6.10 and 6.11. Although the traffic sign in Fig. 6.10 attracts the first FOA in both laser

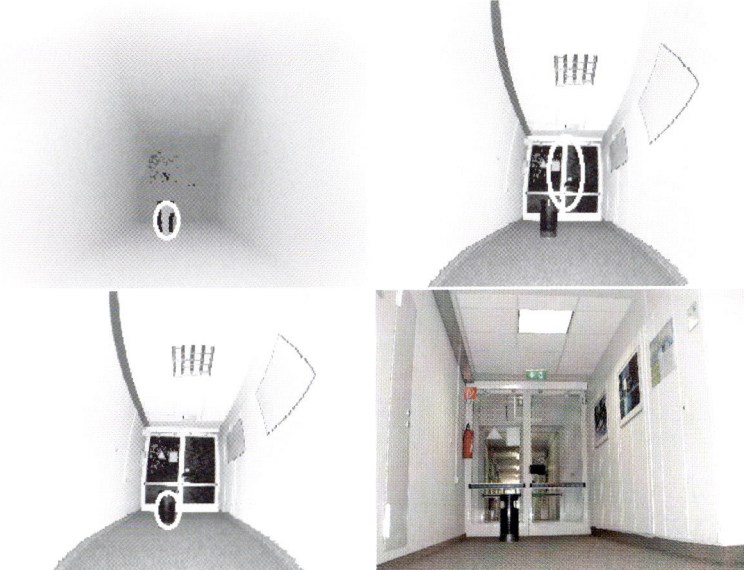

Fig. 6.8. The foci in laser data show some advantages of the depth mode. In reading order: depth image, reflection image, combined image, camera image. The rubbish bin is salient only in the range data. Here, the stronger influence of the depth image causes the first focus to point to the rubbish bin in the combined image, too

Fig. 6.9. The foci in laser data show some advantages of the depth mode. In reading order: depth image, reflection image, combined image, camera image. The open door is salient only in the range data

Fig. 6.10. The foci in laser data show some advantages of the reflection mode. In reading order: depth image, reflection image, combined image, camera image. The handicapped person sign is salient only in the reflection data

Fig. 6.11. The foci in laser data show some advantages of the reflection mode. In reading order: depth image, reflection image, combined image, camera image. All of the four cars are among the first six focus regions in the reflection data

modes, in the reflection image the 5th FOA is directed to the handicapped person sign on the floor. In the depth data this sign is completely invisible. In the combined data this detection occurs later: the 6th FOA is on the handicapped person sign. Another example is shown in Fig. 6.11. Three of the four cars in the scene are among the first four FOAs in the reflection image and within the first seven FOAs in the combined data. Obviously, the strongly reflecting license plates are the reason for high saliency in these regions. In the depth image, the cars are not focused, because the saliency of the nearer tree is stronger.

These examples show the respective advantages of the two laser modes and their complementary effect, enabling to consider different object properties.

6.3.3 Camera Versus Laser

Usually, computational visual attention systems take camera images as input. In this section, we compare this approach to the here introduced method, considering the respective advantages of the sensors.

We present three different cases: FOAs that are similar in both kinds of sensor data, those that are unique in camera images and those being unique in laser data. Fig. 6.12 shows two examples of scenes where both sensor modalities yield the same results: the traffic signs attract the attention in both scenes. We remark that this is due to different reasons: the camera FOAs are attracted by the color of the traffic sign, the laser FOAs by its depth and reflection properties. Obviously, the design of traffic signs is carefully examined since they attract bottom-up attention of different kinds.

One of the advantages of a camera is its ability to obtain color information. Although laser scanners exist that are able to record color and even temperature information, ours is not. Both scenes in Fig. 6.13 show cases in which color properties alone produced saliencies in image regions (the car in the upper image, the telephone box in the lower one) that would hardly be salient in the laser mode data.

On the other hand, Fig. 6.14 shows objects that are only focused in the laser images. The person (top) and the rubbish bin (bottom) are only focused in the laser image. The bottom image is a good example of a scene showing advantages of both, camera and laser. Whereas the focus in the laser data is on the rubbish bin — an interesting region during obstacle avoidance or cleaning up — it is in the camera image on fire extinguisher and emergency exit signs — important regions in security-relevant tasks.

Since each sensor enables the detection of different object attributes, best results should be achieved by a combination of both sensors, inducing a much richer variety of salient regions; this remains subject for future work.

Fig. 6.12. Foci showing the same regions in camera and in laser data. Some FOAs on camera images (left) and laser images, combined from depth and reflection data (right). The FOAs are attracted due to different object properties: by color and intensity in the camera images and by depth contrast and reflection properties in the laser data

6.4 Discussion

In this chapter, we have introduced an extension of VOCUS to several sensor modalities: the Bimodal Laser-based Attention System (BILAS). The bimodal input data for the attention system, depth and reflection, were provided by a 3D laser scanner. Both data modes were processed independently considering different saliencies for the respective modes.

We have tested our system on both indoor and outdoor real-world scenes. The results show that range and reflection values complement each other: some objects are salient in depth but not in reflection data and vice versa. The comparison between the 3D laser scanner and a camera as input sensors exhibited that their data also contain complementary features. In camera images, regions may be salient due to color contrast, which is not existent in laser data. On the other hand, laser data allow the detection of salient regions that cannot be identified in camera data. Best results will be achieved by a combination of laser and camera data, a topic we consider for future work. Due to the distortions of the laser data and the different fields of view of laser and camera, this fusion is not a trivial task and has to be examined

Fig. 6.13. The foci show some advantages of camera images over laser data: the red car (top) and the red telephone box (bottom) are only focused in the camera images (left), but not in laser data (right)

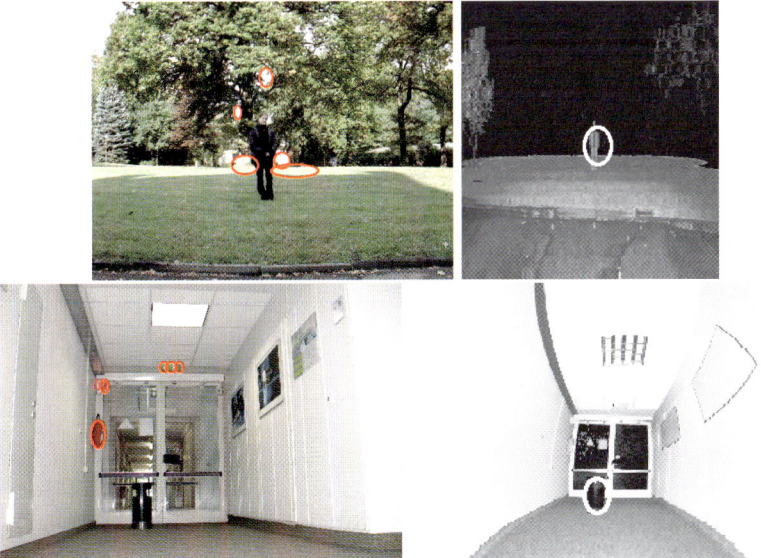

Fig. 6.14. The foci show some advantages of the laser data: the person (top) and the rubbish bin (bottom) are only focused in the laser data (right), but not in camera images (left). The bottom example shows the respective advantages of the sensors: the FOA in the laser data is on the rubbish bin whereas the FOAs in the camera image are on the fire extinguisher and the emergency exit sign

carefully [Sequeira et al., 1999]. First results can be found in [Pervölz et al., 2004].

Considering two sensor modes is a first step for the integration of multiple sensors in an attention system. The same way the two laser modes are fused, the system can be augmented to combine information of arbitrary sensors that provide the possibility to locate the sensor information in the environment. Not only camera and laser data, also auditory information could be depicted in a map and searched for salient regions provided that the direction of the sounds are known. Another possibility is to use infrared cameras to facilitate the detection of humans, a task we consider for future work [Hennig, 2004]. However, the integration of different sensor information requires careful examination.

An advantage of the laser scanner data is that it is independent of illumination variances. Different lighting conditions are a big problem in computer vision applications that rely on camera images. The laser scanner can be applied even in complete darkness, yielding the same results and providing a visual impression of the scene based on the reflection data. This can be an advantage in applications like surveillance in which the robot has to operate at night.

A limiting factor for the application of a scanning device in robot control is the low scan speed. The minimum speed of the scanner is 1.7 seconds for a low resolution 3D scan. Therefore, data from other sensors have to be used for robot navigation in quickly changing environments. On the other hand, the 3D scanner is well-suited for applications in low dynamics environments, like security inspection tasks in facility maintenance, interior survey of buildings and 3D digitalization. A much faster way to acquire range and reflection values are 3D laser "cameras", that use a sensor array to measure these values in parallel.

Several research prototypes of 3D "cameras" are known, e.g., the CSEM range camera [URL, 14], the PMD camera [URL, 15], and the 3D camera at KTH [Carlsson et al., 1999], At the moment, these cameras are still expensive, are mostly restricted to shorter ranges and very low resolutions, and usually yield results that are less precise than those of a laser scanner, but in future such devices might be the sensor of choice for such systems as the one presented here. The application of our system to data from a 3D camera is straightforward: the depth information is extracted and rendered into an image as described in 6.1.2, the color information forms a second image, replacing the reflectance data of our system. This approach has also the advantage of corresponding values and it furthermore provides color information and mainly undistorted data. One approach of applying attentional mechanisms to the data of a 3D camera is presented in [Ouerhani and Hügli, 2000].

In this chapter, we focus on the bottom-up computation of saliencies. Obviously, the next step will be the combination of this approach with the top-down guidance of the previous chapter, a topic we leave for future work. Note that one weight vector has to be computed for each sensor mode. Inevitably, the search will be less successful than the experiments in chapter 5 since it is hard to detect targets only from the two features intensity and orientation. Nevertheless, it might be possible to distinguish obstacles (bright regions in range data) and passages (dark regions in range data). Best results are to be expected from performing goal-directed search on the data from several sensor modes.

7

Attentive Classification

According to [Neisser, 1967], object recognition in human perception is done in two steps: first, attentional processes select a region of interest, and second, complex object recognition is restricted to these regions. In the previous chapters, we introduced the computational attention system VOCUS that performs the first of these steps. In this chapter, we realize the second step: VOCUS is combined with a well-known classifier [Viola and Jones, 2004] resulting in a complete recognition system. This approach is called *attentive classification* (cf. Fig. 7.1).

Although an attention system means a certain overhead in computation, its usage usually pays off since reliable and general object recognition is a complex high level vision task that is usually computationally expensive. The more general the recognizer — enabling recognition of objects of different shapes, poses, scales, and illuminations — the more important is a pre-selection of regions of interest. We discuss in which cases the recognition is sped up by the combined system and in which cases the recognition quality is improved. Several experiments illustrate this behavior. As an alternative approach, we tried the object recognition with Lowe's SIFT keypoint detector [Lowe, 2004, URL, 13] but since this was unsuccessful in first experiments, we elaborate on this approach only briefly.

The combination of attention with object recognition is suggesting and has gained interest recently. Several groups have been working on this using different recognition modules but the combination was always restricted to bottom-up attention systems. The combination of top-down attention and object recognition has not been investigated before. Additionally, to our knowledge a detailed examination of the time and quality gain has not been done before. One example of a combination of attention and recognition is presented in [Miau and Itti, 2001]. They combine an attentional module with the biologically motivated hierarchical model for object recognition HMAX [Riesenhuber and Poggio, 1999]. Since the model simulates the complex structure of early vision in cortex, it is limited in its capabilities. The objects to be detected are ellipses and rectangles in artificially constructed images. The authors extend

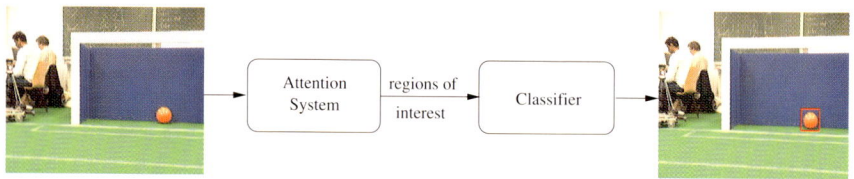

Fig. 7.1. Attentive Classification: the recognition system consists of an attention system providing object candidates and a classification system verifying the hypothesis. The combination yields a flexible and robust system

their approach in [Miau et al., 2001] using a support vector machine algorithm for the detection of pedestrians on attentionally focused image regions. In [Walther et al., 2004, Walther et al., 2005] a visual attention system is combined with Lowe's SIFT Keypoint Detector [Lowe, 2004, URL, 13]. In their approach, this is successful since they use very complex objects and those which not change viewpoint (a fixed view of the object is pasted into a scene). Since the SIFT Keypoint Detector improves if restricted to a relevant region, Walther et al. achieve an improvement in the detection rate.

In the following — after a brief discussion on object recognition in general — we introduce the classifier of Viola and Jones in section 7.1. In section 7.1.2, we touch lightly on object recognition with Lowe's SIFT Keypoint Detector. The combination of the attention and the recognition system is presented in section 7.2. In section 7.3, we show various results on the recognition of objects in both laser and camera data with the pure bottom-up system as well as with the top-down modulated system. We show how the time and the quality of performance are improved in different cases. Finally, section 7.4 concludes the chapter.

7.1 Object Recognition

General object recognition is not solved at all in computer vision [Forsyth and Ponce, 2003]. To illustrate this, it is necessary to regard what humans are able to do: Humans are very good at recognizing objects. We can name many thousands of different objects, categorize them spontaneously into groups, range new objects into these groups, redetect them in arbitrary orientations, from different viewpoints, under most difficult illumination conditions, and if they are partially occluded.

Humans also are able to recognize objects on different hierarchy levels, that means to recognize a poodle as poodle but also as a dog, a mammal, an animal, and a creature. Which level is appropriate in a particular application seems to be intuitively clear to us. Furthermore, we are able to generalize, that means to recognize different kinds of chairs, such with one leg and with four ones as well as such with or without armrests, also if we have never before seen this instance. Finally, we are able to learn new object categories from a small number of examples.

Managing these conditions is extremely difficult for computational object recognition systems. What it makes even more difficult is the question what an object actually is. Is a name plate an object? Is the logo inside the name plate an object? Is the wall an object? Is wind an object? We ignore this ontological question here and consider such things as objects that have an own designation, that are coherent and limited in spatial extent, and that have some feature values that are detectable by vision. In this view, a name plate is an object, also the logo inside, but not the wall — it is not limited in spatial extent — and not wind — it is not directly detectable by vision.

Although an optimal object recognizer does not exist, there are some good approaches that fit special kinds of recognition tasks. A common approach is to do *template matching*, that means looking for image windows that have a simple shape and stylized content. A system that tests whether a template is present in an image or not is called a *classifier*. It takes a feature set as an input and produces a class label. The classifier of choice for our experiments was the one of Viola and Jones [Viola and Jones, 2004] since it is one of the best current classifiers concerning detection and false detection rate. It will be introduced in the following. The classifier works fine on complex objects representable by several edge and line features but has difficulties with simple objects. In section 7.3.2, we show how the combination with the attention system helps to improve the recognition of such simple objects on the example of detecting balls for robot soccer.

We also did some experiments with Lowe's SIFT Keypoint Detector [Lowe, 2004, URL, 13], but found that our targets provide in general not enough stable features to enable a reliable recognition. This is shown in 7.1.2.

7.1.1 The Viola-Jones Classifier

In this section, we introduce the classifier of Viola and Jones that was originally built for face detection. It was first described in [Viola and Jones, 2001] and revised in [Viola and Jones, 2004]. The classifier works on gray-scale images, considering the composition of objects from simple features. Here, we will give only a rough overview of the classifier; more details can be found in appendix B.

Learning Features

The idea of Viola-Jones's classification method is to learn how a target object is composed of several basic features. For example, if the target is an office chair it is learned that chairs have a vertical line in the lower middle (the chair leg) and one horizontal line in the middle (the seat). If these (and many other) features are present in an image to a certain degree, the target is said to be detected. Fig. 7.2 shows the basic features the classifier considers. The

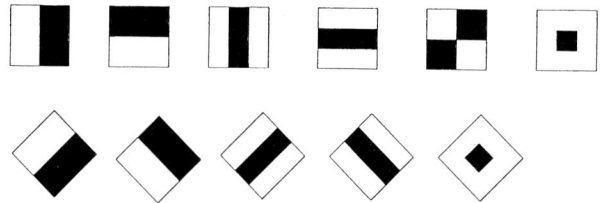

Fig. 7.2. Haar-like feature detection masks used by the Viola-Jones classifier for the detection of edge, line, and blob features [Viola and Jones, 2004]

features are called Haar-like, since they follow the same structure as the Haar basis, i.e., step functions introduced by Alfred Haar to define wavelets. They are also used in [Lienhart and Maydt, 2002, Papageorgiou et al., 1998, Treptow and Zell, 2004, Viola and Jones, 2004].

The computation of features is usually time consuming, especially if they are computed on different scales, but in this approach they are effectively calculated using *integral images* (cf. appendix B). After once creating an integral image in linear time with respect to the number of pixels, a rectangular feature value of arbitrary size is computed with only 4 references. This enables the fast computation of the features and a simple and fast resizing of features to detect objects of different sizes.

A learning technique, the Gentle Ada Boost Algorithm [Freund and Schapire, 1996], is used to select a set of simple features to achieve a given detection and error rate. In a derivative, not the simple features are used for classification and learning, but CARTs (Classification and Regression Tree) (cf. appendix B). These binary trees enable to learn objects with different characteristics, e.g., objects from different viewpoints or with different patterns (cf. section 7.3.2).

The Cascade

The performance of a single classifier, i.e., a set of simple features, is not suitable for object classification, since it produces a high hit rate, e.g., 0.999, but also a high error rate, e.g., 0.5. Nevertheless, the hit rate is much higher than the error rate. To enable an effective recognition, the relevant classifiers are arranged in a cascade, i.e., a degenerated decision tree, which consists of several stages. Each stage contains several features, the more important a feature, the earlier the stage in which it occurs. During recognition, in every stage of the cascade a decision is made whether the image contains the object or not. If the features of the stage are present to a certain degree in the image, the next stage is investigated. If not, the process stops. This enables an efficient processing: many image regions are checked solely by the first stages and only the target regions or regions similar to the target are investigated by more stages. This process also enables a high quality of recognition since the error

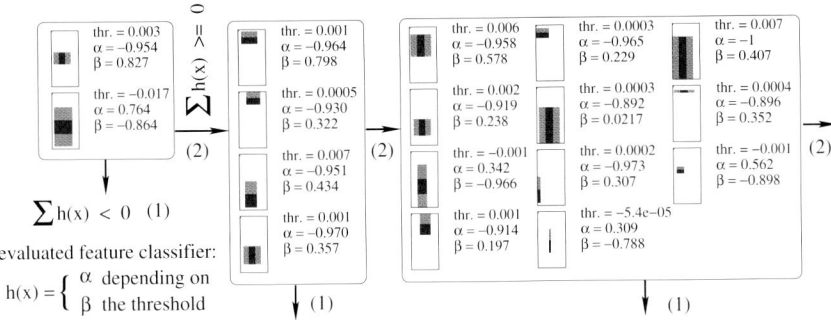

Fig. 7.3. The first three stages of a cascade of classifiers for an office chair in depth data. Every stage contains several simple classifiers that use Haar-like features. α and β are the outputs of the fitted simple feature classifiers that depend on the assigned weights, the expected error, and the classifier size [Viola and Jones, 2004] (cf. appendix B)

rate, multiplied in each stage, approaches zero. Fig. 7.3 shows the first three stages of a cascade that was built for learning an office chair in laser range images (cf. Fig. 7.4). One can see that the first stage contains one vertical and one horizontal line, both in the middle of the search rectangle. These features correspond to the leg and to the seat of the chair and are the two most important features for this object.

The Recognition

After a cascade is learned for the target object, the recognition in a test image is done as follows: a search window is laid on the test image (usually starting at the upper left corner) and it is checked with the cascade whether this region contains the object. Then the search window is shifted one or several pixels to the right and the region is checked again (cf. Fig. 7.4, left). This is done for the whole image, beginning with a search window of a specified small size (e.g. 20 x 40 pixels for chairs). Next, the detector is enlarged by rescaling the features to find objects on larger scales.

Investigating one region after the other in the classical approach has to be done since no information on the target location exists. In our approach, we already have regions of interest providing a hypothesis for the target object. Therefore, only the region of interest is investigated which is determined by the focus of attention (cf. Fig. 7.4, right); details follow in section 7.2.

Classification in Laser Images

We trained the Viola-Jones classifier not only on camera data but also on the images obtained from the 3D laser scanner (cf. section 6.1.1): the classifier

Fig. 7.4. Search windows (green rectangles) of the Viola-Jones Classifier on a test image. Left: in the classical approach, the whole image is searched for objects. Right: in our approach, only the region of interest, determined by the focus of attention (red ellipse), is investigated

was trained on images of two kinds of object: office chairs and the robot Kurt3D. Training was performed on the range as well as on the reflection data. The classification results in section 7.3.1 show that object recognition is also possible in laser data. To achieve a single result from both modes, the results of each cascade were combined by a logical "and", resulting in an output that only considers objects as detected that occur in both laser modes. Fig. 7.5 shows how this method reduces false detections. We chose the logical "and" to combine the results of the laser modes because our targets were detectable in both modes. The operation enabled a reduction of false detections. Note that in other cases a different operation might be useful, e.g., a logical "or". In this case, the detection rate increases, but also the false detection rate.

One advantage of the laser data is that it is independent of illumination, thus less training images are required. On the other hand, recognition in laser data is sometimes difficult because less information leads to several false detections. This problem is mostly overcome by the combination of range and reflection cascades. Besides the independence of illumination, the laser data has another advantage: the misclassification of shadows, mirrored objects, and wall paintings is avoided since these do not occur in the laser data. Fig. 7.6 shows this: in the scene showing a robot and a poster of a robot, only the real robot is detected.

7.1.2 Lowe's SIFT Keypoint Detector

We also did some experiments with Lowe's SIFT Keypoint Detector (SIFT: Scale Invariant Feature Transform) [Lowe, 2004, URL, 13]. This is a powerful and stable recognizer that enables the detection of complex objects or whole scenes by matching the arrangement of *keypoints* (also called SIFT features). These keypoints are invariant to image scaling and rotation, and partially invariant to change in illumination and 3D camera viewpoint. Roughly spoken, the keypoints are extrema in scale-space that have to stand several additional

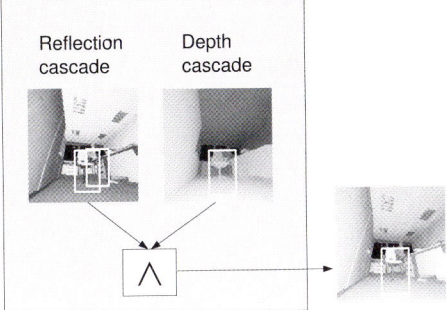

Fig. 7.5. Classification in bimodal laser data: the classification cascades of both laser modes are combined by a logical "and", resulting in an output only considering objects as detected that occur in both laser modes

Fig. 7.6. A camera image of the robot next to a poster showing a robot (top). In the laser data of the same scene, the poster is not visible due to the infrared light and the range information (bottom); this prevents misclassification: only the real robot is detected

tests, e.g., rejecting unstable extrema with low contrast. The matches are identified by finding the 2 nearest neighbors of each keypoint from the first image among those in the second image, and only accepting a match if the distance to the closest neighbor is less than 0.6 of that to the second closest neighbor. The threshold of 0.6 can be adjusted upwards to select more matches or downwards to select only the most reliable ones. An example taken from the

Fig. 7.7. Testing Lowe's SIFT Keypoint Detector [Lowe, 2004, URL, 13] for a complex target (basmati rice box). From left to right: 1) Training image. 2) 572 keypoints on training image. 3) Test image. 4) Test image in which 38 keypoints match. For such complex target objects, the recognition is successful even if the target if presented from different viewpoints (original images from [URL, 13])

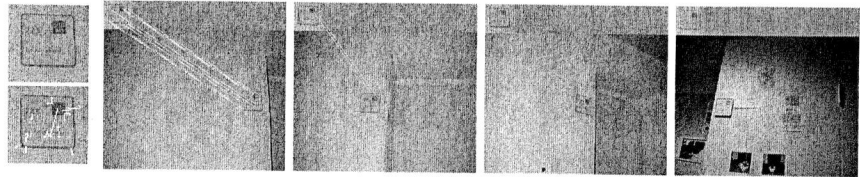

Fig. 7.8. Testing Lowe's SIFT Keypoint Detector [Lowe, 2004, URL, 13] for a simple target (name plate). From left to right: 1) Training image (top) and 17 keypoints on training image (bottom). 2) Search target in the image from which the training image was cut. 3) Test image in which only 2 keypoints match. 4,5) Two test images in which no keypoints match. For such simple target objects, the recognition is difficult even for slight changes in viewpoint and fails completely for larger changes

online data on David Lowe's web pages [URL, 13] is shown in Fig. 7.7. The target object, a basmati rice box, has a complex texture which enables the detection of many keypoints: 572 keypoints are detected. This allows a redetection in the test image on the right: 38 keypoints are successfully matched. An application in which this approach shows good results is the recognition of building facades.

One condition for this approach is "that it generates large numbers of features that densely cover the image over the full range of scales and locations" [Lowe, 2004]. Unfortunately, we found that this is not the case for our targets: these provide in general not enough stable features to enable a reliable recognition. This is shown in Fig. 7.8. For the target object "name plate"(left) only 17 keypoints are detected that may be used for matching with a test object. When the target was searched in the training image itself, the recognition was successful (second left): 15 matches were found. But when it was searched in other test images, nearly no matches were found: in a simple test image (third left), only two matches were found, in more difficult test images (right and second right), nothing was found. For targets with even less features, e.g., the highlighter or key fob of chapter 5 or the balls of section 7.3.2, the recognition is probably even worse. Therefore, it seems that this approach is not adequate for our case.

Walther et al. [Walther et al., 2004, Walther et al., 2005] did also experiments in which they combine a visual attention system with the SIFT Keypoint Detector. In their experiments, this yielded satisfying results because the objects were sufficiently complex and because in most experiments they paste the object into an image scene so that it appears always from the same viewpoint which simplifies the recognition significantly.

7.2 Attentive Classification

Attentive classification means the combination of a fast attention system, applied to the whole scene, with a powerful classifier, restricted to a region of interest (cf. Fig. 7.1). This is an effective way to improve the quality and time performance of vision systems: the attention system points to a region of interest but is not able to determine which object is in this region (bottom-up) or whether a searched target is actually present (top-down). On the other hand, a general classifier needs a lot of time if applied to the whole image. Restricting the classification to the region of interest is much more effective and also improves the quality of recognition in certain cases as will be shown in section 7.3. The more complex and general a recognition system, the more useful is an attentional front-end concentrating the processing on special regions.

The attention system may be used in a pure bottom-up mode or it may search for a target in top-down mode. These are two principally different approaches: the bottom-up system is used in an exploration mode; no special target is given. The system shall favor salient objects or it shall recognize as many objects as possible but does not have the time to cope with all objects. So in the bottom-up mode, the attention system finds regions of interest and the classifier determines the identity of the fixated region. Instead in the top-down mode, the system is searching for a target which is known by the attention as well as by the classification module. Thus, the attention system generates an object hypothesis which is verified or falsified by the classifier.

If the task of a vision system is exploration and recognition of several objects in a scene and there is not enough time to analyze all image regions in detail, a priority has to be set. A simple priority that is usually set in such a case is to scan the scene from upper left to lower right to recognize the first object in the database, then find the second one and so on. Alternatively, the first search window may be searched for all of the objects, then the second window and so on. If time is rare, the first approach has the effect that the objects at the end of the database are never recognized while the second approach has the effect that objects in the lower right corner of the scene are ignored. A much better approach is to detect objects in order of their saliency (attentive classification). The attention system computes a sequence of image regions in order of their saliency. The first region in this sequence is investigated by the classifier for each object in the database and the next salient region is only investigated after recognizing the object — or deciding that the object is not known. Of course, this approach also misses some objects — the non-salient ones — but since this is inevitable due to the lack of time, the missing of non-salient objects is the lesser evil.

There is another application scenario, in which recognizing only salient objects is even preferred to the recognition of all objects: if a system is very complex and knows about a wide variety of object classes it might be useful to not consider everything in the environment. This is also true for humans: not every object in the environment is noticed but mainly salient and/or task-relevant objects are recognized. The socket in the corner will probably not be noticed if you look around in a new entered room unless you need power supply. Here, it is sensible to have an attention system narrowing down the choice of regions for recognition. One application in robotics in which this behavior is useful is the creation of semantic 3D maps, that means maps that contain information about the objects in the environment. Surely, it is not wanted to include every object in the map since this would overload the map and make it confusing — if the map is considered for interaction with humans — or leads to computational problems because of the high amount of data. The attention system is able to restrict the processing to those image regions that are worth to be investigated.

Since a focus of attention is often not on a whole object but on its border or on parts of it, not only the focused region is investigated by the classifier, but a larger region surrounding the focus (cf. Fig. 7.4). In our experiments it turned out that choosing a region which is four times as large as the expected size of the target object yielded good results. For example, for name plates we chose a region of 54×54 pixels on test images of size 512×384. This is about 2% of the image area. Inside this region, the search windows were placed so that the middle of the search window lies inside the region. For name plates, investigating this small region was enough since name plates did not exceed a certain size in our image sets. These images were taken by the author so it would have been possible to take a close up view of a name plate in which it appears much larger. This is not possible in the future application in which a robot will take the pictures since the fixed camera is not able to get closer to the name plate. For other objects, e.g., for the chairs in the laser data, it may be necessary to determine a larger region. If the object may fill the whole image, region size has to be equal to image size.

When the attentive classification is applied to laser instead of camera data, the procedure is roughly the same (cf. Fig. 7.9). The main difference is that both the attention system and the classifier operate not only on one but on two images: range and reflection data. The combination of the classification results

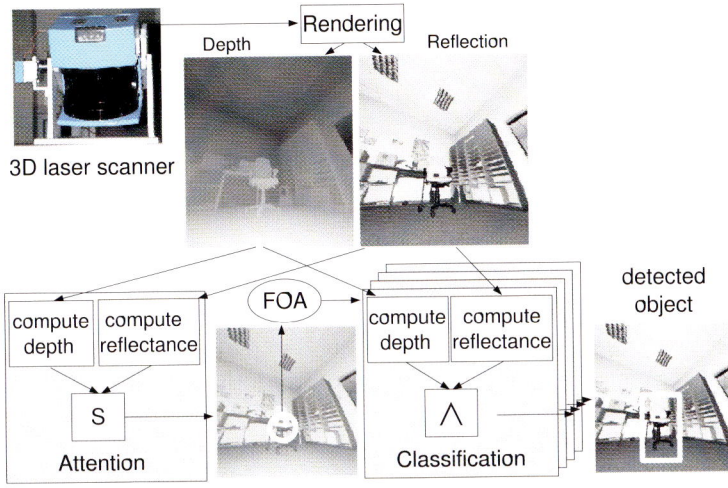

Fig. 7.9. Attentive classification on laser data: two laser modes, depth and reflection, are provided by the 3D laser scanner, rendered into images and fed into the attention and the classification system. The attention system fuses conspicuities of both modes in one saliency map (S) and generates a focus of attention (FOA) which is fed into the classification system. The classifier searches for objects of predefined classes in the neighborhood of the FOA in both laser images and combines the results by a logical "and". The rectangle in the result image (right) depicts a detected object

for each mode by a logical "and" narrows down the number of detections and reduces the amount of false detections.

In the following, we discuss the performance gain achieved in different applications. We start with debating the time savings, especially occurring for the bottom-up system, and after that we argue in which cases the quality is improved by eliminating false detections.

7.2.1 Time Performance

The time saving achieved with the combination of attention and classification depends on the complexity of the classifier as well as on the number of objects that are of interest in a special scene. If the classifier is highly complex and determining the object identity is a time consuming task — more time consuming than the attentional computations — there is no doubt that the combination with the attention system yields a gain in time performance.

But what if the classifier itself is extremely fast, as the Viola-Jones Classifier? In this case the time saving depends on the number of object classes that have to be considered: if only one type of object has to be detected, it might be useful to stick to the classifier and ignore the attention system. But for a complex vision system, knowing 5, 10, or even hundreds of objects it is extremely useful to search for all of these objects merely in a pre-specified region. This time saving usually occurs when the bottom-up attention system is used which determines a region of interest and many classifiers are used to determine the identity of what is in this region.

Here, we analyze the time performance for the bottom-up attentive classification on laser data. On 300×300 pixel images, the attentive classification at a region of interest needs on average 60 ms, compared to 200 ms for an uninformed search across the whole image (Pentium-IV-2400). So the focused classification needs only 30% of the time of the exhaustive one. Note that for other objects like name plates this percentage is even lower since a smaller image region is investigated. The attention system requires 230 ms to compute a focus for both modes; hence, for m object classes the exhaustive search needs $m * 200$ ms versus $230 + m * 60$ ms for the attentive search. Therefore, already for two different object classes the turning point is reached: the exhaustive search needs 400 ms, whereas the attentive search requires only 350 ms. The time saving increases proportionally with the number of objects, and for 5 objects the attentive classification is already twice as fast as the exhaustive classification as is shown in Fig. 7.10.

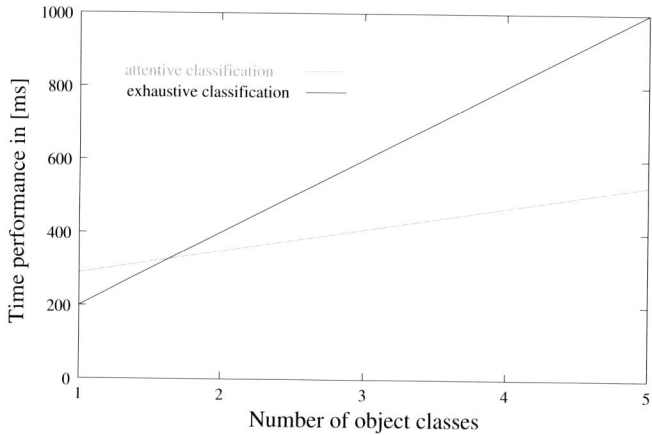

Fig. 7.10. The time saving of bottom-up attentive classification depends on the number of object classes: the more classes, the higher the time saving in the attentive approach. Already for 5 classes, the attentive classification is nearly twice as fast as the exhaustive classification

If the attention system is applied to color camera images, the required time increases since the color computations are time consuming. Instead, the classifier works only on gray-scale images, thus the required time does not increase. Therefore, the turning point is reached at a later point. On the other hand, the use of color allows to consider other object properties enabling a better classification quality (cf. section 7.2.2).

The top-down attention system is applied if a target object is known. This means it is clear which object is searched and which classifier should be applied. Hence, a time saving is only achieved if, firstly, the classifier is more time consuming than the attention system or, secondly, several objects have to be searched in the same scene. In the latter case, the top-down attention system has to determine a new region of interest for each object class, but this does not mean that the whole computation needs to be repeated. For each object class, the weighting of the feature maps with the target's weights vector, the computation of excitation, inhibition, and top-down saliency map have to be performed. But the computation of the image pyramids, the conversion to the LAB color space, and the computation of the feature maps need to be performed only once for a scene. Since these are the most expensive computations, the time increases only slightly for several object classes and the combination with classification pays off.

7.2.2 Quality Performance

The attentive classification increases the performance not only in time but in many cases also in quality. The pre-selection of regions with potentially higher interest than the rest of the image is a quality choice by definition (regions of interest have usually a higher quality than regions of no interest). This has different effects in bottom-up and top-down mode. In bottom-up mode, this is useful if time has to be saved or if only a few objects shall be considered. If, for example, the five most important objects in a scene shall be localized, the bottom-up system of attention may help to select them. Other improvements of recognition quality with help of a bottom-up attention system were reported in [Walther et al., 2004, Walther et al., 2005]. They were using Lowe's SIFT Keypoint Detector [Lowe, 2004, URL, 13] that improves if restricted to a relevant region, so they achieve an improvement in the detection rate. This is not possible for the Viola-Jones Classifier which achieves the same results if focused on the target as if searching the whole image.

In top-down mode, another aspect of quality improvement reveals: the elimination of false detections. Combining attention and classification means to take the intersection of the results of both systems; this diminishes the detection rate as well as the number of false detections. Therefore, an improvement of quality is achieved in cases in which both systems have a reasonable detection rate — which stays almost the same — and the classifier produces many false detections — which are significantly reduced. This is usually the case for simple objects like balls. In section 7.3.2, we will show how the quality of recognition is essentially improved by using the attention system as front end to the classifier.

7.3 Experiments and Results

In this section, we present some experiments of the attentive classification system. We begin with using VOCUS in a bottom-up mode as front end, followed by investigating the combination with the top-down mode.

7.3.1 Bottom-Up Attentive Classification

In a first step, we use the bottom-up mode of VOCUS for the attentive classification[1]. The experiments were performed on laser data. This approach allows the recognition of the most salient objects in a scene what is useful in complex systems that know a wide variety of objects but do not have the time to analyze all objects in a scene. The attention system provides the priority of which region to analyze first.

In the following, we first show the performance of the classifier when trained on laser data before we combine it with the attentional front-end.

Classifier:

The classifier was trained on the objects chairs and the robot Kurt3D in laser images (300 × 300 pixels). We rendered 200 training images with chairs from 46 scans and 1083 training images with the robot from 200 scans (the rendering is explained in [Nüchter et al., 2005]). Additionally, we provided 738 negative example images to the classifier from which a multiple of sub-images is created automatically. The test set consists of 31 chair and 33 robot images for each laser mode yielding 128 test images, disjoint from the training set. There were 33 chairs and 33 robots in the scenes: some images contained two chairs but in each image there was at most one robot. Note that in this test the classifier was applied to the whole images.

We determined the detection and false detection rates for images of both laser modes independently and then for the combination of both approaches. Table 7.1 summarizes the results. It shows that the detection rate for each mode reached about 90% and there were some false detections: usually only 1 or 2, but there happened to occur 10 false detections for one test set. When the modes were combined, the number of false detections was reduced to zero while the detection rates changed only slightly (see also [Nüchter et al., 2004]).

The classifier is still successful if the object is partially occluded (see Fig. 7.12, middle). However, severely occluded objects are not detected (see Fig. 7.11); the amount of occlusion still enabling detection depends on the learned object class and has to be investigated further. In Fig. 7.12 middle, the chair is not only partially occluded, it is also presented sidewards and still recognized. Of course, it depends on the object if this is possible. In the case of the chair this is possible because the main features in the cascade belong to the seat and the chair leg. These features are still present in the rotated

---

[1] The results of this section were also published in [Frintrop et al., 2004b].

Table 7.1. Detections and false detections of the Viola-Jones classifier applied to 31 chair and 33 robot images. While the detection rate stays about the same for the combination of both laser modes, the false detections are reduced to zero

object class	# of obj.	detections			false detections		
		reflection image	depth image	**combined**	reflection image	depth image	**combined**
chair	33	30	29	**29**	2	2	**0**
robot	33	29	29	**29**	10	1	**0**

Fig. 7.11. Image of a chair with strong occlusion. In this example, a recognition with the Viola-Jones Classifier was not possible

version of the chair. The robustness of the classifier according to rotations was tested in more detail for the object class robot. We recorded scans of the robot rotated by 10° at a time. It showed that a robot rotated by 30° is still recognized (Fig. 7.13, right), but it is not if it is rotated more. To enable a recognition under an even greater change of orientation, a rotated version of the robot has to be trained. The same is true for a robot presented the other way round. The training of objects of different orientations can be done with the CARTs mentioned on page 152.

Classifier + Attention system:

When classifying objects at regions of interest, it depends on both systems what is recognized and the result is the intersection of the results of both systems run separately. The classifier detects all focused objects with the same reliability like when applied to the whole scene. Note that if no focus points to an object, this object is not detected. This conforms to our goal to detect only salient objects in the order of decreasing saliency. As discussed in chapter 4, it is hard to evaluate the quality of bottom-up FOAs, thus here we concentrate on presenting some examples of focused and classified objects in laser data in Fig. 7.12 and 7.13. The objects are successfully detected even

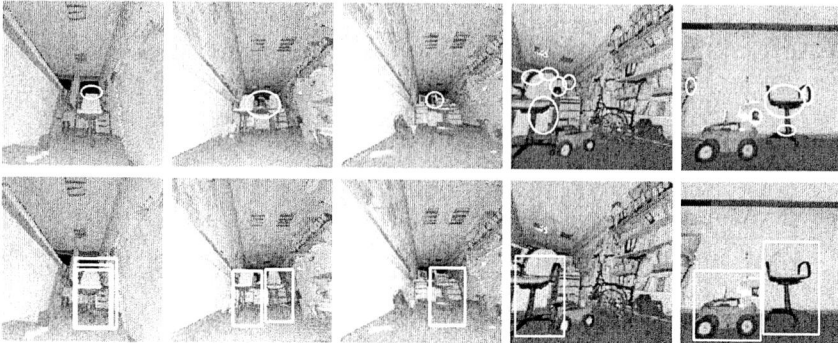

Fig. 7.12. Attentive classification in laser data. Top row: the first resp. the first 5 foci of attention computed on depth and reflection data. Bottom row: classified objects in the focus regions. Left to right: 1) Chair is detected even if the focus is at its border; 2) detection of two chairs; 3) chair is detected although it is presented sidewards and partially occluded; 4) only the chair is focused, therefore the chair but not the robot is classified; 5) both objects are focused and classified

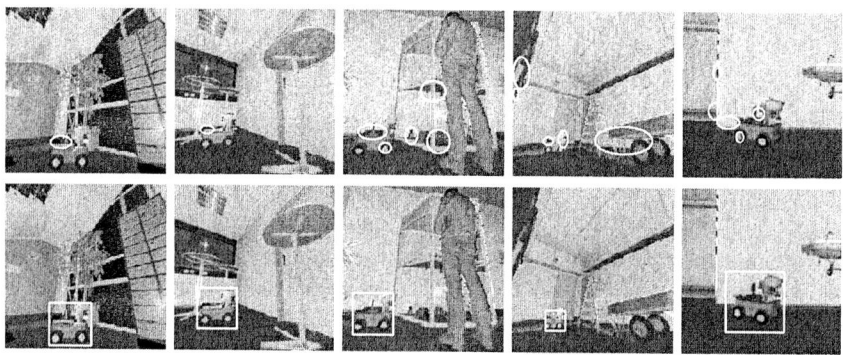

Fig. 7.13. Attentive classification in laser data. Top row: the first resp. the first 5 foci of attention computed on depth and reflection data. Bottom row: classified objects in the focus regions. Right: a robot rotated by 30° is still detected

if the focus is at the object's border (Fig. 7.12, left) since a sufficiently large search region around the focus was chosen.

7.3.2 Top-Down Attentive Classification

If the system is searching for a target instead of exploring the environment, it is clear which classifier has to be applied; there is no use of applying many different classifiers to the image. So in this approach, the attention system provides a hypothesis for the target location which is then verified or falsified by the classification system. The experiments in this section aim at showing the improvement in quality rather than in time; the conditions for an improvement in time were discussed in section 7.2.1.

We investigated the search performance for two different targets: name plates and balls. The experiments show a very different behavior: the name plates are hard to detect by the attention system but rather successfully by the classifier. A combination declines the detection quality. In contrast, balls are easily detected by the attention system but the classifier has difficulties distinguishing them from other round image regions resulting in many false detections. In this case, the combinations yields a significant increase in detection quality.

Experiment 1: Name Plates

Classifier:

The Viola-Jones classifier was trained with 1079 images of name plates. We tested the system with 54 untrained images, applying the search windows to the whole images. Each image contained exactly one name plate. The results are shown in Tab. 7.2; they show that the detection of name plates with the classifier is quite successful: only two name plates are missed and there were 9 false detections. Some examples of the classification results are depicted in Fig. 7.14.

Table 7.2. Classification results for name plates when investigating the whole images (exhaustive classification)

Target	# test im.	Detected	Not Detected	False Detections
name plate	54	52	2	9

Attention system:

As we have shown in chapter 5, the detection of name plates with the top-down attention system is quite difficult due to many similar regions in the surrounding. Table 7.3 shows the detection results for different numbers of foci. In a majority of images (62%), the detection was very successful and the name plate was found by the first focus. But the other images were more difficult resulting in higher hit numbers.

From these results, we already expect that the recognition of name plates with attentive classification yields no gain in quality performance: if few focus regions are considered, too many targets are missed and if many are considered, the false detections will probably not be diminished. This expectation is verified in the next section.

Fig. 7.14. Classifying name plates with the classifier of [Viola and Jones, 2004]. First row: perfect classification. Second row: one miss, 4 false detections and one double detection

Table 7.3. Detection results of VOCUS when searching for name plates. Different numbers of FOAs are considered

Target	# test im	# FOAs	Detected	Not Detected	Average hit number
Name plate	54	1	34	20	1.00
Name plate	54	5	46	8	1.48
Name plate	54	10	51	3	2.16

Classification + Attention system:

One example of attentive classification is shown in Fig. 7.15. The top-down attention focuses on the name plate and the classifier — restricted to this region — detects it without a false positive. This however is only achieved if merely the first focus region is considered. In this case, the number of false de-

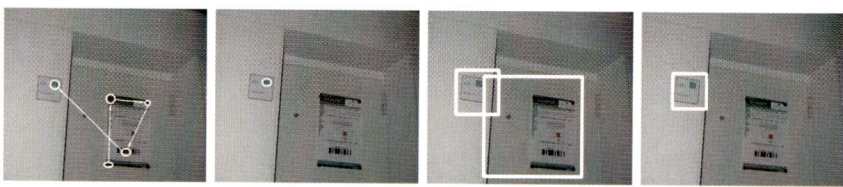

Fig. 7.15. Searching for name plates. From left to right: 1) The first 5 FOAs by pure bottom-up attention, the 5th FOA is on the name plate. 2) The 1st FOA by top-down attention searching for name plates. 3) A false detection found by the classifier while scanning the whole image. 4) No false detection occurs when concentrating on the first region of interest found by the attention module

tections is diminished to 3 (see Tab. 7.4). On the other hand, in 20 images the name plate is missed. This seems unacceptable, so what happens if more focus regions are investigated? It turned out that in this case more name plates are detected but the number of false detections increases too, unfortunately to a number higher than the one for pure classification: this is possible because in this approach, the false detections are counted for each focus separately. Therefore, often the same region yields two or more false detections for different foci. It would be possible to diminish these false detections by checking whether a detection is in the same region as a previous one. Nevertheless, the number of false detections would remain high and would only diminish to about the number of false detections in exhaustive classification.

These results show that our expectation was correct: the combination of both systems yields no gain in quality and if the task is to search only for name plates, it is more sensible to use only the classifier without the attention system. But if several objects have to be detected in the same scene or if a more complex and time-consuming recognition module is used, the favoring of regions provided by the attention system is still useful because of the gain in time performance.

Table 7.4. Results of attentive classification when searching for name plates. The detection rate is the same as in Tab. 7.3, i.e., the 2 targets not detected by the classifier were also not detected by the attention system. See text for further explanations

Target	# test im.	# foci	Detected	Not Detected	False Detections
name plate	54	1	34	20	3
name plate	54	5	46	8	18
name plate	54	10	51	3	31

Experiment 2: Balls

In this experiment, we detect balls for a RoboCup scenario (the Robot World Cup Soccer Games and Conferences [URL, 16]). Until now, balls for RoboCup were of a bright red, simplifying the detection significantly and resulting in algorithms usually based on color. In future, the color coding will be removed to achieve a more realistic setting.

We propose an approach that enables the detection of arbitrary balls; it consists of a training phase — taking place once in advance —, an adaptation phase — taking place immediately before the game when the kind of ball is known —, and a detection phase during the game. In the training phase, the classifier learns the shape of balls considering balls of different sizes, colors, and surface patterns. In the adaptation phase, the top-down attention system is quickly adapted to the actual ball by learning ball-dependent features

Fig. 7.16. Left: image of a RoboCup scene including the three kinds of balls that were used for training the classifier. Right: the corresponding edge image generated with a Sobel filter. The classifier was trained on such images

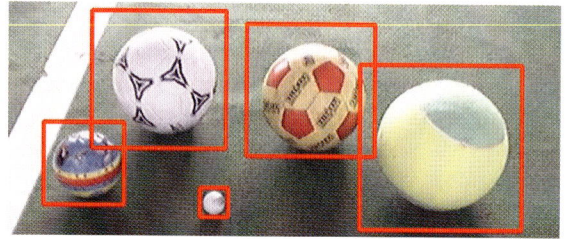

Fig. 7.17. Five different kinds of balls are detected by the classifier

from a few training images. In the detection phase, first, the attention system computes regions of interest by weighting the image features with the learned weights. Second, the classifier is applied to these regions, verifying the object hypotheses.

Classifier (Training phase):

The training and testing of the classifier for balls was done by my colleagues Sara Mitri and Kai Pervölz[2]. They showed in [Mitri et al., 2004] that the classifier, when trained on different balls in the original image data, performed bad because the object is too simple and contains few features. In various experiments they investigated that the performance was significantly improved if edge filters were applied before training. Thus, they used a Sobel filter (cf. appendix A) to obtain edge images as the one in Fig. 7.16 (right) which was then put into the classifier for training. To obtain useful edge images from the color images, the filter was applied to each channel of the colored image separately and then a threshold t was used to include any pixel in any of the 3 color channels that exceeded t in the output image. As shown in [Mitri et al., 2004], this yielded much better edge images than the application of the filter to the image converted into gray-scale.

---

[2] Thank you for marking all these balls!

The ball detection cascade was learned with 1000 images (640 × 480 pixel) showing complex scenes with up to three soccer balls of different colors and patterns. The three balls for training are shown in Fig. 7.16, left. To enable the detection of different kinds of balls, the training was done with CARTs. Fig. 7.17 shows the detection results on five different kinds of balls. Since only the upper two balls (white and yellow/red ball) were used for learning, the image demonstrates the classifier's ability to generalize to different kinds of balls.

For each kind of ball, 60 images were tested, making 180 test images altogether. Table 7.5 shows the detection and false detection rates for each kind of balls. The detection rate of the classifier is adjustable with the number of stages, i.e., a lower number of stages of the cascade increases the number of detections, but also the amount of false detections; with more stages, the detection rate diminishes but there are also few false detections.

The table shows that ball recognition is still a difficult problem: there are many false detections for all kinds of balls since the classifier learns mainly the round shape of the balls and so it is difficult to differentiate between soccer balls and other spherical image regions. At least 12 stages are needed to diminish the number of false detections to 80 for 180 images what is still a lot. But for this number of stages, the detection rate is reduced to 60%. As we will show in the next section, combining the attention system with the classifier trained with few stages improves the results significantly: restricting the region of interest with the top-down modulated attention system helps to strongly reduce the false detections with only a slightly diminished detection rate.

Attention (Adaptation phase):

In the robot soccer scenario, the adaptation phase takes place immediately before a game starts, i.e., when the actual kind of ball to be used is known. This ball is trained on the spot with the top-down attention system from a few (here: 2) training examples. We used the algorithm of Fig. 5.9 to choose some suitable training images from a training image set of 10 images (for VOCUS, we converted the images to half of their size: 320 × 240 pixels). It turned out that two training images were sufficient to yield a local optimum in performance.

In Table 7.6 we show the results of the top-down attention system when searching for balls while considering the first 5 foci. It reveals that in all cases the search is very successful. Obviously, the design of the balls is well chosen to distinguish it from its environment. Most successful is the detection of the red ball: in all of the test images, the ball was immediately detected with the first focus. But even the white ball, although missed in 7% of the examples, is on average detected with the 1.7th focus. What refrains us from using only the attention system is that this system does not distinguish between targets and non-targets. It is not able to detect if there is no ball in the scene; instead, in this case the system points to the regions that are most similar.

Table 7.5. Classification results of the cascade of classifiers depending on the used number of stages. The cascade with 10 stages (bold face) was used for the experiments with the attentive classification

	# stages	# test im.	Detections	Not Detected	False Detections
red ball			52	8	114
white ball	9	60	48	12	70
yel/red ball			57	3	108
Total		180	157	23	292
red ball			**45**	**15**	**52**
white ball	**10**	**60**	**44**	**16**	**45**
yel/red ball			**57**	**3**	**63**
Total		**180**	**146**	**34**	**160**
red ball			45	15	51
white ball	11	60	42	18	47
yel/red ball			56	4	65
Total		180	143	37	163
red ball			44	16	26
white ball	12	60	29	31	31
yel/red ball			37	23	23
Total		180	110	70	80

Table 7.6. Detection results of VOCUS when searching for different balls. In each image, the first 5 focused regions are considered

Target	# test im	Detected	Not Detected	Average hit number
Red Ball	60	60	0	1.0
White Ball	60	56	4	1.7
Yel/red Ball	60	60	0	1.1
Total	180	176	4	1.3

Attentive Classification (Detection phase):

In the combined approach, first the balls are searched with the top-down modulated attention system, and second the first five FOA regions are investigated by the classifier. Therefore, the output is the intersection of both result sets: the detected balls must be found both by the attention algorithm as well as by the classifier.

The results of the attentive classification are shown in Table 7.7. It shows that the false detections are significantly reduced in the combined approach versus pure classification to 23 from 160 while the detections remain nearly stable (141 vs. 146). This is much better than the performance of the classifier with more stages: for 12 stages, the number of false detections was 80, with 110 detections.

Several of the results are depicted in Fig. 7.18 – Fig. 7.20. In the first row of each figure, we show one example in which the results are the same for exhaustive and attentive classification. In the other examples, we focus on more interesting cases in which the combination of the systems yields a difference, e.g., the cases in which false detections are diminished.

When looking closer at the results of the different kinds of balls, it reveals that the performance is different for each kind: for red balls, the detection rate remains stable whereas the false detection rate is diminished significantly from 52 to 1. For white balls, the detection rate shrinks slightly from 44 to 41 and the 45 false detections are completely eliminated. Most false detections occur for the yellow/red ball: 20 of the 63 false detections remain. It is interesting that although for the white ball many of the first 5 foci do not point to the ball but to other regions, the false detections are completely eliminated. Obviously, these regions and the false detections of the classifier were disjoint. Instead, for the yellow ball several false detections remain: in these cases, the foci pointed to regions which were also misclassified by the classifier.

Table 7.7. Comparison of the exhaustive classification with the attentive classification. We used the classification cascade with 10 stages. Column 2 (attention) shows the average hit number (cf. Def. 1). It shows that the false detections are significantly reduces in the attentive approach while the detection rate remains nearly stable

	# im.	Attention Av. hit nb.	Classifier only Detect.	Classifier only False Detect.	Attentive Classification Detect.	Attentive Classification False Detect.
red ball	60	1.0	45	52	45	1
white ball	60	1.7	44	45	40	0
yel/red ball	60	1.1	57	63	57	20
Total	180	1.25	146	160	142	23

7.4 Discussion

In this chapter, we examined the combination of the attention system with a classifier, an approach which we called attentive classification. This method represents an important step towards effective general object recognition since it constrains complex and time-consuming computations to restricted parts of the data.

Against common understanding, often not the complex objects are the ones causing problems in recognition, but the simple ones. The simpler an object, the more difficult it is to distinguish it from other regions in a scene. Since recognition systems usually focus on recognizing special features, e.g., they focus on gray-scale edge features, the risk is high that these features are

Fig. 7.18. Detecting red balls. Left: classifier only. Middle: first 5 FOAs of VOCUS in top-down mode. Right: attentive classification; most false detections are eliminated

Fig. 7.19. Detecting white balls. Left: classifier only. Middle: first 5 FOAs of VOCUS in top-down mode. Right: attentive classification; most false detections are eliminated

Fig. 7.20. Detecting yellow/red balls. Left: classifier only. Middle: first 5 FOAs of VOCUS in top-down mode. Right: attentive classification; most false detections are eliminated

not sufficient to recognize the target successfully. We illustrated this behavior for the example of detecting name plates with Lowe's SIFT Keypoint Detector [Lowe, 2004, URL, 13] and on the examples of detecting balls with the Viola-Jones classifier. The same problems occur for objects like the highlighter or the key fob of chapter 5. We have shown how the combination with the attention system enables a significant improvement of the detection results for simple objects. However, it may be noted that an expansion of a recognizer to process color information may yield similar results. Though, this would lack the advantage of the fast adaptability of the system to color.

The presented approach is a straightforward way to provide the attention system with a module which verifies the generated object hypothesis. It shall be noted that it is a technical solution resulting from the need to achieve a solution which is as robust and fast as possible. In more biologically motivated systems, attention and classification are more intertwined and share resources. That means, the extracted features give a first hint about the object which is then verified more and more by combining more complex detection results. It is interesting to develop this approach further as for example done in [Hamker, 2005] and in [Navalpakkam et al., 2005] but unfortunately at the moment these methods have very low quality in detection and false detection rate and are only able to distinguish object properties very roughly. The classification by Viola and Jones yields high quality results which was the reason for us to choose it. However, it would be an interesting idea to develop a high quality recognizer based on the early features that were already computed by the visual attention system, a subject we leave for future work.

8

Conclusion

8.1 Summary

In this thesis, we have introduced the new computational attention system VOCUS for the efficient and robust detection of regions of interest in images. The approach regards object recognition as a two step process: first, the fast attention system detects regions of interest in the whole image and second, a classifier recognizes the content in the specified region. This separation enables an efficient processing since complex object recognition is restricted to a small image region.

The selection of an image region is determined by two kinds of influences: bottom-up and top-down cues. This contrasts with existing approaches which usually consider only bottom-up influences. Bottom-up cues are determined by local contrasts and by the uniqueness of a feature. Top-down cues depend on the features of a pre-specified target. In VOCUS, both cues are considered and the saliencies are fused in a global saliency map. The strength of bottom-up versus top-down is adjustable according to the task. From this saliency map, the most salient region is extracted and serves as the focus of attention. If a target is available, its features are learned in a fast and user-friendly way by marking the target in a test scene. Robustness is achieved by computing the average values from several training images. We have presented a new selection algorithm that chooses the most suitable training examples from an image set. It turned out that usually less than five training images suffice to achieve robust detection results. We have shown that VOCUS is applicable to real-world scenes and is highly robust: it works fine for complex scenes, for different backgrounds and distractors, under viewpoint changes and illumination variances. On average, one of the first three foci of attention is on the target which allows considerable savings in processing time. We have shown that VOCUS outperforms other approaches clearly with respect to robustness and accuracy.

Furthermore, we have demonstrated that the application of attentional mechanisms need not be restricted to camera data: regarding other sensors helps to consider additional object properties. We have shown that the attentional mechanisms are also applicable to data from a 3D laser scanner which provides range as well as reflection values. Both modes complement each other: some objects are salient in the depth but not in the reflection data and vice versa. We have introduced the new bimodal attention system BILAS, an extension of VOCUS that fuses the information from both laser modes to achieve a single region of interest. The consideration of several sensors and their fusion enables an increase in detection quality and in robustness. Moreover, we have demonstrated that the laser data also complement camera data: whereas the laser data fit well to detect range discontinuities and variations in reflection, the camera data provide color information.

Finally, we have combined VOCUS with a classifier that was trained to recognize several objects — an approach that we have called attentive classification. The combination of a top-down modulated attention system with a classifier had not been done before. We have examined how the time and quality performances change by the combination of the systems. On the example of detecting objects in laser data we have demonstrated that the time saving increases with the number of known object classes in the data base. Already for two object classes, the attentive classification outperforms the pure classifier. On the example of detecting balls for RoboCup, we have pointed out that the quality performance may be significantly improved, too, by the combination of both systems. Especially simple objects like balls, which contain few features to distinguish them from distractors, are much better found by the new approach: the false detections are reduced by 85% while the detection rate remains nearly stable.

8.2 Strengths and Limitations

The presented computational attention system inherits the main advantages of the human attention system: it is generally applicable to every scene and not tuned to special applications as many recognition systems are. It operates equally well on artificial images, e.g., graphical displays used in perceptual psychology, and on natural scenes, on indoor and on outdoor images, on office environments and traffic scenes. It is robust to small changes in viewpoint and illumination, and, when operating in search mode, a new target object can be easily trained by presenting just a few example images. Even learning weights from a single training image yields good results. Furthermore, the structure of the system is highly parallel and thus, although currently implemented in a serial way, well suited to real-time computations on dedicated hardware.

As the strengths, likewise the limitations are inherited from the human attention system. An example is the fact that salient objects are easier found than inconspicuous ones. Although usually an important and useful aspect, this might be annoying if the target of interest is inconspicuous. Everybody has probably once faced the problem of finding a dropped gray key on a gray floor.

Another limitation is due to the complexity of the mechanisms in the human brain. This complexity usually allows only an approximation of human perception on a computer. Therefore, each research group focuses on particular aspects and no attention system includes all aspects of human perception. Building independent and re-usable modules for the distinct parts, for example the feature computations, and eager exchange among researchers may be a solution. However, note that this modularization is not in accordance with the highly intertwined architecture of the brain in which every part interacts with many other regions in a complex, still not yet fully understood way.

8.3 Future Work

The field of visual attention is wide and there are still loads of open questions. Many of these come from the fields of psychology and neuro-science: which are the basic features of early processing in the brain? Is the processing of the features separated or not? How do top-down cues bias the processing in detail? How do lateral connections influence the processing? How is the feature binding achieved? These and many more issues have to be solved in the future and their examination will help to better understand human perception. This will hopefully also facilitate the construction of improved computational attention and recognition systems.

On the other hand, there are several technical aspects by which the presented approach may be improved and extended. A first step in increasing the usefulness of VOCUS in robotic tasks will be to make it real-time capable. Since the feature computations are the costliest part of the system, they have to be sped up first of all. The parallel arrangement of the feature channels suggests a parallel implementation on dedicated hardware as done in [Ouerhani and Hügli, 2003c]. But since currently the code is not yet optimized, a high performance gain will also be achieved by software optimizations.

Another important aspect in real-world applications and especially in robotics is dynamics. Instead of computing the saliencies independently for each frame, it would be useful to profit from previous detections for example by tracking salient regions. Also including motion as a feature is an important step to facilitate the detection of moving objects. Note also that several difficult questions arise when dealing with dynamics that do not occur for static scenes and are usually not explained by existing models. For example, how is the inhibition of return realized and what are the parameters that make the focus of attention jump? The focus should not jump to a new position in each frame but it should also not stick to a once selected region forever. Here, a compromise has to be found.

When using attentional mechanisms in robot control, it is suggestive to consider not only camera images but also information from other available sensors. We have shown that for instance the data of a 3D laser scanner is suitable for the application of attentional mechanisms. Likewise, 3D cameras, infrared cameras, or even auditory information may be utilized. We have demonstrated how the saliencies of different sensor modes can be fused. A subtle part when dealing with different sensors will be calibrating the sensors to achieve a correlation between scene points or regions.

One of the most challenging tasks for future work will be to analyze the interplay between attention and object recognition. We have investigated how a system profits from the combination of an attentional front-end and a recognizing back-end, but both systems operate independently in our approach. To our knowledge, the same is true for all existing approaches that combine attention and recognition. Desirable would be a more intertwined system in which, for example, the recognition phase uses the same features as the attention stage. This would speed up the system and should be the next step towards a unified holistic approach for object recognition.

Let us finally return to the example that opened this work: recall that you tried to find your friend with the yellow hat in a carnival crowd. In the future, perhaps a robot will accompany you and your friend. You ask it where your friend has gone and it will be the robot's attentional module that will locate the yellow hat in the crowd before recognizing your friend and showing you the best way to reach her.

A

Basics of Computer Vision

Here, we will describe some of the techniques and methods of computer vision that are used in this work. The description is intended for the reader who is not familiar with computer vision. It is far from being an exhaustive introduction into the field. For further reading please refer to [Forsyth and Ponce, 2003, Gonzales and Woods, 1992, Phillips, 1994]. Note also that many of the presented techniques are provided by the Open Source Computer Vision Library OpenCV [OpenCV, 2004].

A.1 Digital Filters

A common technique in computer vision to extract information from an image is to apply digital filters to the image. These filters are *masks* (also called *filter kernels*) which are applied to the image by a method called *convolution*. A digital filter extracts particular information from an image, for example the high frequencies of the image: the edges. If the high frequencies are preserved an edge image is obtained, if the high frequencies are removed the result is a smoothed image. In the following, we first explain the method of discrete convolution before we elaborate on several digital filters.

A.1.1 Discrete Convolution

Discrete convolution is the main operation in digital image processing. With this operation, digital filters are applied to the image to extract the desired information. Convolution is applicable for one dimensional and for two dimensional functions as well as for continuous and discrete functions. We concentrate here on the two dimensional discrete case. In the continuous case, the integrals instead of the sums are determined [Gonzales and Woods, 1992]. Convolution is also known as *linear filtering* since the process is linear: first, the output for the sum of two images is the same as the sum of the outputs

The Convolution Operation Sequence

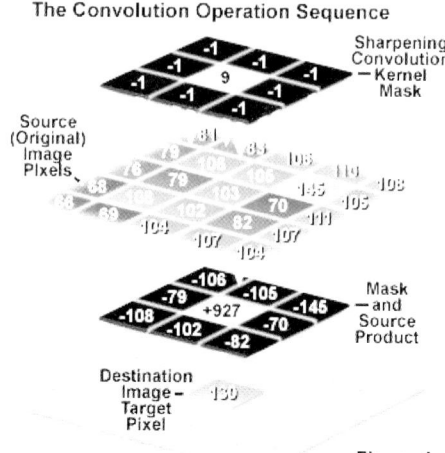

Figure 1

Fig. A.1. Convolution. An original image is convolved with a filter mask for sharpening (edge detection). The mask is laid over the target pixel of the input image. Each component is multiplied with the corresponding pixel; the result is depicted here in the "mask and source product". Finally, the sum of these products gives the pixel value in the destination image (Fig. from [URL, 08])

obtained for the images separately and, second, the response to a scaled image is a scaled version of the response to the original image.

For convolving an image I with an $n \times n$ filter mask M (usually $n = 2k+1$ for $k > 0$), the following procedure is applied to each pixel: place the mask on the pixel and multiply each component of M with the corresponding pixel. Then sum the products and place the result in the center point of the image (see Fig. A.1) [Phillips, 1994]. Usually, the resulting pixel is also scaled to match the displayable intensity range. This procedure is repeated for every pixel of the input image by "moving" the mask over the image. That means, for the input image I and an 3×3 filter mask M, we obtain the following pixel value O_{ij} of the output image O:

$$O_{ij} = \begin{matrix} I_{(i-1)(j-1)} * M_{11} & + I_{(i-1)j} * M_{12} & + I_{(i-1)(j+1)} * M_{13} & + \\ I_{i(j-1)} * M_{21} & + I_{ij} * M_{22} & + I_{i(j+1)} * M_{23} & + \\ I_{(i+1)(j-1)} * M_{31} & + I_{(i+1)j} * M_{32} & + I_{(i+1)(j+1)} * M_{33} & + \end{matrix} \quad \text{(A.1)}$$

A common notation for convolving I with M is: $O = I * * M$ (two dimensional convolution); in the one dimensional case, it is $O = I * M$. The general form of two dimensional discrete convolution is:

$$O_{ij} = k_1 \sum_{x=-k}^{k} \sum_{y=-l}^{l} M(x,y) I(i+x, j+y) + k_0, \quad \text{(A.2)}$$

with k_0 and k_1 are constants for a scaling to the displayable intensity range [Hermes and Winter, 2003].

Usually, small filter masks are chosen (3×3 or 5×5) since it is rather time consuming to convolve an image with larger masks (the complexity is $O(nm)$ where n is the number of pixels in the image and m is the number of entries of the filter mask). The effect is that only small patches of the images are considered and for example a strong smoothing of an image is not possible. One possibility to regard larger filter kernels is to transform the image as well as the filter kernel into the frequency domain (with fast Fourier transform) and multiply the image with the kernel since convolution in the spatial domain is equivalent to multiplication in the frequency domain. However, this approach is also costly, thus as an alternative, another method is usually applied: the use of image pyramids (cf. sect. A.1.5).

Worth to note in the context of convolution is the *border problem*: the above procedure of moving the filter mask over the image is problematic for the image borders since the mask overlaps the image and equation A.2 can not be applied. There are different solutions of this problem:

- The border pixels of the image are cut of. This results in a slightly smaller output image. Usually, this is no problem, but if the mask is large or if the image is iteratively convolved, this procedure leads easily to very small images.
- The border pixels of the input image are copied into the output image.
- The image is periodically continued, that means the left border is considered to be adjacent to the right border, and the upper adjacent to the lower border.
- The overlapping entries of the mask are ignored and the weighted sum is restricted to the existing pixels. This is the most exact solution but requires a special treatment of the border pixels.

In our computations, we use the last solution.

A.1.2 Smoothing

Smoothing an image is used for blurring and for noise reduction. It is also referred to as *low-pass filtering* since the high frequencies are removed. The smoothing is done by convolving the image with a mask in which all values are positive. The simplest case is to use a mask in which all values are 1:

$$M = \begin{pmatrix} 1 & 1 & 1 \\ 1 & 1 & 1 \\ 1 & 1 & 1 \end{pmatrix} \tag{A.3}$$

To prevent the resulting values to exceed the intensity range, the resulting value is divided by 9 (i.e., $k_1 = 1/9$ in equation A.2). Convolving an image with this mask has the effect of assigning each pixel the average value from its local neighborhood.

Usually, smoothing is done with a more sophisticated filter mask: the *Gaussian filter*. This mask adopts its values from a Gaussian, resulting in a smoothing that considers the center region more strongly than the surround. An example of a 3×3 Gaussian filter mask is:

$$M = \begin{pmatrix} 1\ 2\ 1 \\ 2\ 4\ 2 \\ 1\ 2\ 1 \end{pmatrix} \tag{A.4}$$

with a factor $k_1 = 1/16$.

A.1.3 Edge and Bar Detection

Detecting edges in images is also done by convolution. It is also referred to as *high-pass filtering* since the high frequencies, the edges, are preserved. Edge detecting filter masks amplify the slope of the edge. Either a certain direction is preferred, for example horizontal edges, or all discontinuities in intensity are detected that means edges of arbitrary directions. The first kind of filters has zeros in the edge direction, positive values on the one side and negative values on the other. Thereby it enhances image regions with low values on one and high values on the other side. Edges of a particular direction are also called *bars*, whereas the direction-sensitive edge detection is also known as *bar detection*. The number of masks used for edge detection is almost unlimited. Some well known examples of direction-sensitive masks are the *Prewitt Operator*:

$$P_x = \begin{pmatrix} 1\ 0\ -1 \\ 1\ 0\ -1 \\ 1\ 0\ -1 \end{pmatrix} \quad \text{and} \quad P_y = \begin{pmatrix} 1\ \ 1\ \ 1 \\ 0\ \ 0\ \ 0 \\ -1\ -1\ -1 \end{pmatrix} \tag{A.5}$$

with a factor $k_1 = 1/6$, and the *Sobel Operator*:

$$S_x = \begin{pmatrix} 1\ 0\ -1 \\ 2\ 0\ -2 \\ 1\ 0\ -1 \end{pmatrix} \quad \text{and} \quad S_y = \begin{pmatrix} 1\ \ 2\ \ 1 \\ 0\ \ 0\ \ 0 \\ -1\ -2\ -1 \end{pmatrix} \tag{A.6}$$

with a factor $k_1 = 1/8$. P_x and S_x find vertical and P_y and S_y horizontal edges. Equally, the numbers may be arranged to achieve the detection of diagonal edges. An example of a filter masks that detects edges of arbitrary directions is the *Laplace Operator*:

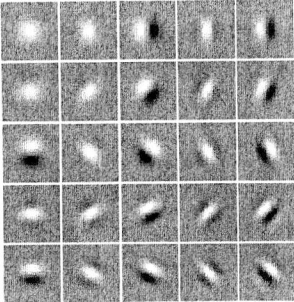

Fig. A.2. A set of Gabor filters for different spatial frequencies; Mid-grey values represent zero, dark values represent negative numbers and bright values represent positive numbers (Fig. from [URL, 17])

$$M = \begin{pmatrix} 0 & -1 & 0 \\ -1 & 4 & -1 \\ 0 & -1 & 0 \end{pmatrix} \tag{A.7}$$

It responds strongly to regions, in which the value of the center region differs from its surrounding. Therefore, it responds strongly to edges but even more to single outlier pixels, making the operator highly sensitive to noise.

If image orientations of a certain direction have to be obtained, a good method is to use *Gabor filters*. A Gabor filter responds strongly to image regions which have a particular spatial frequency and orientation. Their behavior is similar to the response of orientation sensitive cells in the human cortex. Mathematically, the Gabor filter kernels are the product of a symmetric Gaussian with an oriented sinusoid. They come in pairs, one recovers symmetric components in a particular direction, the other recovers antisymmetric components. The form of the symmetric kernel is

$$G_{sym}(x, y) = cos(k_x x + k_y y)\ exp - \left(\frac{x^2 + y^2}{2\sigma^2}\right), \tag{A.8}$$

and of the antisymmetric kernel

$$G_{anitsym}(x, y) = sin(k_0 x + k_1 y)\ exp - \left(\frac{x^2 + y^2}{2\sigma^2}\right), \tag{A.9}$$

where (k_x, k_y) give the spatial frequency to which the filter responds most strongly, and σ is the scale of the filter [Forsyth and Ponce, 2003]. Fig. A.2 shows some examples of Gabor filter kernels for different spatial frequencies.

A.1.4 Morphological Filtering

Morphological filter operations deal with the shape of image regions. These operations work usually on binary images with one or several regions of a

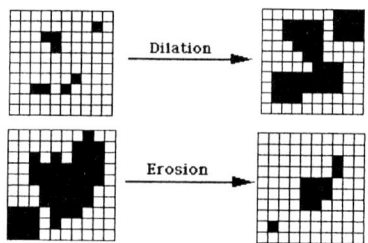

Fig. A.3. The morphological filter operations dilation and erosion. Dilation enlarges image regions whereas erosion shrinks them

particular intensity value and background pixels with the value zero. In the following, we assume that the regions have the value 1. We focus here on the two operations *dilation* and *erosion*, since only dilation is used in this work and erosion is its counterpart. Note that there are other morphological filters, for example *opening* and *closing* or *thinning* and *skeletonization*. These are explained for example in [Gonzales and Woods, 1992] or [Phillips, 1994].

Dilation and erosion are both *neighbor operations*, that means the value of a pixel is changed according to the value of its neighbors. The operations are used to smooth the shape of regions, join broken or discontinuous shapes, or to separate touching regions.

Dilation

Dilation makes a region larger by adding pixels around its edges. This can be done by defining a threshold t and setting a zero pixel to 1 if the number of differing neighbors exceeds t [Phillips, 1994]. If $t = 0$, all pixels in the 3×3 neighborhood of a region pixel are set to 1. This case is shown in Fig. A.3, top.

Erosion

Erosion is the counterpart of dilation and makes a region smaller. The technique is equivalent to dilation: if the number of zero neighbors of a region pixel exceeds a threshold t the region pixel is set to zero too [Phillips, 1994]. If $t = 0$, all border pixels of a region are eliminated. This case is shown in Fig. A.3, bottom.

A.1.5 Image Pyramids

A common technique in computer vision to extract information on different scales is the use of image pyramids [Tanimoto and Pavlidis, 1975, Burt, 1980]. The idea is that applying large filter masks to an image is very costly, so a

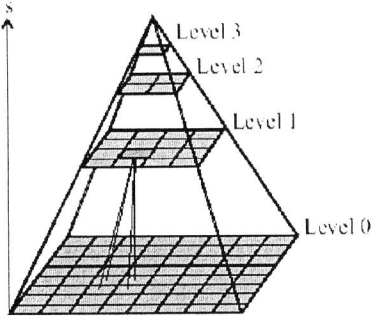

Fig. A.4. An image pyramid with four levels

better approach is to shrink the image and apply small filters to each shrunken image version. An image pyramid is simply a collection of representations of an image of different sizes (see Fig. A.4). Usually, each layer of the pyramid is half the width and height of the previous layer.

The easiest way to obtain an image pyramid is to take every kth pixel (typically every 2nd pixel) from layer n to obtain layer $n + 1$. This method is called *resampling, subsampling* or *downsampling*. Since *Nyquist's theorem* states that the sampling frequency must be at least twice the highest frequency present for a signal to be reconstructed from a sampled version, this approach might lead to problems, namely to an effect called *aliasing* [Forsyth and Ponce, 2003]. Aliasing means that a signal which is sampled too slowly will be misrepresented by the samples since high spatial frequencies will appear as low spatial frequencies. An example is a chessboard: imagine that each field of the board is represented by one pixel. If you take now every 2nd pixel for subsampling, the resulting image is only white or black (depending on the pixel you start with). Aliasing can be avoided by filtering the image so that spatial frequencies above the new sampling frequency are removed. This is done by smoothing. Therefore, a common procedure is to first smooth the image with a Gaussian filter and then subsample it. The resulting image pyramid is called *Gaussian Pyramid*. An example of a Gaussian pyramid was depicted in Fig. 4.2.

Another important pyramid is the *Laplacian Pyramid*. It consists of bandpass filtered versions of the input image: each stage of the pyramid is constructed by subtracting two corresponding adjacent levels of the Gaussian pyramid. Thereby, the smoothed "lowpass" image is subtracted from the original "highpass" image resulting in a bandpass image which contains most of the image's important textural features such as edges. The Laplacian pyramid is named as such because the process is approximately equivalent to convolving the image with the Laplacian of the Gaussian smoothing filter.

From the Laplacian pyramid, an *oriented Laplacian pyramid* is obtained by applying Gabor filters of different directions to each level of the pyra-

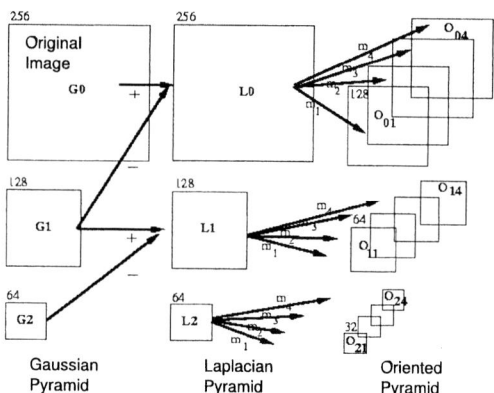

Fig. A.5. To obtain an oriented pyramid O, first a Gaussian pyramid G is computed from the input image, second a Laplacian pyramid L is obtained from the Gaussian pyramid by subtracting two adjacent levels and, finally, Gabor filters of 4 directions are applied to each level of the Laplacian pyramid. O_{ij} denotes the ith level of the pyramid with orientations of direction j (Fig. reprinted with permission from [Greenspan et al., 1994]. ©1994 IEEE)

mid [Greenspan et al., 1994]. In other words, an oriented pyramid consists of several pyramids of edge images, one for each direction. This method was applied to obtain the orientation scale maps on page 61 by considering 4 orientations: $0°, 45°, 90°, 135°$. In Fig. A.5 we show how an oriented pyramid is obtained.

A.2 Color Spaces

Colors are organized in so called color spaces. These spaces are three dimensional since three parameters are sufficient to define almost all colors we perceive. One of the most common color spaces is the RGB color space which is represented as a cube (the RGB cube, see Fig. A.6, left). A color is produced by adding different quantities of the three components red, green, and blue. Another important color space is HSV (H = hue, S = saturation, V = value (luminance)). It can be thought of as a RGB cube tipped up onto one corner. This color space is more intuitive and enables to regard colors independently of their intensity (V) by just ignoring one parameter.

In 1931, an international committee, the CIE (Commission Internationale de l'Eclairage), defined the color space CIE XYZ in which all possible colors that could be made by mixing red, green and blue light sources can be represented using only positive values of X, Y and Z. These colors are arranged in a three-dimensional coordinate system in which Y stands for luminance whereas X and Z give coloring information. Usually, colors are not specified

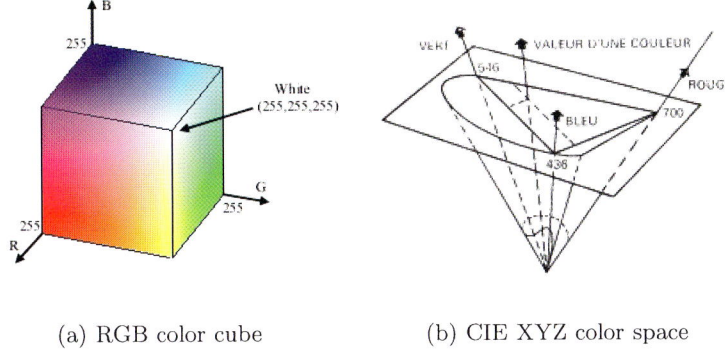

(a) RGB color cube   (b) CIE XYZ color space

Fig. A.6. (a) the RGB cube. Colors are expressed by a red (R), a green (G), and a blue (B) component (Fig. from [URL, 09]). (b) the CIE XYZ color space (Fig. from [URL, 10])

in XYZ coordinates but in *chromaticity coordinates* which are independent of the luminance (hue and saturation taken together are called chromaticity). The shape of the represented colors in a two-dimensional space forms a horseshoe with white in the middle and the colors, with increasing saturation, are arranged circularly around this point. The CIE XYZ color space is depicted in Fig. A.6, right. The XYZ coordinates are obtained from RGB by the following equation:

$$\begin{pmatrix} X \\ Y \\ Z \end{pmatrix} = \begin{pmatrix} X_r & X_g & X_b \\ Y_r & Y_g & Y_b \\ Z_r & Z_g & Z_b \end{pmatrix} * \begin{pmatrix} R \\ G \\ B \end{pmatrix} \qquad (A.10)$$

where X_r, X_g and X_b are the weights applied to the monitor's RGB colors to find X, and so on [Foley et al., 1990]. In this work, we used the following values which are from the converting function of the OpenCV library [OpenCV, 2004]:

$$\begin{pmatrix} X \\ Y \\ Z \end{pmatrix} = \begin{pmatrix} 0.412411 & 0.357585 & 0.180454 \\ 0.212649 & 0.715169 & 0.072182 \\ 0.019332 & 0.119195 & 0.950390 \end{pmatrix} * \begin{pmatrix} R \\ G \\ B \end{pmatrix} \qquad (A.11)$$

In 1976, the CIE defined two new color spaces to achieve more accurate models: the CIE LUV color space (also $L^*u^*v^*$) and the CIE LAB color space (also $L^*a^*b^*$) [Hunt, 1991]. These color spaces are substantially *uniform*, that means, if the distance between two colors in coordinate space is below some threshold, a human observer is not able to distinguish the colors, and the perceived difference between two colors depends on the distance of the colors in the color space, regardless of where in the space the colors are (note that this is not true for other color spaces, for example the HSV or the XYZ color space!).

We concentrate here on the CIE LAB color space, which is well suited for our application since it represents colors similar to human perception. The three parameters in the model represent the luminance of the color (L, the smallest L yields black), its position between red and green (A, the smallest A yields green) and its position between yellow and blue (B, the smallest B yields blue). A rendering of the CIE LAB space is shown in Figure A.7. The coordinates of a color in LAB are obtained as a nonlinear mapping of the XYZ coordinates:

$$L = 116 \left(\frac{Y}{Y_n} \right)^{1/3} - 16 \tag{A.12}$$

$$a = 500 \left[\left(\frac{X}{X_n} \right)^{1/3} - \left(\frac{Y}{Y_n} \right)^{1/3} \right] \tag{A.13}$$

$$b = 200 \left[\left(\frac{Y}{Y_n} \right)^{1/3} - \left(\frac{Z}{Z_n} \right)^{1/3} \right], \tag{A.14}$$

where X_n, Y_n and Z_n are the XYZ coordinates of a reference white patch [Forsyth and Ponce, 2003, Hunt, 1991].

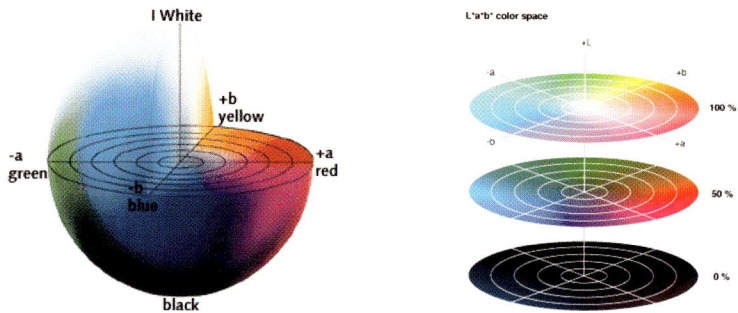

Fig. A.7. The CIE LAB color space. The space is spanned by the axes L (luminance), A (red-green), and B (blue-yellow). On the right, three disks for constant luminance. In chapter 4, we regard the middle disk for the computation of the color maps (Figures from [URL, 11] and [URL, 12])

A.3 Segmentation

Segmentation is the process of dividing an image into regions. It is the first step in the process of image analysis. In contrast to image processing, in image analysis the image is not altered but its content is analyzed. The basic idea of segmentation is to group similar pixels together into regions. Similarity is defined due to intensity, texture, or other properties. Autonomous segmentation is one of the most difficult tasks in image analysis since it is difficult to decide which pixels belong to the same region.

There are many techniques for segmentation (see for example [Gonzales and Woods, 1992] or [Phillips, 1994]). Here, we focus on the simple approach of *seeded region growing* which was used in chapter 4 to determine the most salient region in the saliency map. It starts with a set of "seed" points and from these it grows regions by appending to each seed those neighboring pixels that have similar properties such as intensity, color, or texture. There are two difficulties with this approach. The first is how to select the seeds. The output of the segmentation depends highly on this selection. Fortunately in the application of determining the most salient region, the choice of the (single) seed is obvious: it is simply the brightest pixel in the saliency map. The second difficulty is the selection of the similarity criteria. One solution is to consider all pixels that are neighbored to the seed and differ from it less than p percent according to one or several properties. When determining the most salient region in the saliency map, we accepted all pixels that differed in intensity at most 25% from the seed.

B

The Viola-Jones Classifier

Here, we present the details of the classification method of Viola & Jones that was introduced in chapter 7. The classifier was also described in our publications [Frintrop et al., 2004b] and [Mitri et al., 2005]. Further details can be found in the original papers [Lienhart and Maydt, 2002, Viola and Jones, 2004].

B.1 Feature Detection Using Integral Images

The idea of the classification method is to learn how a target object is composed of several basic features which were depicted in Fig. 7.2. The features are called Haar-like, since they follow the same structure as the Haar basis, i.e., step functions introduced by Alfred Haar to define wavelets. They are also used in [Lienhart and Maydt, 2002, Papageorgiou et al., 1998, Treptow and Zell, 2004, Viola and Jones, 2004]. The set of possible features in an area that is investigated by the classifier is very large, for example for an object detector of 30×30 pixels, there are 642592 possible features (see [Lienhart and Maydt, 2002] for calculation details). A single feature is effectively computed on input images using integral images [Viola and Jones, 2004], also known as summed area tables [Lienhart and Maydt, 2002]. An integral image I is an intermediate representation for the image and contains the sum of gray scale pixel values of image N with height y and width x, i.e.,

$$I(x, y) = \sum_{x'=0}^{x} \sum_{y'=0}^{y} N(x', y').$$ (B.1)

A visualization is depicted in Fig. B.1, left. The integral image is computed recursively by the formula:

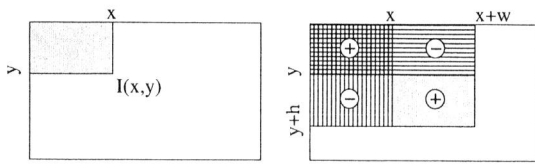

Fig. B.1. Left: The integral image contains at $I(x, y)$ the sum of the pixel values in the shaded region. Right: the computation of the average value in the shaded region is based on four operations on the four depicted rectangles according to eq. B.3

$$I(x, y) = I(x, y - 1) + I(x - 1, y) + N(x, y) - I(x - 1, y - 1) \quad \text{(B.2)}$$

with $I(-1, y) = I(x, -1) = I(-1, -1) = 0$. The computation requires only one scan over the input data. This intermediate representation $I(x, y)$ allows the computation of a rectangle feature value at (x, y) with height h and width w using four references (see Fig. B.1 (right)):

$$F(x, y, h, w) = I(x + w, y + h) - I(x, y + h) \quad \text{(B.3)}$$
$$-I(x + w, y) + I(x, y).$$

For the computation of the rotated features, Lienhart et. al. introduced rotated summed area tables that contain the sum of the pixels of the rectangle rotated by $45°$ with the bottom-most corner at (x, y) and extending till the boundaries of the image (see Fig. B.2) [Lienhart and Maydt, 2002]:

$$I_r(x, y) = \sum_{x'=0}^{x} \sum_{y'=0}^{x - |x' - y|} N(x', y'). \quad \text{(B.4)}$$

The rotated integral image I_r is computed recursively, i.e.,

$$I_r(x, y) = I_r(x - 1, y - 1) + I_r(x + 1, y - 1) \quad \text{(B.5)}$$
$$-I_r(x, y - 2) + N(x, y) + N(x, y - 1)$$

using the start values $I_r(-1, y) = I_r(x, -1) = I_r(x, -2) = I_r(-1, -1) = I_r(-1, -2) = 0$. Four table lookups are required to compute the pixel sum of any rotated rectangle with the formula:

$$F_r(x, y, h, w) = I_r(x + w - h, y + w + h - 1) + I_r(x, y - 1) \quad \text{(B.6)}$$
$$-I_r(x - h, y + h - 1) - I_r(x + w, y + w - 1)$$

Since the features are compositions of rectangles, they are computed with several lookups and subtractions weighted with the area of the black and white rectangles.

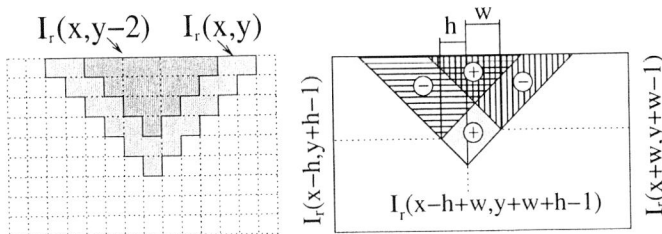

Fig. B.2. Left: calculation of the rotated integral image I_r. Right: four lookups in the rotated integral image are required to compute the feature value a rotated feature F_r

To detect a feature, a threshold is required. This threshold is automatically determined during a fitting process, such that a minimum number of examples are misclassified. Furthermore, the return values (α, β) of the feature are determined, such that the error on the examples is minimized. The examples are given in a set of images that are classified as positive or negative samples. The set is also used in the learning phase that is briefly described next.

B.2 Learning Classification Functions

A learning technique, the Gentle Ada Boost Algorithm [Freund and Schapire, 1996], is used to select a set of simple features to achieve a given detection and error rate. In a derivative, not the simple features are used for classification and learning, but CARTs.

B.2.1 CARTs: Classification and Regression Trees

For all possible features, a Classification and Regression Tree (CART) is created. CART analysis is a form of binary recursive partitioning. Each node is split into two child nodes, in which case the original node is called a parent node. The term recursive refers to the fact that the binary partitioning process is applied over and over to reach a given number of splits (4 in this case). In order to find the best possible split features, all possible splits are calculated, as well as all possible return values to be used in a split node. The program seeks to maximize the average "purity" of the two child nodes using the misclassification error measure. Fig. B.3 (left) shows a CART classifier.

B.2.2 Gentle Ada Boost for CARTs

The Gentle Ada Boost Algorithm [Freund and Schapire, 1996] is used to select a set of simple CARTs to achieve a given detection and error rate [Lienhart

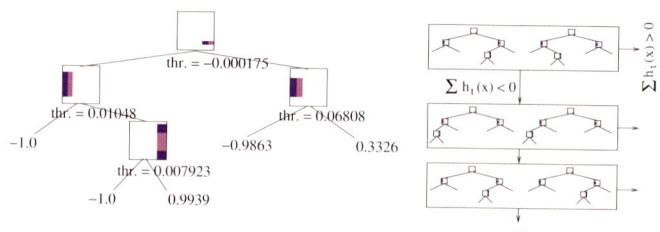

Fig. B.3. Left: A Classification and Regression Tree (CART) with 4 splits. According to the specific filter applied to the image input section x, the output of the tree $h_t(x)$ is calculated, depending on the threshold values. Right: A cascade of CARTs. $h_t(x)$ is determined depending on the path through the tree

and Maydt, 2002]. In the following, a detection is referred to as a hit and an error as a false alarm.

The learning is based on N weighted training examples $(x_1, y_1), \ldots, (x_N, y_N)$, where x_i are the images and $y_i \in \{-1, 1\}, i \in \{1, \ldots, N\}$ the classified output. At the beginning of the learning phase the weights w_i are initialized with $w_i = 1/N$. The following three steps are repeated to select CARTs until a given detection rate d is reached:

1. Every classifier, i.e., a CART, is fit to the data. Hereby the error e is calculated with respect to the weights w_i.
2. The best CART h_t is chosen for the classification function. The counter t is incremented.
3. The weights are updated with $w_i := w_i \cdot e^{-y_i h_t(x_i)}$ and renormalized.

The final output of the classifier is $\text{sign}(\sum_{t=1}^{T} h_t(x)) > 0$, with $h_t(x)$ the weighted return value of the CART. Next, a cascade based on these classifiers is built.

B.3 The Cascade of Classifiers

The performance of a single classifier is not suitable for object classification, since it produces a high hit rate, e.g., 0.999, but also a high error rate, e.g., 0.5. Nevertheless, the hit rate is much higher than the error rate. To construct an overall good classifier, several classifiers are arranged in a cascade, i.e., a degenerated decision tree. In every stage of the cascade, a decision is made whether the image contains the object or not. This computation reduces both rates. Since the hit rate is close to one, their multiplication results also in a value close to one, while the multiplication of the smaller error rates approaches zero. Furthermore, this speeds up the whole classification process.

An overall effective cascade is learned by a simple iterative method. For every stage the classification function $h_t(x)$ is learned until the required hit rate is reached. The process continues with the next stage using the correct classified positive and the currently misclassified negative examples. The number of CARTs used in each classifier may increase with additional stages. In Fig. 7.3 we showed a cascade with simple features, in Fig. B.3 we present a cascade of CARTs.

C

Explanation of Color Figures

Here, we display some of the color figures used in this monograph with bold printed and labeled colors to enable the recognition of the colors also in gray-scale print-outs or for people with visual color perception defects.

Fig. C.1. Color explanation for some test images. Left: the original images. Right: bold and labeled colors

References

[Aloimonos et al., 1988] Aloimonos, Y., Weiss, I., and Bandopadhay, A. (1988). Active vision. *International Journal of Computer Vision (IJCV)*, 1(4):333–356.

[Backer, 2004] Backer, G. (2004). *Modellierung visueller Aufmerksamkeit im Computer-Sehen: Ein zweistufiges Selektionsmodell für ein Aktives Sehsystem.* PhD thesis, Universität Hamburg, Germany.

[Backer and Mertsching, 2000] Backer, G. and Mertsching, B. (2000). Integrating depth and motion into the attentional control of an active vision system. In Baratoff, G. and Neumann, H., editors, *Dynamische Perzeption. Workshop der GI-Fachgruppe 1.0.4 Bildverstehen, Ulm, November 2000*, pages 69–74. Infix.

[Backer et al., 2001] Backer, G., Mertsching, B., and Bollmann, M. (2001). Data- and model-driven gaze control for an active-vision system. *IEEE Transactions on Pattern Analysis and Machine Intelligence (PAMI)*, 23(12):1415–1429.

[Balkenius, 2000] Balkenius, C. (2000). Attention, habituation and conditioning: Towards a computational model. *Cognitive Science Quarterly*, 1(2):171–214.

[Balkenius, 2002] Balkenius, C. (2002). Emotion and learning in context: From biology to robotics. In *IK Kursunterlagen (Interdisziplinäres Kolleg 2002, Günne, Germany)*, pages 156–174.

[Baluja and Pomerleau, 1995] Baluja, S. and Pomerleau, D. (1995). Using the representation in a neural network's hidden layer for task-specific focus of attention. In *Proc. of the 1995 International Joint Conference on Artificial Intelligence (IJCAI '95)*, pages 133–141, Montreal, Canada.

[Baluja and Pomerleau, 1997] Baluja, S. and Pomerleau, D. (1997). Expectation-based selective attention for visual monitoring and control of a robot vehicle. *Robotics and Autonomous Systems*, 22(3-4):329–344.

[Bichot, 2001] Bichot, N. P. (2001). Attention, eye movements, and neurons: Linking physiology and behavior. In Jenkin, M. and Harris, L. R., editors, *Vision and Attention*, chapter 11. Springer Verlag.

[Bollmann, 1999] Bollmann, M. (1999). *Entwicklung einer Aufmerksamkeitssteuerung für ein aktives Sehsystem.* PhD thesis, Universität Hamburg, Germany.

[Bollmann et al., 1999] Bollmann, M., Hoischen, R., Jesikiewicz, M., Justkowski, C., and Mertsching, B. (1999). Playing domino: A case study for an active vision system. In Christensen, H., editor, *Computer Vision Systems*, pages 392–411. Springer.

[Breazeal, 1999] Breazeal, C. (1999). A context-dependent attention system for a social robot. In *Proc. of the Sixteenth International Joint Conference on Artifical Intelligence (IJCAI 99)*, pages 1146–1151, Stockholm, Sweden.

[Bundesen, 1990] Bundesen, C. (1990). A theory of visual attention. *Psychological Review*, 97:523–547.

[Bundesen, 1998] Bundesen, C. (1998). A computational theory of visual attention. *Philosophical Transactions of the Royal Society of London, Series B*, 353:1271–1281.

[Burt, 1980] Burt, P. J. (1980). Tree and pyramid structures for coding hexagonally sampled binary images. *Computer Graphics and Image Processing*, 14(3):802–809.

[Carlsson et al., 1999] Carlsson, T. E., Gustafsson, J., and Nilsson, B. (1999). Development of a 3D camera. In Benton, S. A., editor, *Practical Holography XIII*, volume 3637 of *Proc. SPIE*, pages 218–224.

[Cave, 1999] Cave, K. R. (1999). The FeatureGate model of visual selection. *Psychological Research*, 62:182–194.

[Cave and Wolfe, 1990] Cave, K. R. and Wolfe, J. M. (1990). Modeling the role of parallel processing in visual search. *Cognitive Psychology*, 22(2):225–271.

[Chung et al., 2002] Chung, D., Hirata, R., Mundhenk, T. N., Ng, J., Peters, R. J., Pichon, E., Tsui, A., Ventrice, T., Walther, D., Williams, P., and Itti, L. (2002). A new robotics platform for neuromorphic vision: Beobots. In Bülthoff, H. H., Lee, S.-W., Poggio, T., and Wallraven, C., editors, *Proc. 2nd Workshop on Biologically Motivated Computer Vision (BMCV '02)*, volume 2525, pages 558–566, Conference: Tübingen, Germany. Springer Verlag, Lecture Notes in Computer Science (LNCS).

[Clark and Ferrier, 1989] Clark, J. J. and Ferrier, N. J. (1989). Control of visual attention in mobile robots. In *IEEE Conference on Robotics and Automation*, pages 826–831.

[Corbetta, 1990] Corbetta, M. (1990). Frontoparietal cortical networks for directing attention and the eye to visual locations: Identical, independent, or overlapping neural systems? *Proc. of the National Academy of Sciences of the United States of America*, 95:831–838.

[Corbetta and Shulman, 2002] Corbetta, M. and Shulman, G. L. (2002). Control of goal-directed and stimulus-driven attention in the brain. *Nature Reviews*, 3(3):201–215.

[Desimone and Duncan, 1995] Desimone, R. and Duncan, J. (1995). Neural mechanisms of selective visual attention. *Annual Reviews of Neuroscience*, 18:193–222.

[Deubel and Schneider, 1996] Deubel, H. and Schneider, W. X. (1996). Saccade target selection and object recognition: Evidence for a common attentional mechanism. *Vision Research*, 36(12):1827–1837.

[Draper and Lionelle, 2003] Draper, B. and Lionelle, A. (2003). Evaluation of selective attention under similarity transforms. In *Proc. of the International Workshop on Attention and Performance in Computer Vision (WAPCV '03)*, pages 31–38, Graz, Austria.

[Driscoll et al., 1998] Driscoll, J. A., Peters, R. A., and Cave, K. R. (1998). A visual attention network for a humanoid robot. In *Proc. of the International Conference on Intelligent Robots and Systems (IROS '98)*, pages 1968–1974.

[Egeth and Yantis, 1997] Egeth, H. E. and Yantis, S. (1997). Visual attention: control, representation, and time course. *Annual Review of Psychology*, 48:269–297.

[Enoch, 1959] Enoch, J. (1959). Natural tendencies in visual search of a complex display. Visual search techniques. *NAS/NRC Publication*, 171:187–193.

[Eriksen and James, 1986] Eriksen, C. W. and James, J. D. S. (1986). Visual attention within and around the field of focal attention: A zoom lens model. *Perception and Psychophysics*, 40:225–240.

[Findlay and Gilchrist, 2001] Findlay, J. M. and Gilchrist, I. D. (2001). Active vision perspective. In Jenkin, M. and Harris, L. R., editors, *Vision & Attention*, chapter 5, pages 83–103. Springer Verlag.

[Findlay and Walker, 1999] Findlay, J. M. and Walker, R. (1999). A model of saccade generation based on parallel processing and competitive inhibition. *Behavioral and Brain Sciences*, 22:661–721.

[Foley et al., 1990] Foley, J. D., van Dam, A., Feiner, S. K., and Hughes, J. F. (1990). *Computer Graphics, Principles and Practice*. Addison-Wesley Publishing Company, 2nd edition.

[Forsyth and Ponce, 2003] Forsyth, D. A. and Ponce, J. (2003). *Computer Vision: A Modern Approach*. Prentice Hall, Berkeley.

[Fraundorfer and Bischof, 2003] Fraundorfer, F. and Bischof, H. (2003). Utilizing saliency operators for image matching. In *Proc. of the International Workshop on Attention and Performance in Computer Vision (WAPCV '03)*, pages 17–24, Graz, Austria.

[Freund and Schapire, 1996] Freund, Y. and Schapire, R. E. (1996). Experiments with a new boosting algorithm. In *Machine Learning: Proc. of the 13th International Conference*, pages 148 – 156.

[Frintrop et al., 2005a] Frintrop, S., Backer, G., and Rome, E. (2005a). Goal-directed search with a top-down modulated computational attention system. In *Proc. of the Annual meeting of the German Association for Pattern Recognition (Jahrestagung der Deutschen Arbeitsgemeinschaft für Mustererkennung) DAGM 2005*, Lecture Notes in Computer Science (LNCS), pages 117–124, Conference: Wien, Austria. Springer.

[Frintrop et al., 2005b] Frintrop, S., Backer, G., and Rome, E. (2005b). Selecting what is important: Training visual attention. In *Proc. of the 28th German Conference on Artificial Intelligence (KI 2005)*, Lecture Notes in Computer Science (LNCS), pages 351–365, Conference: Koblenz, Germany. Springer.

[Frintrop et al., 2004a] Frintrop, S., Nüchter, A., and Surmann, H. (2004a). Visual attention for object recognition in spatial 3D data. In *International Workshop on Attention and Performance in Computer Vision (WAPCV '04)*, pages 75–82, Conference: Prag, Czech Republic.

[Frintrop et al., 2004b] Frintrop, S., Nüchter, A., Surmann, H., and Hertzberg, J. (2004b). Saliency-based object recognition in 3D data. In *Proc. of the International Conference on Intelligent Robots and Systems (IROS '04)*, pages 2167 – 2172, Conference: Sendai, Japan.

[Frintrop et al., 2003a] Frintrop, S., Rome, E., Nüchter, A., and Surmann, H. (2003a). Applying attentional mechanisms to bi-modal 3D laser data. In *International Workshop on Attention and Performance in Computer Vision (WAPCV '03)*, pages 25–30, Conference: Graz, Austria.

[Frintrop et al., 2003b] Frintrop, S., Rome, E., Nüchter, A., and Surmann, H. (2003b). An attentive, multi-modal laser "eye". In Crowley, J., Piater, J., Vincze, M., and Paletta, L., editors, *Proc. of 3rd International Conference on Computer Vision Systems (ICVS '03)*, pages 202–211, Conference: Graz, Austria. Springer, Berlin, LNCS 2626.

[Frintrop et al., 2005c] Frintrop, S., Rome, E., Nüchter, A., and Surmann, H. (2005c). A bimodal laser-based attention system. *Journal of Computer Vision and Image Understanding (CVIU), Special Issue on Attention and Performance in Computer Vision*, 100(1-2):124–151.

[Fritz et al., 2004] Fritz, G., Seifert, C., and Paletta, L. (2004). Attentive object detection using an information theoretic saliency measure. In Paletta, L., Tsotsos, J. K., Rome, E., and Humphreys, G. W., editors, *Proc. of the 2nd international workshop on attention and performance in computational vision (WAPCV '04)*, pages 136–143, Conference: Prague, Czech Republic.

[Garey and Johnson, 1979] Garey, M. and Johnson, D. S. (1979). *Computers and Intractability, A Guide to the Theory of NP-Completeness*. Freeman, San Francisco.

[Gegenfurtner, 2003] Gegenfurtner, K. R. (2003). Cortical mechanisms of colour vision. *Nature Reviews Neuroscience*, 4:563–572.

[Gonzales and Woods, 1992] Gonzales, R. C. and Woods, R. E. (1992). *Digital image processing*. Addison-Wesley Publishing Company, Reading, Massachusetts.

[Gottlieb et al., 1998] Gottlieb, J. P., Kusunoki, M., and Goldberg, M. E. (1998). The representation of visual salience in monkey parietal cortex. *Nature*, 391:481–484.

[Greenspan et al., 1994] Greenspan, H., Belongie, S., Goodman, R., Perona, P., Rakshit, S., and Anderson, C. (1994). Overcomplete steerable pyramid filters and rotation invariance. In *Proc. IEEE Computer Vision and Pattern Recognition (CVPR)*, pages 222–228, Conference: Seattle, Washington.

[Hamker, 1998] Hamker, F. H. (1998). *Visuelle Aufmerksamkeit und lebenslanges Lernen im Wahrnehmungs-Handlungs-Zyklus*. PhD thesis, TU Ilmenau, Germany.

[Hamker, 2000] Hamker, F. H. (2000). Distributed competition in directed attention. In Baratoff, G. and Neumann, H., editors, *Proc. in Artificial Intelligence*, volume 9, pages 39–44, Berlin. AKA, Akademische Verlagsgesellschaft.

[Hamker, 2004] Hamker, F. H. (2004). Modeling attention: From computational neuroscience to computer vision. In Paletta, L., Tsotsos, J. K., Rome, E., and Humphreys, G. W., editors, *Proc.of the 2nd International Workshop on Attention and Performance in Computational Vision (WAPCV '04)*, pages 59–66, Conference: Prague, Czech Republic.

[Hamker, 2005] Hamker, F. H. (2005). The emergence of attention by population-based inference and its role in distributed processing and cognitive control of vision. *Journal of Computer Vision and Image Understanding (CVIU), Special Issue on Attention and Performance*, 100(1-2):64–106.

[Heidemann et al., 2004] Heidemann, G., Rae, R., Bekel, H., Bax, I., and Ritter, H. (2004). Integrating context-free and context-dependent attentional mechanisms for gestural object reference. *Machine Vision and Applications*, 16(1):64–73.

[Heinke and Humphreys, 2004] Heinke, D. and Humphreys, G. W. (2004). Computational models of visual selective attention. A review. In Houghton, G., editor, *Connectionist models in psychology*, pages 273 – 312. Psychology Press.

[Heinke et al., 2002] Heinke, D., Humphreys, G. W., and diVirgilo, G. (2002). Modeling visual search experiments: Selective attention for identification model (SAIM). *Neurocomputing*, 44:817–822.

[Hennig, 2004] Hennig, M. (2004). Integrierte Kommunikationsplattform zur Beobachtung und Steuerung von (teil-)autonomen mobilen Robotern. Diplomarbeit, Fraunhofer Institut für Autonome Intelligente Systeme / Technische Universität Dresden, Dresden.

[Hermes and Winter, 2003] Hermes, T. and Winter, A. (2003). A short trip from pixels to objects. In *Course material to the Interdisciplinary College 2003: Applications, Brains, Computers*, pages 71–90. Günne, Germany.

[Humphreys and Müller, 1993] Humphreys, G. W. and Müller, H. J. (1993). Search via recursive rejection (SERR): A connectionist model of visual search. *Cognitive Psychology*, 25:43–110.

[Hunt, 1991] Hunt, R. W. G. (1991). *Measuring colour*. Ellis Horwood Limited, Chichester, West Sussex, England.

[Itti, 2002] Itti, L. (2002). Real-time high-performance attention focusing in outdoors color video streams. In Rogowitz, B. and Pappas, T. N., editors, *Proc. SPIE Human Vision and Electronic Imaging IV (HVEI '02)*, pages 235–243.

[Itti, 2003] Itti, L. (2003). The Beobot platform for embedded real-time neuromorphic vision. In Dietterich, T. G., Becker, S., and Ghahramani, Z., editors, *Advances in Neural Information Processing Systems, Vol. 15, Hardware Demo Track*. MIT Press, Cambridge, MA.

[Itti and Koch, 2001a] Itti, L. and Koch, C. (2001a). Computational modeling of visual attention. *Nature Reviews Neuroscience*, 2(3):194–203.

[Itti and Koch, 2001b] Itti, L. and Koch, C. (2001b). Feature combination strategies for saliency-based visual attention systems. *Journal of Electronic Imaging*, 10(1):161–169.

[Itti et al., 1998] Itti, L., Koch, C., and Niebur, E. (1998). A model of saliency-based visual attention for rapid scene analysis. *IEEE Transactions on Pattern Analysis and Machine Intelligence (PAMI)*, 20(11):1254–1259.

[James, 1890] James, W. (1890). *The Principles of Psychology*. Dover Publications, New York.

[Johansson et al., 2001] Johansson, R., Westling, G., Backstrom, A., and Flanagan, J. (2001). Eye-hand coordination in object manipulation. *The Journal of Neuroscience*, 21(17):6917–6932.

[Jonides, 1981] Jonides, J. (1981). Voluntary versus automatic control over the mind's eye movements. In Long, A. D., editor, *Attention and Performance IX*, pages 187–203. Lawrence Erlbaum Associates, Hillsadale, NJ.

[Jonides and Gleitman, 1972] Jonides, J. and Gleitman, H. (1972). A conceptual category effect in visual search: 0 as a letter or digit. *Perception & Psychophysics*, 12:457–460.

[Kaiser, 1996] Kaiser, P. K. (1996). *The Joy of Visual Perception*. Online Book, http://www.yorku.ca/eye/thejoy.htm.

[Kandel et al., 1996] Kandel, E. R., Schwartz, J. H., and Jessell, T. M., editors (1996). *Essentials of Neural Science and Behavior*. McGraw-Hill/Appleton & Lange.

[Kastner and Ungerleider, 2001] Kastner, S. and Ungerleider, L. G. (2001). The neural basis of biased competition in human visual cortex. *Neuropsychologia*, 39:1263–1276.

[Koch and Ullman, 1985] Koch, C. and Ullman, S. (1985). Shifts in selective visual attention: towards the underlying neural circuitry. *Human Neurobiology*, 4(4):219–227.

[Kröse and Julesz, 1989] Kröse, B. and Julesz, B. (1989). The control and speed of shifts of attention. *Vision Research*, 29(11):1607–1619.

[Lee et al., 2003] Lee, K., Buxton, H., and Feng, J. (2003). Selective attention for cue-guided search using a spiking neural network. In *Proc. of the International Workshop on Attention and Performance in Computer Vision (WAPCV '03)*, pages 55–62, Graz, Austria.

[Lennie et al., 1990] Lennie, P., Krauskopf, J., and Sclar, G. (1990). Chromatic mechanisms in striate cortex of macaque. *Journal of Neuroscience*, 10:649–669.

[Levin, 1996] Levin, D. (1996). Classifying faces by race: the structure of face categories. *Journal of Experimental Psychology: Learning, Memory, & Recognition*, 22:1364–1382.

[Lienhart and Maydt, 2002] Lienhart, R. and Maydt, J. (2002). An Extended Set of Haar-like Features for Rapid Object Detection. In *Proc. of the IEEE Conf. on Image Processing (ICIP '02)*, pages 155–162, New York, USA.

[Livingstone and Hubel, 1987] Livingstone, M. S. and Hubel, D. H. (1987). Psychophysical evidence for separate channels for the perception of form, color, movement, and depth. *Journal of Neuroscience*, 7(11):3416–3468.

[Logan, 1996] Logan, G. D. (1996). The CODE theory of visual attention: an integration of space-based and object-based attention. *Psychological Review*, 103:603–649.

[Lowe, 2004] Lowe, D. G. (2004). Distinctive image features from scale-invariant keypoints. *International Journal of Computer Vision (IJCV)*, 60(2):91–110.

[Maki et al., 1996] Maki, A., Nordlund, P., and Eklundh, J.-O. (1996). A computational model of depth-based attention. In *Proc. of International Conference on Pattern Recognition (ICPR '96)*, volume 7472, page 734.

[Maki et al., 2000] Maki, A., Nordlund, P., and Eklundh, J.-O. (2000). Attentional scene segmentation: Integrating depth and motion. *Computer Vision and Image Understanding (CVIU)*, 78(3):351–373.

[Mannan et al., 1997] Mannan, S. K., Ruddock, K. H., and Wooding, D. (1997). Fixation sequences made during visual examination of briefly presented 2D images. *Spatial Vision*, 11(2):157–178.

[Maunsell, 1995] Maunsell, J. H. R. (1995). The brain's visual world: representation of visual targets in cerebral cortex. *Science*, 270:764–769.

[Mazer and Gallant, 2003] Mazer, J. A. and Gallant, J. L. (2003). Goal-related activity in V4 during free viewing visual search. Evidence for a ventral stream visual salience map. *Neuron*, 40(6):1241–50.

[Mertsching et al., 1999] Mertsching, B., Bollmann, M., Hoischen, R., and Schmalz, S. (1999). The neural active vision system NAVIS. In Jähne, B., Haussecke, H., and Geissler, P., editors, *Handbook of Computer Vision and Applications*, volume 3, pages 543–568. Academic Press.

[Miau and Itti, 2001] Miau, F. and Itti, L. (2001). A neural model combining attentional orienting to object recognition: Preliminary explorations on the interplay between where and what. In *Proc. IEEE Engineering in Medicine and Biology Society (EMBS)*, pages 789–792.

[Miau et al., 2001] Miau, F., Papageorgiou, C., and Itti, L. (2001). Neuromorphic algorithms for computer vision and attention. In *Proc. SPIE 46 Annual International Symposium on Optical Science and Technology*, volume 4479, pages 12–23.

[Milanese, 1993] Milanese, R. (1993). *Detecting Salient Regions in an Image: From Biological Evidence to Computer Implementation*. PhD thesis, University of Geneva, Switzerland.

[Milanese et al., 1994] Milanese, R., Wechsler, H., Gil, S., Bost, J., and Pun, T. (1994). Integration of bottom-up and top-down cues for visual attention using non-linear relaxation. In *Proc. of the IEEE Conference on Computer Vision and Pattern Recognition (CVPR '94)*, pages 781–785.

[Mitri et al., 2005] Mitri, S., Frintrop, S., Pervölz, K., Surmann, H., and Nüchter, A. (2005). Robust object detection at regions of interest with an application in ball recognition. In *IEEE 2005 Proc. of the International Conference on Robotics and Automation (ICRA '05)*, pages 126–131, Conference: Barcelona, Spain.

[Mitri et al., 2004] Mitri, S., Pervölz, K., Nüchter, A., and Surmann, H. (2004). Fast color-independent ball detection for mobile autonomous robots. In *Proc. of IEEE Mechatronics & Robotics (Mechrob '04)*, pages 900–905, Conference: Aachen, Germany.

[Mozer, 1987] Mozer, M. C. (1987). Early parallel processing in reading: a connectionist approach. In Coltheart, M., editor, *Attention and performance XII: The psychology of reading*, pages 83–104. Hove, UK: Lawrence Erlbaum Associated Ltd.

[Nakayama and Silverman, 1986] Nakayama, K. and Silverman, G. H. (1986). Serial and parallel processing of visual feature conjunctions. *Nature*, 320:264–265.

[Navalpakkam and Itti, 2002] Navalpakkam, V. and Itti, L. (2002). A goal oriented attention guidance model. In Bülthoff, H. H., Lee, S.-W., Poggio, T., and Wallraven, C., editors, *Proc. 2nd Workshop on Biologically Motivated Computer Vision (BMCV '02)*, volume 2525, pages 453–461, Conference: Tübingen, Germany. Springer Verlag, Lecture Notes in Computer Science (LNCS).

[Navalpakkam and Itti, 2003] Navalpakkam, V. and Itti, L. (2003). Sharing resources: Buy attention, get object recognition. In *Proc. of the International Workshop on Attention and Performance in Computer Vision (WAPCV '03)*, pages 73–79, Graz, Austria.

[Navalpakkam et al., 2004] Navalpakkam, V., Rebesco, J., and Itti, L. (2004). Modeling the influence of knowledge of the target and distractors on visual search. *Journal of Vision*, 4(8):690.

[Navalpakkam et al., 2005] Navalpakkam, V., Rebesco, J., and Itti, L. (2005). Modeling the influence of task on attention. *Vision Research*, 45(2):205–231.

[Neisser, 1967] Neisser, U. (1967). *Cognitive Psychology*. Appleton-Century-Crofts, New York.

[Nickerson et al., 1998] Nickerson, S. B., Jasiobedzki, P., Wilkes, D., Jenkin, M., Milios, E., Tsotsos, J. K., Jepson, A., and Bains, O. N. (1998). The ARK project: Autonomous mobile robots for known industrial environments. *Robotics and Autonomous Systems*, 25(1-2):83–104.

[Nothdurft, 1993] Nothdurft, H. C. (1993). The role of features in preattentive vision: Comparison of orientation, motion and color cues. *Vision Research*, 33:1937–1958.

[Nüchter et al., 2005] Nüchter, A., Lingemann, K., Hertzberg, J., and Surmann, H. (2005). Accurate object localization in 3D laser range scans. In *Proceedings of the 12th International Conference on Advanced Robotics (ICAR '05)*, pages 665–672.

[Nüchter et al., 2004] Nüchter, A., Surmann, H., and Hertzberg, J. (2004). Automatic Classification of Objects in 3D Laser Range Scans. In *Proc. 8th Conference on Intelligent Autonomous Systems (IAS '04)*, pages 963–970, Amsterdam, The Netherlands. IOS Press.

[Oliva et al., 2003] Oliva, A., Torralba, A., Castelhano, M. S., and Henderson, J. M. (2003). Top-down control of visual attention in object detection. In *International Conference on Image Processing (ICIP)*, pages 253–256, Conference: Barcelona, Spain.

[Olshausen et al., 1993] Olshausen, B., Anderson, C., and van Essen, D. (1993). A neurobiological model of visual attention and invariant pattern recognition based on dynamic routing of information. *Journal of Neuroscience*, 13(11):4700–4719.

[OpenCV, 2004] OpenCV (2004). OpenCV: Intel Open Source Computer Vision Library. Version: beta 4. http://www.intel.com/research/mrl/research/opencv/.

[Ouerhani, 2003] Ouerhani, N. (2003). *Visual Attention: From Bio-Inspired Modeling to Real-Time Implementation*. PhD thesis, Institut de Microtechnique Université de Neuchâtel, Switzerland.

[Ouerhani et al., 2002] Ouerhani, N., Archip, N., Hügli, H., and Erard, P. J. (2002). A color image segmentation method based on seeded region growing and visual attention. *Int. Journal of Image Processing and Communication*, 8(1):3–11.

[Ouerhani et al., 2001] Ouerhani, N., Bracamonte, J., Hügli, H., Ansorge, M., and Pellandini, F. (2001). Adaptive color image compression based on visual attention. In *Proc. of the International Conference of Image Analysis and Processing (ICIAP '01)*, pages 416–421. IEEE Computer Society Press.

[Ouerhani and Hügli, 2000] Ouerhani, N. and Hügli, H. (2000). Computing visual attention from scene depth. In *Proc. of the 15th International Conference on Pattern Recognition (ICPR 2000)*, volume 1, pages 375–378. IEEE Computer Society Press.

[Ouerhani and Hügli, 2003a] Ouerhani, N. and Hügli, H. (2003a). MAPS: multi-scale attention-based presegmentation of color images. In *4th International Conference on Scale-Space Theories in Computer Vision*, volume 2695, pages 537–549. Springer Verlag, Lecture Notes in Computer Science (LNCS).

[Ouerhani and Hügli, 2003b] Ouerhani, N. and Hügli, H. (2003b). A model of dynamic visual attention for object tracking in natural image sequences. In *International Conference on Artificial and Natural Neural Network (IWANN)*, volume 2686, pages 702–709. Springer Verlag, Lecture Notes in Computer Science (LNCS).

[Ouerhani and Hügli, 2003c] Ouerhani, N. and Hügli, H. (2003c). Real time visual attention on a massively parallel SIMD architecture. *International Journal of Real-time Imaging, Elsevier Computer Science*, 9(3):189–196.

[Ouerhani and Hügli, 2004] Ouerhani, N. and Hügli, H. (2004). AttentiRobot: a visual attention-based landmark selection approach for mobile robot navigation. In Paletta, L., Tsotsos, J. K., Rome, E., and Humphreys, G. W., editors, *Proc. of the 2nd international workshop on attention and performance in computational vision (WAPCV '04)*, pages 83–89, Conference: Prague, Czech Republic.

[Ouerhani et al., 2004] Ouerhani, N., von Wartburg, R., Hügli, H., and Müri, R. (2004). Empirical validation of the saliency-based model of visual attention. *Electronic Letters on Computer Vision and Image Analysis*, 3(1):13–24.

[Palmer, 1999] Palmer, S. E. (1999). *Vision Science, Photons to Phenomenology*. The MIT Press, Cambridge, MA.

[Papageorgiou et al., 1998] Papageorgiou, C., Oren, M., and Poggio, T. (1998). A general framework for object detection. In *Proc. of the 6th International Conference on Computer Vision (ICCV '98)*, pages 555–562, Conference: Bombay, India.

[Parkhurst et al., 2002] Parkhurst, D., Law, K., and Niebur, E. (2002). Modeling the role of salience in the allocation of overt visual attention. *Vision Research*, 42(1):107–123.

[Pashler, 1997] Pashler, H. (1997). *The Psychology of Attention*. MIT Press, Cambridge, MA.

[Pervölz et al., 2004] Pervölz, K., Nüchter, A., Surmann, H., and Hertzberg, J. (2004). Automatic reconstruction of colored 3D models. In *Proc. of Robotik 2004*, pages 215–222, Munich, Germany. VDI-Berichte 1841.

[Pessoa and Exel, 1999] Pessoa, L. and Exel, S. (1999). Attentional strategies for object recognition. In Mira, J. and Sachez-Andres, J., editors, *Proc. of the International Work-Conference on Artificial and Natural Neural Networks (IWANN '99)*, volume 1606 of *Lecture Notes in Computer Science (LNCS)*, pages 850–859, Alicante, Spain. Springer.

[Phaf et al., 1990] Phaf, R. H., van der Heijden, A. H. C., and Hudson, P. T. W. (1990). SLAM: A connectionist model for attention in visual selection tasks. *Cognitive Psychology*, 22:273–341.

[Phillips, 1994] Phillips, D. (1994). *Image Processing in C: Analyzing and Enhancing Digital Images*. R & D Publications, Inc. Lawrence, Kansas.

[Posner, 1980] Posner, M. I. (1980). Orienting of attention. *Quarterly Journal of Experimental Psychology*, 32:3–25.

[Posner and Petersen, 1990] Posner, M. I. and Petersen, S. E. (1990). The attentional system of the human brain. *Annual Review of Neuroscience*, 13:25–42.

[Postma, 1994] Postma, E. (1994). *SCAN: A Neural Model of Covert Attention*. PhD thesis, Rijksuniversiteit Limburg, Wageningen.

[Rae, 2000] Rae, R. (2000). *Gestikbasierte Mensch-Maschine-Kommunikation auf der Grundlage visueller Aufmerksamkeit und Adaptivität*. PhD thesis, Technische Fakultät der Universität Bielefeld, Germany.

[Ramström and Christensen, 2002] Ramström, O. and Christensen, H. I. (2002). Visual attention using game theory. In Bülthoff, H. H., Lee, S.-W., Poggio, T., and Wallraven, C., editors, *Proc. 2nd Workshop on Biologically Motivated Computer Vision (BMCV '02)*, volume 2525, pages 462–471, Conference: Tübingen, Germany. Springer Verlag, Lecture Notes in Computer Science (LNCS).

[Ramström and Christensen, 2004] Ramström, O. and Christensen, H. I. (2004). Object based visual attention: Searching for objects defined by size. In Paletta, L., Tsotsos, J. K., Rome, E., and Humphreys, G. W., editors, *Proc. of the 2nd International Workshop on Attention and Performance in Computational Vision (WAPCV '04)*, pages 9–16, Conference: Prague, Czech Republic.

[Rao et al., 2002] Rao, R., Zelinsky, G., Hayhoe, M., and Ballard, D. (2002). Eye movements in iconic visual search. *Vision Research*, 42:1447–1463.

[Remington and Pierce, 1984] Remington, R. and Pierce, L. (1984). Moving attention: evidence for time-invariant shifts of visual selective attention. *Perception & Psychophysics*, 35(4):393–399.

[Rensink, 2000] Rensink, R. A. (2000). The dynamic representation of scenes. *Visual Cognition*, 7:17–42.

[Rensink, 2002] Rensink, R. A. (2002). Internal vs. external information in visual perception. In *Proc. of the Second International Symposium on Smart Graphics*, pages 63–70, Hawthorne, NY, USA.

[Rensink et al., 1997] Rensink, R. A., O'Regan, J. K., and Clark, J. J. (1997). To see or not to see: The need for attention to perceive changes in scenes. *Psychological Science*, 8:368–373.

[Riesenhuber and Poggio, 1999] Riesenhuber, M. and Poggio, T. (1999). Hierarchical models of object recognition in cortex. *Nature Neuroscience*, 2(11):1019–1025.

[Sabra, 1989] Sabra, A. I. (1989). *The Optics of Ibn Al-Haytham*. The Warburg Institute, University of London.

[Salah et al., 2002] Salah, A., Alpaydin, E., and Akrun, L. (2002). A selective attention based method for visual pattern recognition with application to handwritten digit recognition and face recognition. *IEEE Transactions on Pattern Analysis and Machine Intelligence (PAMI)*, 24(3):420–425.

[Scheier and Egner, 1997] Scheier, C. and Egner, S. (1997). Visual attention in a mobile robot. In *Proc. of the IEEE International Symposium on Industrial Electronics*, pages 48–53.

[Schmid et al., 2000] Schmid, C., Mohr, R., and Bauckhage, C. (2000). Evaluation of interest point detectors. *International Journal of Computer Vision (IJCV)*, 37(2):151–172.

[Sequeira et al., 1999] Sequeira, V., Ng, K., Wolfart, E., Goncalves, J., and Hogg, D. (1999). Automated 3D reconstruction of interiors with multiple scan–views. In *Proc. of SPIE, Electronic Imaging '99, The Society for Imaging Science and Technology /SPIE's 11th Annual Symposium*, pages 106–117, Conference: San Jose, CA, USA.

[Simons and Levin, 1997] Simons, D. J. and Levin, D. T. (1997). Change blindness. *Trends in Cognitive Sciences*, 1:261–267.

[Simons and Levin, 1998] Simons, D. J. and Levin, D. T. (1998). Failure to detect changes to people in a real-world interaction. *Psychonomic Bulletin & Review*, 5:644–649.

[Styles, 1997] Styles, E. A. (1997). *The Psychology of Attention*. Psychology Press Ltd, East Sussex, UK.

[Sun and Fisher, 2003] Sun, Y. and Fisher, R. (2003). Object-based visual attention for computer vision. *Artificial Intelligence*, 146(1):77–123.

[Surmann et al., 2001] Surmann, H., Lingemann, K., Nüchter, A., and Hertzberg, J. (2001). A 3D laser range finder for autonomous mobile robots. In *Proc. 32nd International Symposium on Robotics (ISR 2001)*, pages 153–158, Seoul, South Korea.

[Tanimoto and Pavlidis, 1975] Tanimoto, S. and Pavlidis, T. (1975). A hierarchical data structure for image processing. *Computer Graphics and Image Processing*, 4:104–119.

[Theeuwes, 2004] Theeuwes, J. (2004). Top-down search strategies cannot override attentional capture. *Psychonomic Bulletin & Review*, 11:65–70.

[Torralba, 2003] Torralba, A. (2003). Modeling global scene factors in attention. *Journal of Optical Society of America A. Special Issue on Bayesian and Statistical Approaches to Vision*, 20(7):1407–1418.

[Treisman, 1993] Treisman, A. M. (1993). The perception of features and objects. In Baddeley, A. and Weiskrantz, L., editors, *Attention: Selection, awareness, and control*, pages 5–35. Clarendon Press, Oxford.

[Treisman and Gelade, 1980] Treisman, A. M. and Gelade, G. (1980). A feature integration theory of attention. *Cognitive Psychology*, 12:97–136.

[Treisman and Gormican, 1988] Treisman, A. M. and Gormican, S. (1988). Feature analysis in early vision: Evidence from search asymmetries. *Psychological Review*, 95(1):15–48.

[Treptow and Zell, 2004] Treptow, A. and Zell, A. (2004). Real-time object tracking for soccer-robots without color information. *Robotics and Autonomous Systems*, 48(1):41–48.

[Tsotsos, 1990] Tsotsos, J. K. (1990). Analyzing vision at the complexity level. *Behavioral and Brain Sciences*, 13(3):423–445.

[Tsotsos, 1993] Tsotsos, J. K. (1993). An inhibitory beam for attentional selection. In Harris, L. R. and Jenkin, M., editors, *Spatial Vision in Humans and Robots*, pages 313–331. Cambridge University Press.

[Tsotsos, 2001] Tsotsos, J. K. (2001). Complexity, vision, and attention. In Jenkin, M. and Harris, L. R., editors, *Vision and Attention*, chapter 6. Springer Verlag.

[Tsotsos et al., 1995] Tsotsos, J. K., Culhane, S. M., Wai, W. Y. K., Lai, Y., Davis, N., and Nuflo, F. (1995). Modeling visual attention via selective tuning. *Artificial Intelligence*, 78(1-2):507–545.

[Tsotsos et al., 2005] Tsotsos, J. K., Liu, Y., Martinez-Trujillo, J. C., Pomplun, M., Simine, E., and Zhou, K. (to appear 2005). Attenting to visual motion. *Journal of Computer Vision and Image Understanding (CVIU), Special Issue on Attention and Performance*.

[Tsotsos et al., 1998] Tsotsos, J. K., Verghese, G., Stevenson, S., Black, M., Metaxas, D., Culhane, S., Dickinson, S., Jenkin, M., Jepson, A., Milios, E., Nuflo, F., Ye, Y., and Mann, R. (1998). PLAYBOT: A visually-guided robot to assist physically disabled children in play. *Image and Vision Computing 16, Special Issue on Vision for the Disabled*, pages 275–292.

[Ungerleider and Mishkin, 1982] Ungerleider, L. and Mishkin, M. (1982). Two cortical visual systems. In Ingle, D., Goodale, M., and Mansfield, R., editors, *Analysis of visual behavior*, pages 549–586. MIT Press.

[URL, 01] URL (01). Kyle Cave: Visual Perception and Cognition. http://www.ecs.soton.ac.uk/~kc/py202/attention.htm.

[URL, 02] URL (02). Jacob L. Driesen: Neuropsychology, Medical Psychology, and Neuroscience Website. http://www.driesen.com.

[URL, 03] URL (03). Color Vision and Art. http://webexhibits.org/colorart/ganglion.html.

[URL, 04] URL (04). Philosophy and cognitive science. http://philosophy.hku.hk/courses/cogsci/ncc.php.

[URL, 05] URL (05). iLab at the University of Southern California. http://ilab.usc.edu/.

[URL, 06] URL (06). iLab Neuromorphic Vision C++ Toolkit Screenshots. http://ilab.usc.edu/toolkit/screenshots.shtml.

[URL, 07] URL (07). iLab Image Databases. http://ilab.usc.edu/imgdbs/.

[URL, 08] URL (08). Molecular Expressions. http://micro.magnet.fsu.edu/primer/java/digitalimaging/processing/-kernelmaskoperation/.

[URL, 09] URL (09). The MathWorks. http://www.mathworks.com/access/-helpdesk/help/toolbox/images/colorcube.jpg.

[URL, 10] URL (10). Color Model Museum. http://www.colorcube.com/articles/models/model.htm.

[URL, 11] URL (11). Apple developer connection. http://developer.apple.com/documentation/GraphicsImaging/Conceptual/-ManagingColorSync/IntroCSpaces/chapter_15_section_4.html.

[URL, 12] URL (12). SAP Design Guild. http://www.sapdesignguild.org/resources/glossary_color/index1.html.

[URL, 13] URL (13). David G. Lowe: Demo Software: SIFT Keypoint Detector. http://www.cs.ubc.ca/~lowe/keypoints/.

[URL, 14] URL (14). Solid-State Time-of-Flight Range Camera. http://www.csem.ch/detailed/p_531_3d_cam.htm.

[URL, 15] URL (15). The PMD camera. http://www.pmdtec.com/.

[URL, 16] URL (16). Robot World Cup Soccer Games and Conferences. http://www.robocup.org.

[URL, 17] URL (17). Système d'Evaluation du Taux d'Actualisation de donnees topo-geographiques par Teledetection Spatiale. http://www.sic.rma.ac.be/Projects/ETATS/content.html.

[van der Willigen and von Campenhausen, 2002] van der Willigen, R. F. and von Campenhausen, M. (2002). Audio-oculomotor transformation. In Bülthoff, H. H., Lee, S.-W., Poggio, T. A., and Wallraven, C., editors, *Biologically Motivated Computer Vision*, Second International Workshop, BMCV, Tübingen, Germany. Springer.

[van Oeffelen and Vos, 1982] van Oeffelen, M. P. and Vos, P. G. (1982). Configurational effects on the enumeration of dots: counting by groups. *Memory & Cognition*, 10:396–404.

[Vickery et al., 2005] Vickery, T. J., King, L.-W., and Jiang, Y. (2005). Setting up the target template in visual search. *Journal of Vision*, 5(1):81–92. doi:10.1167/5.1.8.

[Vijayakumar et al., 2001] Vijayakumar, S., Conradt, J., Shibata, T., and Schaal, S. (2001). Overt visual attention for a humanoid robot. In *Proc. International Conference on Intelligence in Robotics and Autonomous Systems (IROS 2001)*, pages 2332–2337, Hawaii.

[Viola and Jones, 2001] Viola, P. and Jones, M. J. (2001). Robust Real-time Object Detection. In *Proc. 2nd Int'l Workshop on Statistical and Computational Theories of Vision – Modeling, Learning, Computing and Sampling*, Conference: Vancouver, Canada.

[Viola and Jones, 2004] Viola, P. and Jones, M. J. (2004). Robust real-time face detection. *International Journal of Computer Vision (IJCV)*, 57(2):137–154.

[Walther et al., 2002] Walther, D., Itti, L., Riesenhuber, M., Poggio, T., and Koch, C. (2002). Attentional selection for object recognition — a gentle way. In Bülthoff, H. H., Lee, S.-W., Poggio, T., and Wallraven, C., editors, *Proc. 2nd Workshop on Biologically Motivated Computer Vision (BMCV '02), Tübingen, Germany*, volume 2525, pages 472–479, Conference: Tübingen, Germany. Springer Verlag, Lecture Notes in Computer Science (LNCS).

[Walther et al., 2004] Walther, D., Rutishauser, U., Koch, C., and Perona, P. (2004). On the usefulness of attention for object recognition. In Paletta, L., Tsotsos, J. K., Rome, E., and Humphreys, G. W., editors, *Proc. of the 2nd international workshop on attention and performance in computational vision (WAPCV '04)*, pages 96–103, Conference: Prague, Czech Republic.

[Walther et al., 2005] Walther, D., Rutishauser, U., Koch, C., and Perona, P. (2005). Selective visual attention enables learning and recognition of multiple objects in cluttered scenes. *Computer Vision and Image Understanding*, 100(1-2):41–63.

[Wang et al., 1994] Wang, Q., Cavanagh, P., and Green, M. (1994). Familiarity and pop-out in visual search. *Perception & Psychophysics*, 56:495–500.

[Watanabe and Shimojo, 2005] Watanabe, K. and Shimojo, S. (2005). Crossmodal attention in event perception. In Itti, L., Rees, G., and Tsotsos, J., editors, *Neurobiology of Attention*, chapter 89, pages 538–546. Elsevier Academic Press.

[Wolfe, 1994] Wolfe, J. M. (1994). Guided search 2.0: A revised model of visual search. *Psychonomic Bulletin and Review*, 1(2):202–238.

[Wolfe, 1998a] Wolfe, J. M. (1998a). Visual search. In Pashler, H., editor, *Attention*, pages 13–74. Hove, U.K.: Psychology Press.

[Wolfe, 1998b] Wolfe, J. M. (1998b). What can 1,000,000 trials tell us about visual search? *Psychological Science*, 9(1):33–39.

[Wolfe, 2001a] Wolfe, J. M. (2001a). Asymmetries in visual search: An introduction. *Perception & Psychophysics*, 63(3):381–389.

[Wolfe, 2001b] Wolfe, J. M. (2001b). Guided search 4.0: A guided search model that does not require memory for rejected distractors. *Journal of Vision, Abstracts of the 2001 VSS Meeting*, 1(3):349a.

[Wolfe et al., 1989] Wolfe, J. M., Cave, K., and Franzel, S. (1989). Guided search: An alternative to the feature integration model for visual search. *Journal of Experimental Psychology: Human Perception and Performance*, 15:419–433.

[Wolfe and Gancarz, 1996] Wolfe, J. M. and Gancarz, G. (1996). Guided search 3.0: Basic and clinical applications of vision science. Dordrecht, Netherlands: Kluwer Academic. 189–192.

[Wolfe et al., 2004] Wolfe, J. M., Horowitz, T., Kenner, N., Hyle, M., and Vasan, N. (2004). How fast can you change your mind? The speed of top-down guidance in visual search. *Vision Research*, 44:1411–1426.

[Zeki, 1993] Zeki, S. (1993). *A Vision of the Brain*. Cambridge, MA: Blackwell Scientific.

Index

Lecture Notes in Artificial Intelligence (LNAI)